In these dark times, *Never Can I Write of Damascus* is a gift to the world, a captivating love letter to the culture and people of Syria (and the Iraqi and Palestinian refugees in their midst), based on the experience of the authors of the torments and glories of their lives and surroundings. This book should be required reading for Americans currently endangered by a public Islamophobic campaign.

—RICHARD FALK
Author of *Chaos and Counterrevolution: After the Arab Spring*

Part travelogue and part social history, *Never Can I Write of Damascus* is an absorbing and educational journey.... It is a testimonial of how individual lives can make a difference over the long run and succeed in bridging gaps in culture and politics that have long been considered insurmountable.

—HALA FATTAH, PhD
Independent scholar, Amman, Jordan

Never can I think of Damascus without thinking of Gabe Huck and Theresa Kubasak and of the stories they tell in this book: of Damascus and its neighborhoods in and around the old city, of learning Arabic and teaching English, of the Iraqi Student Project and its brief, potent flourishing, of Deir Mar Musa al-Habashi and its re-founder, Father Paolo Dall'Oglio (now perhaps martyred by Da'esh in Raqqa), of Palestine and its refugees, of Iraq and its refugees, and now of Syria and its refugees, among whom Gabe and Theresa must be numbered, if only unofficially.

To be a refugee is not a matter merely or only of legal status; it is a state of mind and body and spirit triggered by the forcible displacement of a people from their homes and their history, such as has now happened to the people of Syria. So this is a refugee memoir, a recollection of Syria in a time before. It speaks to all of us who remember the Syria of that time.

—JOSEPH A. GREENE
Harvard University

This book is more than just an intimate view of one of the world's least-known great cities; it is also the story of two Americans trying to understand U.S. policy in Iraq and Syria while doing their part to assist some of those whose families and communities have been destroyed by those policies. If you need confirmation of Margaret Mead's improbable assertion, "Never doubt that a small group of thoughtful, committed citizens can change the world; indeed, it's the only thing that ever has," read *Never Can I Write of Damascus.*"

—DOUG HOSTETTER
Author of *The Bosnian Student Project: A Response to Genocide*

Learning about other societies involves excavation and wandering. Kubasak and Huck introduce the reader to life and its daily rhythms in Damascus. Instead of rushing through, they meander through streets, and report on what they see, hear, smell, and taste. They hear calls to prayer, church bells, cats on rooftops, artisans at work, vegetable sellers, and the joyous festivities of Ramadan. They are the best of what Voices in the Wilderness can offer. They report on life, but also on what is done in their name by the U.S. government in Iraq and Syria. In part, their narrative revives memories of locations (Yarmouk camp) that are today out of place—vanished as a result of conflict and war. Their Syria is about history, culture, resilience, and real people, and not simply as our "other." Their testimony is lyrical and serves as witnessing for peace.

—**NUBAR HOVSEPIAN**
Associate professor of political science at Chapman University

This vivid memoir of Damascene years witnesses the intersection of the Iraqi, Palestinian, and Syrian tragedies. Through their testimony, the authors not only convey their unwavering commitment to the victims, they also show empathy and solidarity amidst endless human suffering.

—**ELIZABETH SUZANNE KASSAB**
Author of *Contemporary Arab Thought:*
Cultural Critique in Comparative Perspective

How else to explain Gabe Huck's and Theresa Kubasak's relationship with Iraqi and Syrian culture other than to say that they fell in love? Yet the romance blossomed, always, during military and economic wars. Their narrative includes blunt assessment of U.S. foreign policies which afflicted and terrorized Iraqi people, helping readers understand the authors' decision to personally make reparations. Dedicated to serving Iraqis who sought refuge in Syria, they created the remarkable Iraqi Student Project. Woven throughout Gabe and Theresa's engrossing story is an essential question: "What if we believed in peace-making?" I gratefully and wholeheartedly recommend this book.

—**KATHY KELLY**
Co-coordinator, Voices for Creative Nonviolence
(formerly Voices in the Wilderness)

This book is both heartwarming and heartbreaking. It provides a look into real life in Syria, which is a wonderfully refreshing counterpoint to the crude stereotypes most outsiders hear. At the same time, it gives us reason to lament the rash blindness that led outsiders to crash into that country and help tear it apart.

—STEPHEN KINZER

Author of *Crescent and Star: Turkey Between Two Worlds*

At a stage of life when many of their contemporaries were ready to retire to Florida, Gabe Huck and Theresa Kubasak had something more ambitious and risky in mind. Troubled by the chaos that their own country's actions had helped to produce in Iraq, these two New York activists decided to embark on a journey of engagement to the heart of the Arab world. In 2005, this led them to Damascus—then inundated with Iraqi refugees. They came with humility: they wanted to learn. They plunged into the study of Arabic and the city around them with surprising energy and persistence. Amidst the pressing tragedies that surrounded them, they found a world of immense depth and fascination. This was the world's oldest continuously inhabited city. Its intricate streets were the focus of a thousand stories.

Displaced Iraqis were desperate for their children to be educated. Gabe and Theresa responded when some asked for help with English and other academic subjects. Then they activated a transnational network that eventually provided free university education in the United States to scores of young Iraqis. But this is not a narrative of Americans rescuing benighted people without history. Rather, it is a story of what two Americans learned—a story that other Americans must read.

—PATRICK VINCENT MCGREEVY

Dean of the Faculty of Arts and Sciences, American University of Beirut

Just World Books
Timely Books for Changing Times

Just World Books exists to expand the discourse in the United States and worldwide on issues of vital international concern. We are committed to building a more just, equitable, and peaceable world. We uphold the equality of all human persons. We aim for our books to contribute to increasing understanding across national, religious, ethnic, and racial lines; to share more broadly the reflections, analyses, and policy prescriptions of pathbreaking activists for peace; and to help to prevent war.

To learn about our existing and upcoming titles or to buy our books, visit our website:

www.JustWorldBooks.com

Also, follow us on Facebook, Twitter, and Instagram!

Our recent titles include:

- *America's Continuing Misadventures in the Middle East*, by Chas W. Freeman
- *Arabia Incognita: Dispatches from Yemen and the Gulf*, edited by Sheila Carapico
- *War Is a Lie*, by David Swanson
- *The General's Son: Journey of an Israeli in Palestine, Second Edition*, by Miko Peled
- *Survival and Conscience: From the Shadows of Nazi Germany to the Jewish Boat to Gaza*, by Lillian Rosengarten
- *The People Make the Peace: Lessons from the Vietnam Antiwar Movement*, edited by Karín Aguilar-San Juan and Frank Joyce
- *Gaza Unsilenced*, edited by Refaat Alareer and Laila El-Haddad
- *Baddawi*, by Leila Abdelrazaq
- *Chaos and Counterrevolution: After the Arab Spring*, by Richard Falk
- *Palestine: The Legitimacy of Hope*, by Richard Falk
- *Chief Complaint: A Country Doctor's Tales of Life in Galilee*, by Hatim Kanaaneh
- *Gaza Writes Back: Short Stories from Young Writers in Gaza, Palestine*, edited by Refaat Alareer
- *The Gaza Kitchen: A Palestinian Culinary Journey*, by Laila El-Haddad and Maggie Schmitt

For John & Michael
Dear friends,
Walk with us through the
streets of Damascus, our
beloved city. Let us
continue to believe
in peace and work for
justice. Blessings,
Theresa
Gabe

Never Can I Write of Damascus

When Syria Became Our Home

Theresa Kubasak and Gabe Huck

Just World Books

Charlottesville, Virginia

Just World Books

Timely Books for Changing Times

Just World Books is an imprint of Just World Publishing, LLC.

Cover design and typesetting by Diana Ghazzawi for Just World Publishing, LLC.
Cover photos by urf.
All interior art and photographs copyright of their creators and used here with permission.

Publisher's Cataloging in Publication
(Provided by Quality Books, Inc.)

Kubasak, Theresa, author.
    Never can I write of Damascus when Syria became our
home / Theresa Kubasak and Gabe Huck.
    pages cm
    LCCN 2015953895
    ISBN 978-1-682570-06-7
    ISBN 978-1-682570-58-6 (epub)
    ISBN 978-1-682570-59-3 (mobi)
    ISBN 978-1-682570-60-9 (PDF)
    1. Kubasak, Theresa. 2. Huck, Gabe. 3. Iraq War,
2003-2011--Refugees. 4. Political activists--Biography.
5. Refugees--Syria. 6. Refugees--Iraq. 7. Refugees--
Palestine. 8. Syria--Social life and customs. 9. Iraq
--Social life and customs. 10. Autobiographies.
I. Huck, Gabe, author. II. Title.
DS79.767.R43K83 2016   956.7044'31
                           QBI16-600050

لا أستطيع أن أكتب عن دمشق،
دون أن يعرش الياسمين
على أصابعي .
ولا أستطيع أن أنطق إسمها،
دون أن يكتظّ فمي بعصير المشمش
والرمان، والتوت، والسفرجل .
ولا أستطيع أن أتذكرها،
دون أن تحطّ على جدار ذاكرتي
ألف حمامة .. وتطير ألف حمامة ..

نزار قباني

Never can I write of Damascus
without my hands becoming
a trellis for her jasmine.

Nor can my mouth utter that name
without savoring the juices of her apricot,
pomegranate, mulberry and quince.

Nor can I remember her
without a thousand doves landing on the wall of my memories...
and a thousand doves take flight...

NIZAR QABBANI

The Khan Pasha, pictured on the cover of this book, is one of the wondrous rooms of Damascus and of the world. Yet walking the spice souq, you might never notice the entrance. The Umayyad Mosque is a short walk away if you measure, but with the spices, sweets, jewelry, and a 900-year-old hammam in between, who measures? Khan Pasha is young, not yet 300 years old, the grandest of these buildings where travelers on the trade routes or the hajj could stay, stable their wagons and animals, meet other traders—and every time they pause at some new spot on the ground floor or the balconies, see the Khan's arches and stones, its geometry and scope anew. The alternation of basalt and limestone, the former plentiful south of Damascus, the latter to the north, was already typical of the area.
Photo by Viktor Hegyi.

Contents

Part 4. Jiser Abyad (2009–2012)

Introduction
Our Road to Damascus

When the wave, then thought of as the "Arab Spring," reached Syria in March 2011, we had been living there for more than five years. The nonviolent protests that spread so quickly in the spring that year met with immediate and blunt violence from the regime, thereby ending an organized and committed effort at peaceful change. Almost five years later, half of Syria's population has fled in search of safety. Some have a nameless moment in the media as they are or are not rescued from boats heading toward a Greek shore. Most of these refugees are not yet 20 years old.

Until we left for Syria in 2005, our labors had been (for Theresa) teaching young children and mentoring those who wanted to become teachers of children, and (for Gabe) directing a small publishing house, founded after the Second Vatican Council to take the conversation about renewal of the Catholic Church to parishes in Chicago and beyond. We are both children of the Sixties. We mourned Malcolm X and Martin Luther King, Jr., the children killed in a Birmingham church, Steve Biko in South Africa, and Archbishop Oscar Romero in Salvador. We kept May Day and Earth Day, voted for Ralph Nader and Winona LaDuke. Our journeys took us—separately at first and then together—to causes when the stakes were high and triumphs were small and infrequent.

We are people of the word and the song; we take action, demonstrate, write articles, go on fasts, get arrested, write letters to editors and politicians, and subscribe to *The Nation*, *Rethinking Schools*, and *New York Review of Books*. Along the way, we made good friends who came from various backgrounds who, like us, had spent years paying attention to those in need. Little by little, all of us were learning to ask why and to whose benefit was this suffering.

THE FURY UNLEASHED by the United States on Iraq in 1990 must have come as a surprise to ordinary Iraqis, because U.S.–Iraq relations throughout the 1980s were anything but hostile. Iraq declared war on Iran in 1980, ostensibly to reclaim border territory it claimed belonged to Iraq. This was during the turmoil of Iran's postrevolutionary period. The United States not only supported Iraq against Iran, but also sold chemical weapons to the Iraqi government. After eight years of war and a million dead, both sides accepted a UN-negotiated ceasefire. Both countries had poured lives and money into the effort and were in debt despite oil revenues.

In working with Iraqis in their late teens and early 20s, none of them yet born when the war ended, we were told the stories that they had heard from their parents and grandparents. They expressed not blame but rather regret for how needless it all was and how powerless civilians on both sides had been to end it. They were familiar with the role of the United States in playing one side against the other. This war was part of every Iraqi family's life: its length, its dead and wounded, its destruction of towns and cities, and its whimper of a conclusion.

Two years after the war ended, Iraq invaded Kuwait, one of its creditors during its destructive and avoidable war with Iran. An official Iraqi explanation for the invasion would no doubt include the charge that Kuwait had engaged in slant drilling, thereby "stealing" Iraqi oil, and that it pumped well above established quotas, thereby bringing the price of oil down (with disastrous consequences for debt-burdened Iraq).

Despite U.S. Ambassador April Glaspie's assertion that the United States had no stake in Iraq-Kuwait relations (what some might see as a green light for invasion—or at the very least a pledge of neutrality), the United States responded promptly and furiously to Iraq's invasion of Kuwait, and urged UN sanctions and a January 1991 deadline for Iraq to end its occupation. When the deadline came, the United States began an air attack.

After six weeks of one-sided U.S. air attacks on Iraqi forces in Kuwait, the ground war began. Within days, all Iraqi forces withdrew from Kuwait, but U.S. and other coalition forces continued to attack. Retreating Iraqi troops were attacked from the ground and the air; their dead bodies and wrecked vehicles extended for miles on what became known as the "highway of death." The United States used artillery firing shells coated with depleted uranium to make them "armor piercing" when striking tanks. (Years later, we saw in Basra and Damascus hospitals the statistics and the photos of children born with birth defects and deformations attributable to the use of depleted uranium.)

American missiles and bombs destroyed much of an infrastructure that served its population. The extent of this bombing had nothing whatsoever to do with Iraq's invasion of Kuwait or with weakening Saddam Hussein's hold on power. The bombing targeted electric power stations, refineries, petrochemical complexes, telecommunications centers, bridges, roads, highways, railroads, hundreds of locomotives and boxcars full of goods, radio and television broadcasting stations, cement plants, and factories producing aluminum, textiles, electric cables, and medical supplies. One of the most notorious U.S. strikes in February 1991 targeted a clearly marked bomb shelter in Amiriya, killing at least 408 civilians. Years later, we visited that spot, which had been turned into a memorial to the victims and a statement about U.S. regard for Iraqi lives.

> The UN Security Council imposed sanctions on Iraq. Soon Iraq found that it was unable to purify the water supply, treat sewage, transport people and goods by land and air, turn on the lights every night, have access to basic medicine, and cross the rivers on bridges that bound homes and jobs together. Yet in the United States, sanctions were being praised by some as a new form of nonviolent action. And even when the cost was irrefutably shown to be unconscionable (half a million dead Iraqi children whose deaths could be attributable to the sanctions), an unperturbed U.S. Secretary of State (Madeleine Albright) casually brushed off the cost in children's lives as "worth it."
>
> The sanctions that were imposed on Iraq in the wake of its invasion of Kuwait in 1990 were unprecedented in UN history and exacted so high a civilian cost that three high-profile officials tasked with overseeing humanitarian aid to that country—Denis Halliday, Hans von Sponeck, and Jutta Burghardt—resigned in protest within roughly one year. In early 2003, several career diplomats would resign in protest of U.S. policy in Iraq.

Syria by Way of Iraq

How and why did we come to live in Syria for seven years? Even a short version has to begin not in Syria, but with the tangled story of Iraq and the United States.

Beginning in 1999, we made four trips to Iraq as part of Voices in the Wilderness delegations. Our purpose was to break the U.S. ban on travel to Iraq and to bear witness to the effects of the brutal UN sanctions that continued to destroy lives and culture in that country. We wanted to witness first, then tell other Americans about the effects of U.S. policies on ordinary Iraqis: shopkeepers, teachers, farmers, artists, the young and the old, city residents and rural communities. After our made-for-TV war to end Iraq's occupation of Kuwait in early 1991, the U.S. government had launched a more brutal but bureaucratic (and thus invisible) attack against Iraq. This never-seen-in-prime-time war was in its tenth year in 1999, and all the casualties were on the Iraqi side. When George W. Bush became president in 2001, his administration wasted little time in developing plans ("shock and awe") to effect regime change in Iraq. With the attacks of September 11, 2001, the plans had only to wait until we began another war—in Afghanistan.

The Iraq we had seen suffering under sanctions exposed the naked imperial power of the United States. Ten weeks before the United States launched its illegal and unprovoked war on Iraq in March 2003, we were in Basra for our third Christmas midnight mass with Iraqi Christians, who chanted the ancient prayers transmitted from generation to generation. In Baghdad, we listened to the *maqam* music at a tiny anthropological museum each Friday evening, loved the smell of freshly baked bread called *samoon* taken out of round ovens, and walked up and up and up on the no-railing spiral ascent on the minaret of the Samarra mosque. But we also noted that the amount of paper bills needed to settle our hotel bill would fill a small suitcase, and we saw too many children begging in the streets. In schools, children played in the mud puddles from a winter rain and were taught in crowded classrooms by teachers who had no chalk. We attended a university literature class where students were reading and discussing Samuel Beckett's *Waiting for Godot.* They too were waiting.

One memory is especially vivid. We had been led through the corridors and into the rooms of a children's hospital in Basra, visiting with patients and those caring for them. No matter how often we came to Iraq's hospitals, we could not become accustomed to what we would see there—not only the lack of anything to sterilize instruments, but what many doctors believed were the effects of the depleted uranium coating on shells and missiles used by the U.S. forces twelve years earlier all through the area north of Kuwait. The birth defects were many and horrible. Parents and hospital personnel were rightly angry about this, not blaming us so much as saying, "We see you coming to look, and you tell us you will talk to your officials at home. But nothing happens. The deformed live or die. Nothing changes this."

Outside one hospital as we lined up to board a van, a medical student we had met inside confronted the two of us, pleading when he could have demanded, "Can you bring me a book?" A textbook? A medical dictionary? Just: a book. He could speak English but he could not receive medical journals in Iraq because of the sanctions. His desire to learn made him a beggar and shamed us.

We can still hear that question. We were in Basra, the very base of the Fertile Crescent, where the alphabet originated as a way to use sounds so words could be written rather than pictures, where paper arrived from China and libraries were built to hold and share the books. Here in their new capital, Baghdad, the early Abbasid caliphs revered knowledge and founded the House of Wisdom, *Beit al-Hikma,* where Jews, Christians, Muslims, and Zoroastrians gathered to translate and preserve and build on the Greek philosophers, the poems and scriptures, the sciences of nature and physics. They would develop an understanding of medicine and healing, of agriculture, of music, of time and astronomy, of philosophy, and of the Greek philosophers. Legend had it that when the Mongols destroyed the handwritten books of Baghdad's libraries in the thirteenth century by tossing them into the Tigris River, the water turned black from ink. And here we were, in the early years of the twenty-first century, being asked by an heir of that tradition for a book.

That was the last time we were in Iraq.

The 2003 invasion of Iraq replaced the tyranny of Saddam Hussein with the U.S. military occupation. The arrogance and incompetence exhibited in the next years brought chaos and daily violence to the people of Iraq. Many fled the country. By 2007, over a million Iraqi refugees had gone to Syria, whose cities had shown hospitality to many refugees over the centuries. Iraqi refugees were not housed in camps; they sought lodging in Damascus and other cities. Jordan also received many Iraqi refugees in those years, though, it seemed, with more bureaucratic and economic restrictions.

As the second year of the U.S. occupation of Iraq began, we decided to leave the United States and move to the Middle East. We would live as close to Iraq as our finances—one Social Security check and one small pension—would permit. That eliminated Amman and Beirut and almost anywhere else near Iraq, but not the cities of Syria. We would study Arabic. And we would also look for something we could do—we did not know what that would be when we moved—to make a token reparation to the Iraqi people for what our government had done to their lives and culture in those last 15 years: the war of 1991 and destruction of Iraq's infrastructure, the imposition of sanctions over a 13-year period on a weakened Iraq with the suffering and the estimated million Iraqi lives lost, then invasion and occupation to be remembered by our use of torture and of mercenaries and of an incompetent administration. This was deliberate, unrelated to any harm done to the United States, supported by lies, and from motives that humiliate all of us.

Making a Home in Damascus

So we came to live in Damascus, perhaps the world's longest continually inhabited city, in the summer of 2005. We undertook this adventure (our first experience living outside the United States for an extended period of time) when Gabe was 64 years old and Theresa was 54. We stayed until August 2012.

WHETHER GOING OURSELVES with a Voices in the Wilderness delegation to Iraq or sending others off at O'Hare Airport in Chicago, we invited friends and anyone passing by to sing with us. This was a "talking" song, Woody Guthrie style, with words we wrote to remind us of this land's history and its suffering now.

Refrain:
    Going to the Fertile Crescent,
    Cradle of civilization,
    Land between two rivers.
    Going to Mesopotamia.

The law of Hammurabi,
The wheel of the Assyrians,
Irrigation and the Sumerians,
Gardens of the Babylonians. (Refrain)

Architecture and geometry,
Mathematics and libraries,
The vaulted arch and cuneiform,
Gilgamesh and epic poetry. (Refrain)

The land of the prophet Jonah,
And Abraham and Sarah,
Ezekiel and Daniel,
People of the holy book. (Refrain)

House of Wisdom, universities,
Translations and calligraphy,
Three religions live in harmony,
And a shining city named for peace. (Refrain)

Land of depleted uranium,
Congenital malformations,
Children dying of leukemia,
Isolated, no economy. (Refrain)

Water sickness and the stolen air,
Endless sanctions, how they grind and tear.
Mass destruction's what we've got here.
For a dozen years the world's not cared.
(Refrain)

For seven years, Syrians welcomed us in their homes and their capital city. We went there, and they took us in, although they didn't have to; they were for us, in Robert Frost's phrase (in "Death of the Hired Man"), the home that we "somehow haven't to deserve." We left Damascus and its residents in 2012 only reluctantly and with great sadness. We write to honor them and to lament the destruction brought on them.

■ ■ ■

Syria's population went from less than one million to nearly 19 million in a century for reasons that certainly have much to do with fertility and increased longevity but also open arms. *"Ahlan wa-sahlan"* (welcome!) comes naturally to the lips of Syrians. And they have welcomed many people needing a safe haven: Armenians fleeing persecution in eastern Turkey in the early twentieth century, Palestinians ethnically cleansed from Palestine by Zionist militias in 1948, Lebanese fleeing Israeli bombardment in 2006. It seemed to us that Syrians practice the sentiments expressed in Emma Lazarus's text—Syria might not have a golden door, but it was welcoming refugees once more. We grew in respect for Syrians and how their country handled these situations.

The number of Iraqi refugees who crossed into Syria in the first years after the U.S. invasion of Iraq in 2003 is estimated at more than a million. Syria, alone among Iraq's neighbors, demanded little more than stopping to receive residency papers from Syria's government. Iraqi children were admitted without charge to Syrian schools. Eventually Syria's struggling economy and the lack of significant financial help from outside caused limits to be placed on the number of Iraqis allowed to enter and find safety in Syria, but by then one in 15 people in Syria was an Iraqi refugee.

Unlike the Syrians who now take refuge in Jordan, Turkey, or Lebanon, Iraqi and earlier refugees in Syria had some say over their lives. Those Syrians who grumbled about Iraqis driving up rents and prices seemed to us far outnumbered by the Syrians who took it in stride, and expected to share and maybe to see the life of Damascus somehow enriched by the newcomers. Neither dignity nor hope had to be left at the border.

Our Damascus is life on the streets. It is shopkeepers sitting, alone or in pairs or groups, always a steaming pot of tea nearby on some sort of gas or electric device. It is men playing backgammon with or without an audience. It is crowds of children off to school and home from school. It is the sellers of street food on corners or the sounds of them calling out to come see what they have as they go through the lanes on bicycles with carts behind or with a donkey pulling the cart—ears of corn boiling away in a kettle nestled in their cart, or perhaps the amazing banana-on-flat-bread garnished with tahini and chocolate sauce and a variety of other toppings, or that cold mulberry juice. Life on Damascus streets is the processions to the cemetery and the public mourning tent near the home. It is the one-man tea service who comes right to your park bench. It is the sellers of books and posters outside the university and the souqs selling vegetables and fruit just in from the Ghouta or two dozen kinds of olives from the Dead Cities area southwest of Aleppo. It is near-professional skateboarders zooming past on the sidewalk. It is the man selling hot *foul* from a great stove on wheels—beans cooking with olive oil and lemon and sprinkled with sumac. It is the homeless cats (and all of them are homeless) who share their city with us. It is coming around a corner and stopping short because you realize you came round it three minutes ago and how did you get here again? It is, for one long season each year, the sight and full fragrance of jasmine, the city's widely and wildly growing flower. It is the men with their rolling garbage cans who pick up after all of us. And until we left Damascus, it was still possible to walk those streets without any trepidation any hour of day or night.

Mark Twain on First Seeing Damascus in 1867

Soon after arriving in Damascus, we understood why Mark Twain described his first sight of that city from Mount Qassiun:

> As the glare of day mellowed into twilight, we looked down upon a picture which is celebrated all over the world. I think I have read about four hundred times that when Mahomet was a simple camel-driver he reached this point and looked down upon Damascus for the first time, and then made a certain renowned remark. He said man could enter only one paradise; he preferred to go to the one above. So he sat down there and feasted his eyes upon the earthly paradise of Damascus, and then went away without entering its gates. They have erected a tower on the hill to mark the spot where he stood.
>
> Damascus is beautiful from the mountain. It is beautiful even to foreigners accustomed to luxuriant vegetation, and I can easily understand how unspeakably beautiful it must be to eyes that are only used to the God-forsaken barrenness and desolation of Syria. I should think a Syrian would go wild with ecstasy when such a picture bursts upon him for the first time....
>
> Leave the matters written of in the first eleven chapters of the Old Testament out, and no recorded event has occurred in the world but Damascus was in existence to receive the news of it. Go back as far as you will into the vague past, there was always a Damascus. In the writings of every century for more than four thousand years, its name has been mentioned and its praises sung. To Damascus, years are only moments, decades are only flitting trifles of time. She measures time, not by days and months and years, but by the empires she has seen rise, and prosper and crumble to ruin. She is a type of immortality. (*The Innocents Abroad*, ch. xliv)

Mark Twain described the city before him when he came to Damascus in 1867. Less than 15 years later, Louis Charles Emile Lortet, a medical doctor and a scientist from Lyon, France, spent much time in Egypt and Greater Syria to study plants and animals, but he also made sketches and etchings that would be collected and published in Paris in 1884. Twain and Lortet would have been among those from the West whose writing and art could be characterized as what Edward Said would call "Orientalism," a Western, romanticized seeing of the "other" that lives on even now. In the excerpt from *Innocents Abroad*, however, Twain speaks with almost reverence for the city he is seeing for the first time.

In Lortet's etching (page 19), we see the Old City in the distance, but Damascus had been growing beyond the city walls for centuries. We see the Umayyad Mosque with its dome and three minarets; the Citadel, the northwest corner of the walled city, is in the foreground. South of the Old City is al-Midan, where pilgrims from north and east and west came to form caravans for the hajj.

Beyond those many minarets of al-Midan we see the northernmost of the three peaks called in the Hebrew scriptures "Mount Hermon," but usually now called Jabal al-Shaikh—its three peaks snow-covered. On the west side of this mountain and not seen here is the Golan Heights, occupied by Israel since 1967 in defiance of repeated UN resolutions.

The land east of these mountains is called the Hauran. The Romans made it the bread basket of their eastern empire. Now there are vineyards and olive groves and, as the highway approaches the Jordanian border at Dara'a, the dark basalt stone is seen much more than the limestone in older buildings (in Bosra especially). See the Damascus Area map on page 29.

Twain and Lortet were seeing Damascus from the slope of Mount Qassiun. In front of them were the homes, schools, mosques, and tombs, including the tomb of Ibn al-Arabi. So this was also and still is a place of pilgrimage.

Just beyond the white minaret near the left edge of Lortet's work is the Yazid Canal and further down slope we see another square minaret that is near the Tora Canal, the earliest effort (around 3000 BCE) to bring the Barada's springtime waters further east and so surround Damascus with orchards and gardens and grains. The forest Twain and Lortet saw as they stood on the slope of Mount Qassiun would soon give way to a larger population and their homes and markets, mosques and schools, and so much more. In fact, that forest becomes what we see in the Central Damascus map on page 32. Where Lortet made his sketches 140 years ago of the trees west of the Old City, we would now see the Opera, the National Museum, the Tekiyye, and the University of Damascus.

The Souq al-Jouma'a (see the map on page 33) begins by that closer minaret and moves southeast, beyond what we see here, staying level along the slope for more than a kilometer of ancient building and the shops and carts of merchants. All this welcomes those who come to find the olives and pomegranates and greens and potatoes from the Ghouta and beyond. This is today a busy souq but it is also still a place of pilgrimage to these tombs and mosques, and still also a place where students come from many countries to study Islam.

For three years, we lived halfway between those two square minarets in Lortet's etching, a five-minute walk downhill to the one on our right in this image, and five minutes walking up the slope to the closer minaret.

In the 1870s, this engraving looks south from the lower slopes of Mount Qassiun and takes in the nearby tombs and mosques and minarets, many already there for centuries. In the distance is the walled Old City centered on the Umayyad Mosque with its three minarets. Far off to the southwest is the hazy shape of Mount Hermon. View of the city of Damascus, from "La Syrie d'aujourd'hui. Voyages dans la Phenicie, le Liban et la Judee. 1875-1880" of Louis Charles Emile Lortet, 1884 (b/w engraving), French School, (19th century) / Private Collection / © Gerard Degeorge / Bridgeman Images

When Lortet published his work in the 1880s in Paris, this "View of the City of Damascus" filled one page of *La Syrie d'aujourd'hui*, "Syria Today." (In our time in Damascus, an English language monthly had that name.) The "Syria" of Lortet's title was that "Greater Syria," not a nation at all, but rather the whole area made up of present-day Lebanon, Palestine (Israel), Jordan, and Syria. All of them divided into smaller provinces and all of them for 400 years part of the Ottoman Empire, ruled from Istanbul. That empire was gone after World War I, to be replaced by mandates giving England and France a colonial-like power still in place when World War II erupted.

We first saw this image when we attended a benefit in 2011 at al-Safina ("The Ark," but really "L'Arche," a movement founded in France in 1964 by Jean Vanier). The Damascus home of al-Safina is one of nearly 150 such centers in all parts of the world, all of them communities where persons with intellectual disabilities live and work within a network of friends. The residents themselves had made a thick paper and printed on it this image of Damascus as it was 130 years ago. This community continues until now, five years after the violence began in Syria.

Making Reparations to the People of Iraq

Our Arabic study was the great adventure of the first two-plus years in Damascus, but from spring of 2007 until we left in 2012, our Damascus days and nights, weeks and months became the Iraqi Student Project (ISP). We thought in terms of reparations, of the young refugees in Damascus unable to attend college, of Iraq's strong tradition of learning, and of our own talents. We also saw that this project would involve many people in the United States. There would be the admissions people in universities, support groups, people to share their homes with a student. And we would involve first-language English people in Damascus, many of them students of Arabic, as volunteer language partners and teachers. We saw ISP as one small thing we could do with much help from friends in Damascus and in the United States.

We knew that U.S. sanctions, the invasion, and the occupation of Iraq had wreaked havoc on that country's higher educational system. Once considered the finest in the Middle East, Iraq's universities were increasingly unable to function under the sanctions and were collapsing in the aftermath of the U.S. invasion and occupation. Thirteen years of blunt sanctions had cut academia off from the outside world and starved Iraqis even of textbooks and visiting professors. Then the U.S. occupation of Iraq that began in 2003 created a situation in which violence flourished. For a range of motives from sectarian to monetary, university professors were being kidnapped and assassinated. Many academics fled from Iraq. For Iraqi refugees in Syria, higher education in Syrian universities was often unaffordable, and few options were available to them. We thought that if we could facilitate the education of these young adults in U.S. universities, they would not only get a good education but also be able to meet American students as equals. And they could tell their peers about what had been done to their country.

We made a point of working simply and openly, from the daily hours of classes taught in our apartment to the field trips in and out of Damascus, to the endless communication with possible schools and possible support group leaders in the United States. We figured such openness was one way to avoid trouble with the Syrian authorities. And equally important, we never asked for payment and never accepted payment for anything we did. We remained unpaid volunteers living month-by-month on that Social Security check. As a not-for-profit incorporated in the state of New York, ISP in the United States raised money for its quite modest needs (e.g., airfare for the Iraqi students leaving Damascus), but we never sought grants from any office of any government. We kept our Syrian visas current, did our bimonthly residency renewals, and left Syria each summer for up to two months.

> ### Odes to Books
>
> Books, you have fought through the years
> to get to the reader's hands.
> Hundreds of years ago
> when the Mongols occupied Iraq,
> the first thing they did was:
> Throw all the books in Baghdad's library
> into the river.
> The Dijlah turned black from the ink in the books.
> But only a few people felt scared and stopped reading.
> The majority didn't stop.
> They kept writing, reading and learning.
>
> —Fatima
>
> Books, you are talking about my life!
>
> —Humam

From spring 2007 until the day we left Syria in summer 2012, our Iraqi Student Project—against odds we happily did not know at the time—became a way for 60 young Iraqi women and men to prepare for and begin college study in the United States. In 2009, we had a few worrisome months when we knew someone in some Syrian office somewhere was looking into what we were doing. Syria, which always made it to the U.S. annual list of states sponsoring terrorism, had reason to be suspicious of anything that involved U.S. citizens living in Damascus for an extended period. But we believe our openness with ISP brought us through this little crisis.

Telling Our Story

Our story is about Iraqis, about Syrians, about our lives in Syria. From 2007 on, our story is entwined with ISP like those old grapevines in Damascus homes that twist around each other as they grow from patches of unpromising soil between the flat stones of the courtyard up to the balconies where they suddenly become a most lovely source of shade and the finest grapes.

WE WERE GUESTS AMONG A PEOPLE for whom welcoming the stranger as a friend is still amazingly natural.

In summer 2006, when we returned to the United States for a few weeks, we would be asked, over and over, "Are you safe there in Syria?" What did that mean in 2006?

- After the way the United States has been treating Iraq and Afghanistan, are you safe in Syria?
- Are you two U.S. citizens safe there after the United States has never missed a year of putting Syria on its "sponsors of terrorism" list? You like living with sponsors of terror? And they must hate us for telling the truth!
- Are you safe in Syria after so many decades of U.S. vetoes of any meaningful censure of Israel? Are you safe in Syria when, after almost 50 years, Israel hasn't returned the Golan to Syria and the United States protects and supports Israel's occupation of Syrian territory?
- Are you safe in Syria when the Syrians know how the United States has made life difficult for Muslims and Arabs, whether residents in the United States or visitors here? Don't they take that out on U.S. visitors to their country?
- Are you safe there when we read and see on the U.S. media that Syria has had a heavy hand in Lebanon and Fox News says that Syria was involved in the assassination in Beirut of Rafic Hariri, who earlier been Lebanon's prime minister? Besides, Syria is Iran's friend and what must that mean? And Hezbollah? And before all that, in the good old Cold War days, wasn't Syria on the side of the Soviet Union?

After being asked "Aren't you afraid there?" by so many friends and strangers during this summer visit to the United States, we still find it hard to understand that so many Americans had this one question. We could answer, of course, with other questions: "Are you safe here in Omaha or Pocatello or Richmond?"

What we thought each time was: Friend, do you remember sixth grade when you studied the Cradle of Civilization, the Fertile Crescent? You were studying what today is called Iraq and Syria: They are the land between the rivers, Mesopotamia. As a Christian or a Jew or a Muslim, don't you feel some attachment for those deserts and mountains and ancient cities and roads where these three religions—and more! — had their beginnings and still carry on?

Did we feel at home? And were we ready to be critical there as we are here in the United States of the government and media and values in Syria? Yes to both.

All through our seven years in Damascus, we wrote long and leisurely letters, 49 of them in all, sent by e-mail to a growing list of friends. For the first two years, we wrote nearly each month. We were trying to communicate about many aspects of our life in Damascus: delights, puzzlements, anger, adventures, characters, good reading. (Our wish that Americans could come to know Syria and Syrians, as we ourselves were beginning to, led to an invitation to visit that many on our list accepted. This would be called Springtime in Syria, a weeklong tour that we organized for several years.) When we began the Iraqi Student Project, the frequency of our letters dropped, and sometimes even the length. This book began with the project of publishing those letters. But the publisher proposed that we write instead a memoir of the Syria years.

The main divisions of this book are named for the areas where we lived. After living for our first Damascus year (2005–2006) in the Old City, we lived for two years in Yarmouk camp (2006–2008). This large area south of the city had become the place where refugees from Palestine from 1948 and 1967 found a home; by the time we lived there, three generations at least had made it their home. Yarmouk was not the only such camp in the Damascus area, but it was probably the largest. The tents of 1948 had long ago given way to cinderblock buildings, which went higher as the exile got longer.

In 2008, we moved again. That summer concluded the first year of the Iraqi Student Project, and 13 young Iraqis went off with scholarships or tuition waivers to U.S. colleges. But Yarmouk was far from being central to the areas where Iraqi refugees were living—those living in Damascus were not in camps—and

"Never Can I Write of Damascus…"

The title of this book is from a poem by Nizar Qabbani (1923-98), a Syrian poet whose work is much loved. The translation into English of the first six lines was done by Iraqi students who were part of our program. The students had seen an exhibit of the work of Iraqi artist Mutea al-Jumaily. One of these paintings was al-Jumaily's large calligraphy celebrating Qabbani's poem.

The translation of the remaining lines on page 7 and of the verse on the final page of this book is by Larry Tucker. Larry also found that this poem, known by so many Arabic speakers, had circulated not in publication with other work by Qabbani but orally and on the internet in the poet's handwritten text. A Syrian friend told us that the Arabic text "is all over the Internet but nothing explains how we all know it."

Shakir Mustafa, a professor of Arabic at Northeastern University in Boston and a member of the board of Iraqi Student Project, wrote the words of the poem in Arabic for this book.

In the New York Times obituary for Nizar Qabbani, the Syrian poet Youssef Karkoutly is quoted: "His poetry was as necessary to our lives as air."

finding a place for ISP to meet was a challenge. So we moved to an apartment in central Damascus that seemed convenient to our students who would be coming there five or more days a week from many directions using public transportation.

We might have stayed on and on there but by the spring of 2009 some neighbor—we don't know who—was not happy with young Iraqis coming and going to our apartment all day. Rather than cause trouble for the owner, we moved further up these lowest slopes of Mount Qassiun. This new neighborhood was not quite so convenient for our students, but we and most of them came to love this area. This neighborhood is called Jiser Abyad, the White Bridge, but the bridge was long gone. The busy street nearest us was carrying cars and buses past the old French Embassy and then left and ever higher. It became the shopping street of a neighborhood called Muhajireen. Above it the houses climbed the suddenly steeper mountainside. The word "Muhajireen" had to do with the first building up of this area as a settlement place for immigrants.

But, we would tell visitors, before you climb left into Muhajireen, take the street on your right as you walk past the walls of the old French Embassy. That's our street. We don't know its name, and we don't have a house number, but walk past the barbershop, the juice counter, then enter the doors between the men's clothing shop and the electrical shop. We're the front apartment on the third floor. Everyone found us. We lived there three years and from there we reluctantly left Damascus at the end of July 2012.

We bring this together now with sorrow for all that has been destroyed since 2011 and with a sense of urgency that readers educate themselves about what the economic, military, and political power of the United States has wrought for Iraqis and Syrians in their homelands and in their exiles. We write simply to tell you what we learned only after living there, things we did not know even though we have been watching since the 1960s as our country makes footprints in other lands. We write about what we saw and heard, to tell of the surprises, the beauty, the wisdom, the everyday life no one ever mentioned to us.

Join us on our journey! *Ahlan wa-sahlan!*

A short walk west from the Old City is Sahat Merjeh, the square where a growing city centered in the last decades of Ottoman times. Some would say Merjeh still is the city center, at least symbolically. Many government buildings are nearby as are a row of competing pastry shops. Photo by Bachar Azmeh.

Maps

The seven pages following are maps that we hope readers will use again and again. Where are we talking about? We want you to envision the larger space of sea, mountains, rivers, and deserts that is sometimes called the Fertile Crescent or the Cradle of Civilization. Then, within that, find the what-and-where of Damascus as it goes with the terrain created by Mount Qassiun's lower slopes. The line where one becomes conscious that we're climbing now would not be a perfect west/east line, but the west is moving slightly south, the east slowly north. But in reality, the mountain makes one's image of what direction is where. The Damascus terrain is also created by the Barada River and the canals that have watered orchards and fields, and so made Damascus a paradise of dwellings and public space. Then comes the desert.

The maps show but do not emphasize national boundaries, most of them just a century old and imposed from outside.

Each map has been given a title and a north-pointing compass. And each map has a caption to indicate scale (e.g., distance from Damascus to Aleppo in miles and kilometers on the map called "The Desert and the Sown"). If you come to know the maps now, they will be a great help and not only in reading our story.

Two mapmaking artists created these maps in all shades and textures of black and white to convey some feel for the larger areas and then for neighborhoods of Damascus. Their maps are not in competition with all that can be found by means of internet, nor can the internet compete with what Jakob and Victoria have created.

—Gabe Huck and Theresa Kubasak

Making these maps was a strange and remarkable experience. We have never visited the places depicted, and in many ways we never can. The day we received the request was the same day we had read about the razing of Mukhayam Yarmouk.

We did not undertake these illustrations lightly, in part because we were moved by the vision and integrity of the authors. We worked with Gabe and Theresa to try to remain faithful to the spirit of the places depicted, as they experienced them. Mapmaking is a political act, and we saw it as our task to make visible the convictions of the authors, and to highlight histories and relationships that have been obscured. At their best, we hope the maps lend some clarity to the marvelous story Gabe and Theresa have lived.

—Victoria Sobel and Jakob Biernat

Measure of Distance: "m" is miles and "km" is kilometers in distances given in the captions for each map. The distances are "as the crow flies." Arrows at the edges show direction to other points that will appear on a map that covers a larger area.

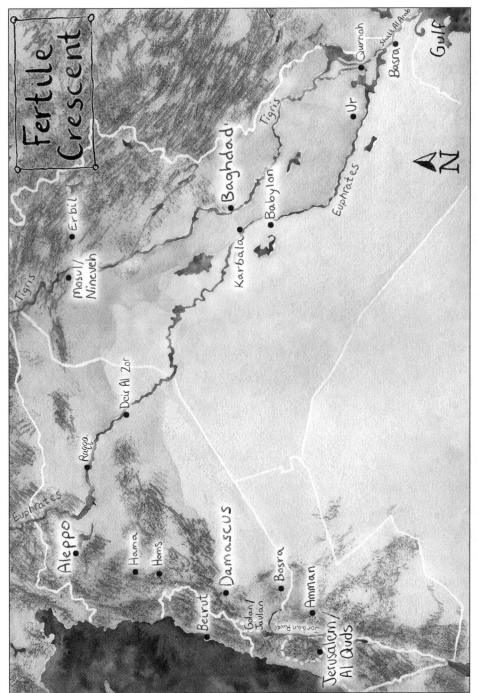

FERTILE CRESCENT. Many of these cities were on the Silk Road from eastern Asia to the Mediterranean, and then beyond either by ship or land. The two great rivers, Tigris and Euphrates, allowed the development of settled life and the empires that came and mostly went. **Distance from Baghdad:** Basra: 278m/447km, Mosul: 356m/414km, Amman: 501m/806k, Damascus: 468m/753k. We made the roundtrip from Amman to Baghdad, traveling in vans, four times during the sanctions against Iraq.

Map by Victoria Sobel and Jakob Biernat.

THE DESERT AND THE SOWN. This is a phrase Gertrude Bell used more than a century ago to introduce to the West what she was learning about the culture, history, and languages of this area. The two nouns, "desert" and "sown," were one way to speak of these areas. Water is crucial, and learning to irrigate and build canals made the Crescent fertile, made Damascus possible. A drought of many years extended through our time in Syria. It gave the edges of "the sown" back to "the desert" and contributed to the anger toward the ruling party when so little was done for those who had lost their livelihood. **Distance from Damascus:** Aleppo: 192m/310km, Beirut and the Mediterranean: 53m/85km, al-Quds/Jerusalem: 134m/216km, Nazareth: 80m/127km.

Map by Victoria Sobel and Jakob Biernat.

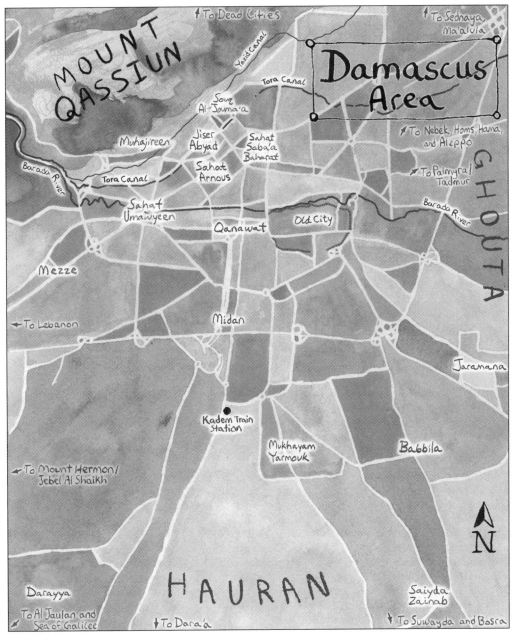

DAMASCUS AREA. The walled Old City is on the southeast edge of the more recent downtown that extends toward Sahat Umawyeen to the west and then on to Mezze or up Mount Qassiun following the Barada River. Along the lowest slopes of Qassiun are areas like Muhajireen and further east the 12th-century Sufi mosques, tombs, and madrasas of the street now called "Souq al-Jouma'a," the Friday Souq. The "Ghouta" is the fertile area of orchards, vines, and vegetables. At the bottom the "Hauran" runs south toward the Jordan border; Mount Hermon/Jabel al-Shaikh is just to the west much of the way. In Roman times, this fertile land was the bread basket of this part of the empire. **Distance:** Jaramana (near Babbila and Mukhayam Yarmouk) to Muhajireen: 2.5m/4km.

Map by Victoria Sobel and Jakob Biernat.

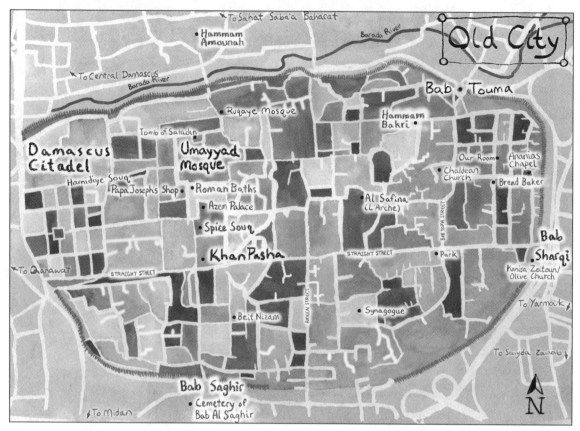

The following labels appear on the map:

To Sahat Saba'a Baharat
Hammam Amounah
Barada River
Old City
Bab · Touma
To Central Damascus
Barada River
· Ruqaye Mosque
Hammam Bakri
Tomb of Saladin
Our Room · Ananias Chapel
Chaldean Church
Damascus Citadel
Umayyad Mosque
· Bread Baker
Hamidiye Souq
Papa Joseph's Shop · · Roman Baths
· Azem Palace
· Al Safina (L'Arche)
BAB TOMA STREET
Bab Sharqi
· Spice Souq
· Park
STRAIGHT STREET
Kanisa Zeitoun/ Olive Church
To Qanawat
Khan Pasha
STRAIGHT STREET
AMEEN STREET
To Yarmouk
· Synagogue
· Beit Nizam
To Saiyda Zainab
N
Bab Saghir
· Cemetery of Bab Al Saghir
To Midan

OLD CITY. Whole books tell of the Old City, but only this map will show where we lived that first year in Damascus. New layers of former buildings are still being found because, unlike Palmyra and many ancient places, for these 4,000 years, as some estimate, Damascus didn't stop being inhabited and the old became the basement of the new, over and over. You will read in this book's introduction (page 11) what Mark Twain wrote in 1867 when he saw Damascus for the first time (page 17). The Umayyad Mosque, a holy place for all Islam, is built on ground that was holy for Christians and for Romans, Greeks, Arameans, and on back. But the Old City is not a museum. Palestinian refugees found homes there in 1948. The building on the cover of this book, Khan Pasha, faces on the spice souq just off Straight Street, and you could walk by a hundred times and never realize such a place was there because spices and sweets line the streets. The poet Nizar Qabbani (whose poetry gave us the name for this book) was buried in the cemetery named for the Bab Saghir ("the little gate") in the south wall of the Old City. **Distance:** The east gate to the Old City, Bab Sharqi, along Straight Street until it ends and one crosses a street to Qanawat: 1m/1.4km.

Map by Victoria Sobel and Jakob Biernat.

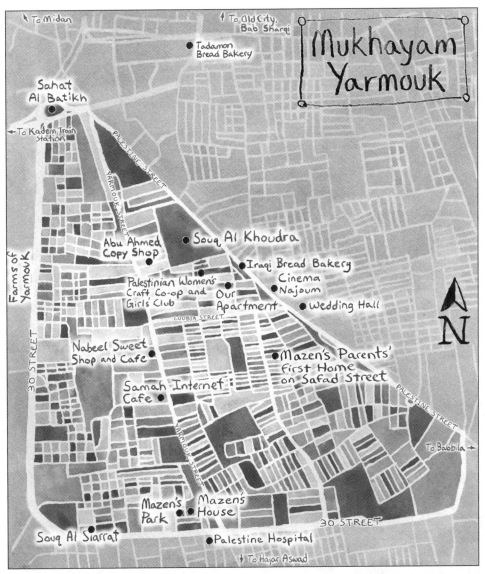

YARMOUK CAMP. This area south of Damascus was not built up until after 1948, when it became one of the largest areas for refugees from Palestine, who lived in camps (the meaning of "mukhayam") and gradually built homes. We lived here two years, including the year we started the Iraqi Student Project. Mazen Rabia, who is interviewed in Chapter 17, was born here. Mazen was our teacher and expert on everything about Damascus. Many of the streets are named after the towns and villages of Palestine, the ancestral homes of those who came here as refugees after the militias of Israel forced the Palestinians to leave. In the current violence between the Syrian military and various militias, no area so close to downtown Damascus has been leveled as has Yarmouk. **Distance:** Sahat al-Batikh (Watermelon Square) along Yarmouk Street south to 30 Street: 1.1m/1.8km. And every inch of it was crowded except for the days of Ramadan when the sun went down and no one was on the street because it was time to break the day-long fast—at home.

Map by Victoria Sobel and Jakob Biernat.

CENTRAL DAMASCUS. We moved to Sahat Arnous neighborhood in summer 2008 so our apartment would be central for the students coming daily from the many directions where Iraqis refugees were living. The next fall we moved further up the slope of Qassiun, and there we stayed the final three years in Damascus. Both locations are on this map, the second one just northeast of the French Embassy. Not as fascinating as the Old City, not as interesting as Yarmouk, but we came to love having Souq al-Jouma'a so close. We loved it not only for being so filled with every good thing, in its season, grown around Damascus, but for the Mosque and Tomb of Ibn al-Arabi and for the many mosques where the call to prayer was chanted at the appointed hours each day. And all the cultural centers were withing an easy walking distance.

Distance measure: Sahat Umawyeen to the National Museum: 0.6m/1 km.

Map by Victoria Sobel and Jakob Biernat.

34

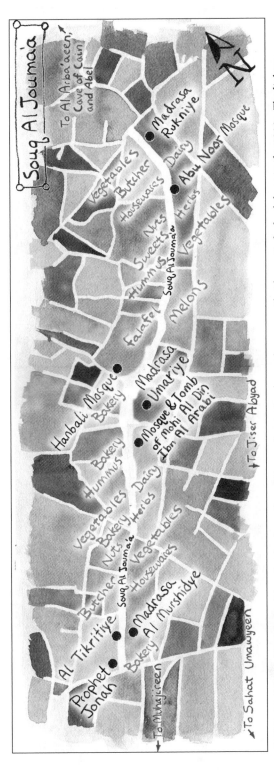

SOUQ AL-JOUMA'A. The darker print locates a few of the madrasas, tombs, and mosques that began to be built here in the 1200s. The lighter words simply list some of what is sold in front of or just inside these buildings. The narrow street is perhaps the busiest and most wonderful souq of Damascus. People climb up from Afeef Street and other areas, or descend along the lanes from their apartments further up the mountain. The souq itself simply stays level on Qassiun's slope. As usual in Damascus markets, it was cash only and merchants were scrupulous when it came to weighing and making change. Few tourists came here. **Distance:** From a tomb on the far west named for the Prophet Jonah to the Madrasa Rukniya: 1m/1.4km—but what a mile! Unless we were there during *iftar* in Ramadan or Fridays before noon prayer, the crowds of grocery shoppers and the tangles when deliveries came in pick-up trucks would make it the mile that lasts and lasts, each step a wonder.

Map by Victoria Sobel and Jakob Biernat.

35

Part 1

The Old City
(2005–2006)

Below this Old City balcony is the park where free public concerts were sponsored by ECHO, a civic organization to promote the arts. Photo by Bachar Azmeh.

1

Learning the City

We arrived in Damascus in August 2005 with two heavy suitcases and no return ticket. We had visited Damascus only briefly in February and had met a few Americans and Syrians, all of whom were welcoming and encouraging. It was affordable and as close to Iraq as we could get. We decided to make it our new home.

That summer, the news in Syria concerned the removal of Syrian military units from Lebanon. Business tycoon and former prime minister of Lebanon Rafic Hariri had been assassinated in Beirut on February 14 of that year. The United States suspected Syria of involvement in Hariri's death and withdrew its ambassador to Syria while insisting that all Syrian military leave Lebanon. They did so, ending a Syrian presence that had begun 30 years earlier and was supported then by the Arab League. The U.S. effort to pin Hariri's death somehow on the Syrian government went on through all the years we lived in Syria. We saw the reaction of Syrians whenever it came up: What sort of investigation has there been when the CIA plots an assassination? The United States did not send another ambassador to Syria until six years later.

Also that summer, thousands of Syrians were protesting what the U.S. invasion and occupation had done to Iraq and its people. This was solidarity with the Iraqi people, not at all a protest against Iraqi refugees who found safety in Syria. During our first few weeks, we learned of Syrians' concern for the drought that had already forced many families to give up their farms "between the desert and the sown" because years of drought were enlarging the desert. This too would continue through the years we lived in Syria. (The failure of the government to assist farmers and the small cities like Dara'a where they were moving was often seen as one factor that triggered the nonviolent protests that began in March 2011.)

During our first week in Damascus, we stayed in the guesthouse of a convent that was a 10-minute walk from the Eastern Gate of the Old City. This convent is one of several locations claiming to be the very place where Saul (Paul in the New Testament) was knocked to the ground, blind; according to the biblical story, a Christian named Ananias laid hands on him "[a]nd immediately something like scales fell from his eyes and his sight was restored." This healing happened, as the scripture says, "on the street called Straight," the Roman east-west "Via Recta" that remains the only really straight street in the Old City.

Then we moved to an apartment (also temporary: a six-week housesitting arrangement) in a neighborhood crawling, sometimes steeply, up the lower slopes of Mount Qassiun. This part of Damascus is called Muhajireen ("immigrants") because it had been developed around the turn of the twentieth century when Muslims from the island of Crete were fleeing Greek control of their homeland, until then part of the Ottoman Empire.

Beit ʿArabee on the Roof

Two months after we arrived in Damascus, we were looking for a place to live in the Bab Touma ("Thomas Gate") area of the Old City. For centuries this has been called the Christian Quarter, though Christians live in many other areas and many non-Christians live in the Bab Touma neighborhood, an area that spreads out within the Old City's walls in both directions from two of the Old City gates, Bab Touma and Bab Sharqi, and includes the eastern portion of Straight Street and all of Bab Touma Street.

In seeking a place to live, we had help from friends. Eldon and Jane were the representatives in Syria of the Mennonite Central Committee, a nonproselytizing and respectful presence that supports local people who are serving their

For almost 3,000 years, successive peoples came to Damascus from all possible directions, and some always stayed on. Who would leave Damascus, with its rivers and canals, its wet winters and cloudless summers and autumns, its mountains to the west and deserts to the east, its fertile soil for growing everything from watermelon to figs and dates, grapes and apricots, sweet Melissa and perfumed jasmine? Goats and sheep could grow fat on the grassy hillsides and find surprising places to graze even in the deserts. For building homes, Damascenes had limestone to the north and basalt to the south, and those cedars of Lebanon just over the mountain. The trade route from the east eventually brought silk; from the south, through pathways along the mountains called Mount Hermon in the Hebrew scriptures and Jabal al-Shaikh today, came the goods being traded by the Egyptians and other peoples of North Africa, by the peoples of Yemen and Ethiopia. And by sea through the Mediterranean ports came trade with Cyprus, Crete, Sardinia, and Sicily, and eventually from Iberia and beyond.

Damascus has a wall and a citadel, but its strength has always been assimilation with or without conversion. Damascus took Greeks and Romans in stride; the vegetable and craft markets must have helped. Centuries later, the city benefited from those mountains that run parallel to the Mediterranean coast; the Crusaders from Europe mostly kept between the sea and the mountains as they spread terror from Constantinople (Istanbul) to Jerusalem in the eleventh century. Their defeat came through the leadership of Saladin (Salih al-Din), whose tomb is near the north wall of the Umayyad Mosque.

From Daughter of Damascus

[T]he old Damascene homes...perhaps more than any other material aspect, reflect the deep-seated values of home and family in Syrian society. Because so much time was spent inside those inner walls, care was taken in the past to make them as much like worldly paradises as possible.... The entire household complex was organized to entice family members into congenial meeting spaces. In winter, people sat in rooms on the upper story that projected above the rest of the house and like a solarium, attracted the sunlight's warmth. In summer, the sitting area was an alcove in the sweet-scented courtyards, open to the sun and air, where the splashing fountains and the foliage of flowers and trees provided a cool and soothing place to relax from the heat and the dust of the outside street.

—From the Introduction to *Daughter of Damascus* by Siham Tergeman, pages xvi–xvii

own communities. Eldon and Jane and their two children, Mary and Tony, had lived in the Bab Touma quarter of the Old City for years by the time we arrived in Damascus. The four of them are fluent in Arabic, English, and French, and could switch easily from one language to another to talk with whoever was a guest at the family table that day.

Eldon assisted us in finding a room on the second level of a *beit 'Arabee*, about a three-minute walk from Bab Touma to the north or a three-minute walk to Straight Street to the south.

A *beit 'Arabee* ("Arab house") refers to a home whose rooms on the ground floor back up against outer walls that form a rectangle and open unto a courtyard. On the level above, the rooms open to a balcony overlooking and surrounding the courtyard. Such homes dominate the Old City and the oldest neighborhoods just outside the north wall of the Old City. Beyond the Old City, one is more likely to find multifamily apartments with small stores on the ground floor facing the commercial streets.

The courtyard is the heart of this type of house. It will usually have a fountain in the center with plants and fruit trees anywhere in the courtyard, and often there are vines that climb to bring grapes and flowers, especially jasmine, onto the level high above. The walls of the Arab house are made of mud and organic material like straw. In some of the homes, every inch of ceiling, walls, floors, and built-in furniture and shelves and cabinets, is the work of craftspeople with myriad skills, including mosaic work in wood or in stone. Present inhabitants may or may not have been able to preserve that work. We saw this style at its best in places open to the public, no longer homes to families but small museums or, more commonly, restaurants where much of the beauty had been restored or replaced. Some "boutique" hotels began to appear as families gave up and sold their *beit 'Arabee* homes to developers who correctly gauged the value and charm of such homes but not the turmoil that would erupt in March 2011.

On the ground level are the parlors, workrooms, kitchen, and the *liwan*, a three-sided room open to the courtyard, usually on the south side so that it never feels the summer sun. The second level has bedrooms that stay warmer in the colder, damp months.

In the Old City, these homes are often hundreds of years old. A narrow lane for pedestrians and carts separates facing rows of houses. Here the calls of street sellers reverberate up and down the lanes, giving the families inside notice that they can come to the door and purchase onions, salad greens, and other vegetables and fruit. A second-story window may open and a basket come down on a rope while amount and price are negotiated between the seller and the resident. These lanes that separate one unbroken row of houses from another are often just wide enough for one small car to pass one pedestrian pressed to the wall, and sometimes just too narrow for any car. The high walls of the homes keep the lanes shaded most of the time, and in some places, old grapevines offer all a green umbrella in the hottest months. The high walls of the homes and the lack of windows at the ground level assure that nothing of the interior is seen or even suggested from outside.

The house's outside wall usually has a single door for entering a home from the lane, and only the door itself might indicate whether this particular house is still kept intact and beautiful in every detail, or if the present generation living there (and perhaps a generation or two before them) could not afford the time for repair of the door or anything else. This sole entrance to the family's space—entirely unseen until one is inside—often stands open during the day. When locked, one looks for some way to ring a bell. Someone inside may release the lock by pulling a rope from some corner of the second level. It was always fascinating to walk slowly and peep into any open doorway. A fragrant fountain, a courtyard with many turtles, or a parakeet in a cage suspended from a lemon tree might be our reward. Or we might see a crowded courtyard with a washer and dryer, old bicycles, and storage boxes covered in plastic.

In Bab Touma, a few of the old homes have been turned into restaurants or small hotels, but many more have for a long time been reshaped a bit to allow small shops to open to the lane or street—wedding gowns made here, sweets prepared and sold there, a tiny grocery store at the corner next to an internet café. A house would stay in the family, it seemed, for many generations, but only some members might live in it (taking up the craft, art, or trade of the past generations) while others moved elsewhere—to apartments elsewhere in the city or to the Gulf countries to find work.

We rented our room on the roof from Umm Karam, who lived with her family on the ground level and handled everything related to the tenants. Her husband, Abu Karam, worked outside the Old City. Umm Karam's daughter was in college and sang in the church choir. Karam was in high school. The grandmother lived with them, a common living arrangement among the families we knew.

We soon learned that referring to adults as "Abu" (father of) or "Umm" (mother of), followed most often by the name of the oldest son, was the common way of speaking of or to parents no matter how old or how many their children. In fact, our friend Eldon was called "Abu Tony" by everyone. We wondered if the given names faded gradually from memory once one became a parent.

Umm Karam rented out two rooms on the second level; a third room was a shared kitchen with bathroom attached. Most rented rooms in Damascus were furnished, sometimes overly furnished. Our stand-alone room was a drafty adobe square. We put the bed diagonally in the east corner with our homework table touching the foot of the bed. The few clothes we had brought with us were kept in a metal cupboard that clanged shut near one of the windows. The room also had an "L"-shaped arrangement of two sofas that we covered with textiles we found in a souq. When winter came, the linoleum flooring became so cold we bought our first Middle Eastern rug; it was large enough to cover the whole floor. In the summer we noticed what Umm Karam did with her carpets and did the same: We took it outside, hosed it down, scrubbed it, dried it, rolled it up, and put it away until the next winter.

From our room on the second level, we could step out to the balcony and look down through the large open space to see the courtyard where Umm Karam and her mother would usually be sitting and plucking parsley leaves for tabouli for the family supper. For many months of fall and then again when summer approached, the vines that climbed up to our level became jasmine, so fragrant especially in the summer evenings. Overhead we could see the circling flocks of doves. Most of them lived on other rooftops where their keepers would wave bright flags to bring them home.

We lived in one upstairs room, and Viktor, a graduate student from Budapest who had come to study Arabic, lived in the other. We found so much to admire in him and other 20-something-year-old students coming from various parts of the world to study Arabic in Damascus. In the internet café, we heard them in their home languages talking to their families. (Home wi-fi was a few years off then.) We heard, or imagined we heard, voice changes when they spoke to the young siblings, to the parents, to the grandparents, whatever the language.

Our shared kitchen was a bit like some summer cabins we'd visited in the United States: a rag-tag assortment of hand-me-down pots and pans, unmatched plates and cups, random tableware. The stove used *mazote* that came in heavy tanks and was sold, except when the supply would suddenly run low,

The window of our room on the roof looks down into the courtyard and the trees grow-
ing below. Jasmine rises up to us curling over our clothesline. Across the tiles from the
clothesline is a small kitchen we shared with Viktor, the Hungarian student who took
many of the photos in this book. Photo by Viktor Hegyi.

from trucks or shops all over the city. Trucks brought refilled containers and
took back empties to be filled again. People found many and amazing ways to
bring the heavy canisters (empty or full made little difference) back and forth
and up and down stairs.

In this kitchen, we learned to make staples of Damascene cuisine like hummus and stuffed grapeleaves and chopped salad with pomegranate dressing
(*fattoush*). Down a short lane was the neighborhood bakery, from which we
bought our daily (government subsidized) bread. We learned to join the crowd
that clustered in the street around the counter window. We could watch as large
batches of dough were mixed and then shaped into balls by hand; then flat circles of dough were put on a conveyer belt that took them into a fiery oven and
then out again—a fragrant circle with the thickness of tortillas to be air-dried
and then stacked and carried home.

In the Old City, we lived without the sounds of the too many motor vehicles
that snarled the streets of Damascus. We had other sounds:

- Cats on the roofs (cats rule Damascus).
- Street sellers calling out their wares, from propane to toilet paper.
- Church bells—real ones!
- Calls to prayer from the mosques, again coming from many sides, sometimes a wonderful confusion of sound with the various ways the chant is done.
- Children at school (a call/response was much in use here in the classroom as we heard whenever walking by schools) and out of school, playing in these narrow streets.
- Weddings and women ululating (whether the wedding was Muslim or Christian).

We felt blessed to live in a place where church bells are real and sounded often. The first one rang about 30 times at 6:30 a.m., and on Sundays, sounds of bells came from all directions. Later we would be far from the nearest church bells, but we came to love the call to prayer, as it marked the coming, the passage, and the end of each day.

To be honest, we must add to our list the not-so-lovely sounds: the amplified sound of the preacher's never-tiring voice from the evangelical Christian church across the street, the boom-boom-boom music the teenagers downstairs played now and then, the amplified sound of recorded bells playing Ave Maria from some church that had no real bells.

But we had another kind of music to our ears from our first day in Damascus: the way Arabic is spoken there. It has music! It is music! It has ways of lifting up tones within and at the end of sentences, patterns that vary from person to person but are a real part of the street music.

THE IMAGES OF PRESIDENT BASHAR AL-ASSAD, of Bashar and his father, of Bashar and his deceased brother, of Bashar along with both father and brother, were simply part of the streets, shops, and vehicles of Damascus. Somewhat more rare were father and brother without Bashar, dating back before Bashar's brother, then the presumed heir, crashed his car and was killed in front of the Damascus airport very early one morning. Bashar was then summoned home from studies in England, and six years later Hafiz died and Bashar was elected to replace him.

This display of leader images wasn't new to us when we came to Syria. On four trips to Iraq between 1999 and the U.S. invasion in 2003, we saw Saddam's image everywhere. But that image wasn't so dull. It takes nothing away from Saddam Hussein's crimes to admit that the man must have understood that if people would be seeing his image hundreds of times each day, he should give them some variety.

In the Iraq we visited before 2003, Saddam's image was everywhere: stamps, statues, money, billboards, pictures in stores, pictures in offices and in cars and in homes. So in Syria we were not surprised to see Assad's image. What was different about Iraq? It was as if some PR firm from the United States had charge of those billboards and posters and pictures and sculptures. They tried not to bore people. They tried to create the image of a many-sided guy you'd really like. Here was Saddam the hunter with his spiffy hat and jacket, and there a pious Saddam kneeling on his prayer rug. There was Saddam the farmer holding a cornucopia of fruit, Saddam the shopper, Saddam the solemn statesman, Saddam the rugged soldier, Saddam the friend of children as he shares a children's book with young friends, Saddam the builder, Saddam the novelist.

He had a thousand outfits, a dozen different haircuts, and hundreds of facial expressions. Perhaps it takes a sense of humor and even a certain lack of ego, a certain humility even, to pose your aging self in all those outfits and look all those silly ways. He clearly didn't have to do it, but he must have been strangely willing to play the fool, to be the clown of the nation he ruled. Also, as our Arabic teacher remarked, as happens here with Assad, when you use the same picture of yourself everyplace and all the time, you disappear.

We do not know whether Saddam ever appeared in public, but the Syrian president was often out and about, perhaps attending a concert with his wife or taking their three young children for a stroll. We saw the president once at the small drama theater at the Opera House where a satirical play had just opened that week to good reviews. The night we went, more people arrived than tickets and seats available. Only one of us was able to be seated, the other was left outdoors. Yet there were four empty seats just a few rows down. As the play was about to begin, the president and his wife entered the theater accompanied by two men in suits. People applauded, Assad turned and waved, and then the couple and their companions claimed those four last seats. Later some in the audience expressed surprise that the first couple wanted to see political satire that evening. We wondered why he didn't have a poster later of husband and wife at the theater together.

When we arrived in Damascus, many seemed still hopeful that the changes in Bashar's first years as president (internet access and satellite reception, a little more room for political parties) would continue. That did not continue. What seemed to be happening, to our outsider eyes, was less and less of the Ba'athist ideal of a socialist state. Now the wealth of the wealthy and the number of the newly wealthy were on the increase. We felt those left behind were often more upset about the loss of a shared ideal than about not being part of the wealthy group. If people were disappointed with Bashar before March 2011, they had hope for a few weeks because somehow, whether Bashar ordered it or not, the more hated insiders, hated for their greed and power, resigned from their places of power. One even spoke of doing penance.

From Syria: A Historical and Architectural Guide

Warwick Ball (in *Syria: A Historical and Architectural Guide*) calls a stroll on Straight Street "walking through history" and "the legendary centre of one of the greatest caravan cities of Asia."

He suggests taking any lane and following it to the next lane:

> Plunge straight into them, and simply wander around exploring them at leisure. One will almost certainly get lost, but that is part of the pleasure—one is in any case never far from a landmark, and a passer-by is always happy to help regain one's bearings. These streets are the most picturesque of Damascus: narrow, winding lanes with houses that jut out at haphazard angles, occasionally even meeting overhead so that one finds oneself walking through a tunnel. Most are away from the bustle of the bazaars and are furthermore usually too narrow for heavy traffic so it is blissfully quiet, even serene: occasional sleepy little neighborhood shops selling household necessities, frequent tea and coffee shops where it is possible to rest worn feet, glimpses of courtyards and shady interiors that have not changed for a thousand years, quiet streets adorned with vines.... (pages 78–79)

Straight Street and Other Walks

We took daily walks to orient ourselves to our new hometown. We sometimes walked on streets that took us straight up the mountain; where the builders of streets and homes could go no further, we turned around and had a panoramic view of the city whose geography we were trying to learn. If we walked down this final slope of Mount Qassiun into the Muhajireen neighborhood, we would soon be passing men wearing suits who were simply standing around keeping an eye out for something. Some of them carried weapons openly. We were told they were not so subtly guarding the embassies in this neighborhood as well as the quite modest family home where the president of Syria, Bashar al-Assad, grew up.

We were impressed that the first family still lived in the house where Bashar grew up and not in the new Presidential Palace on a high plateau looking down on the city. While the modest living quarters of the Assad family impressed us, the omnipresent images of a smiling Bashar all over Damascus did not. Often side-by-side with his father on these posters, bumper stickers, and billboards, Assad's face, either smiling or trying to look serious and in charge, seemed to be everywhere and unavoidable in Damascus. Did many shop owners and car owners display the president's face as part of the way things are done? Were those who chose not to making a statement?

In the Old City of Damascus, one walks on layers upon layers—perhaps 4,000 years—of buildings built and later leveled, then new building using whatever fragments of the previous generation might be helpful. What could not be used in the next era stayed as the new ground level.

One year, we watched week-by-week as Straight Street was closed to vehicle traffic and workers dug down to lay a new underground labyrinth of water pipes, electric cables, and sewers. As this continued, more and more pieces of Straight Street dating to Roman times were brought to the surface; many such

Children in the Old City streets who saw us approaching almost always called out in school-room English, "Welcome to Syria!" Photo by Robert Rosser.

pieces of columns and walls and paving stones eventually were placed in tiny park-like spaces between the vehicles and the pedestrians along Straight Street.

Straight Street joins Bab Sharqi on the east to (almost) Bab al-Jabiya, a mile away. In Roman times, Straight Street wasn't simply a wide paved street for vehicles, but on either side the pedestrian walkways were covered and colonnaded to provide shade from the fierce sun, shelter from winter rains, and safety from the passing vehicles. This sense of building places of beauty and dignity not just for the wealthy but for all is seen in the Roman forums, baths, marketplaces, temples, theaters, and stadiums. Bosra, near Syria's border with Jordan, retains elements of all of these public areas.

At the intersection of Straight Street and Bab Touma Street, we came across a strange little park with many air vents going into the ground. Because of their shapes, we called this "the mushroom park." We discovered eventually that the park had been built over a bomb shelter. ("Who was bombing?" "Probably the French," we were told.) While we lived in Damascus, this large underground place became an art gallery occasionally open to the public. The park itself was much used for sitting and talking by teenagers and the elderly. And us! Across the street from this park, we could buy hot chocolate during the winter, then sit in the park to enjoy it.

A few steps further was a tiny, wonderful shop owned by a pharmacist and his wife. They told us how they waited for his retirement so they could open this room filled with his woodworking creations: frames of various woods and sizes with delicate carving; game boards or whole tables for chess or backgammon; cabinets with many small drawers; and holders or "chairs" for the Qur'an, the traditional hinging together of two elaborately carved boards so that, when opened, an "x" is formed on which the holy book can rest open. Often his pieces had inlaid shells, calligraphy carved into the wood, and combinations of various woods.

Next door, an open zucchini and eggplant stall lured passersby. This wonderful juxtaposition of food and art was echoed often as we walked west on Straight Street: Just past an open vegetable stall and a fish market were two woodworkers making fine implements for the kitchen. And there was a multitude of tiny jewelry places, usually with all the necklaces and earrings and rings in the window, and inside, one or two people making more pieces in silver and gold.

Further west on Straight Street was an outside display of fabric to delight the eye, even in this place where such delights were scattered all over. A clothesline of sorts was suspended across a 30-foot wall and on it were draped colorful quilts, some made of Bedouin dress scraps, some featuring velvets like the dresses women wore in Bosra, others with Palestinian embroidery, or patches of shimmery silks or elaborate brocades.

The Barada River and its canals flow beneath and through the city, trying to make the orchards that remain to the east of Damascus the verdant oasis it once was.
Photo by Bachar Azmeh.

Various crafts are still a pride of Damascus, and some of these workshops are located in the Old City. One can visit while mosaic pieces of various woods are created and become parts of tables and chairs or the mosaic boxes and chess tables, or while wood and metal kitchen tools are formed. The shops of the Old City are not without their "Made in China" products and those who work in crafts often see their children make other choices. The Silk Road is different now.

One can watch artists hammer and engrave copper or brass, forming beautiful trays. The finished products are then perched on wooden puzzle-like legs that unfolded like the wings of an origami crane. On one occasion, we watched an artisan engrave a particularly intricate pattern; we returned the next week to purchase it as a wedding gift. Damascene homes often have these handy, instant tables, and when not in use, the tray can be displayed on the wall.

Damascenes are skilled merchants, but they do it without the glitz, the slogans, the brands, the ever-changing stock, and the specials so characteristic of American malls. To keep a shop here, and in much of Damascus, is often the work of one person and often that person's lifelong work. The merchant knows the stock: Among hundreds of rugs, each one is known.

My River and Your River

Baghdadis would likely insist that *river* be written with quotation marks when it is preceded by "Barada"—thus, the Barada "River." Loving the Tigris (the *Dijlah* in Arabic), flowing widely through their beloved Baghdad, the Barada seemed what we would call a "creek" or a "stream." But modest though it is and nearly dry for months each year, the Barada and the canals that were dug long ago disperse the river's waters, especially when the snow in the mountains is melting, over a wide area of watered gardens, orchards, and fields. The first of them, the Tora Canal, still bears an Aramaean name. More than 30 centuries ago, when Damascus was the capital of the Aramaean empire, people put in the engineering work and the hard labor that allowed the spring floods of the Barada to irrigate a large area rather than make a temporary summer marsh of a much smaller area. Other canals would follow. Without the Barada and other such tiny rivers and their canals, there would be no Damascus, no oasis, no paradise. This fertile land east and south of Damascus, watered by these streams, has long been called the Ghouta, the paradise of green forests and fruit trees that caused Mohammed, as Twain retells the old legend, not to enter the paradise of Damascus.

The Hebrew Bible (2 Kings 5:1–27) tells a fine story about a certain Naaman, a high officer in the Aramaean army. This Naaman is suffering from what might have been leprosy. A young servant girl tells Naaman's wife that Naaman should seek "the prophet who is in Samaria" and request a cure. Naaman, with the blessing of the king of Aram and a letter of introduction to the king of Israel, travels south from Damascus to Samaria, less than 100 miles. The king of Israel, terrified of the power of the northern neighbor, thinks this must be some scheme to find an excuse for war. But word of Naaman's request reaches Elisha the prophet, who sends a message that he will deal with Naaman. So the whole entourage then seeks out the house of Elisha. Elisha sends another message from inside his house: If you wash seven times in the Jordan River "your flesh shall be restored and you shall be clean."

Naaman is furious: "I thought that for me this prophet would surely come out, and stand and call on the name of the Lord his God, and would wave his hand over the spot, and cure the leprosy! Are not the Abana [the very same river as today's Barada] and the Pharpar [perhaps another Damascus stream today called the Banias], the rivers of Damascus, better than all the waters of Israel? Could I not wash in them and be clean?" But Naaman's servants convince him not to turn back to Damascus but at least to give the lowly Jordan River a try. One can almost hear Naaman grumbling, "Oh all right." Of course, Naaman emerges from the Jordan cured. Repentant and grateful, he returns to Damascus.

On many Saturday mornings, our walks took us past the only synagogue still open in the Jewish Quarter. We learned that the majority of Jews emigrated when the government permitted them to do so in the early 1990s; most of them went to the United States, and perhaps as few as 50 remained in Damascus. We walked through the Jewish Quarter often and saw how so many of the old Arab-style homes, empty for two decades or more, are gradually going to pieces. Some of the larger homes were being "developed" as boutique hotels. As Arabic texts from the Qur'an can be found in the tiles or stone of the entrances to many homes in the Old City, so here in the Jewish Quarter we saw Hebrew texts.

We would walk east to west on Straight Street and come to a single remnant of the Roman arches that once honored all who bought, sold, or strolled on Straight Street. After the Roman arch, we would soon be in the area where the street is covered, not by Roman arches of stone but by a barrel vault of tin that is dotted with holes. This was the result of the French again, we were told, putting down one more rebellion in the 25 years they held the "mandate" over Syria from the League of Nations.

Continuing west under this ceiling several stories above, we might or might not resist turning right on the street that leads past the spices and sweets and then the gold souqs to the Umayyad Mosque. Before the covered portion of Straight Street ends, we passed the entrance to other specialty areas like the cotton souq. And down one lane were scores of shops selling perfumes, made to order for those who know what they want. One could judge the quality of their creations by the length of the line waiting to purchase favorite scents.

Ordinarily, whenever we happened onto Straight Street at 11 a.m. or later, the street itself was busy, but it would still be a good walk and more so when, as sometimes happened, parts of it were closed to motor traffic. Automobiles, especially taxis, used Straight Street to avoid the much longer journey around the circumference of the Old City, but for us pedestrians, they didn't belong.

The lanes leading off from Straight Street were often too narrow for traffic, twisting so we would always lose a sense of direction but not a sense of wonder: How did this visual and aural excitement degenerate into modern shopping malls scattered through the world's cities, each with its acres of parking? We looked at many beautiful things in fabric and wood, and we loved just being there where the merchants didn't pressure us even when tourists were few or nonexistent in 2011 and 2012. But it wasn't tourists, at least not tourists from outside the Middle East, who kept Straight Street so busy year-round. Damascenes knew where the items they needed were sold and knew the merchants they wanted to deal with. Children and teens whose schools were nearby in the Old City crossed or walked along Straight Street in chattering groups, sometimes sharing something to eat from a street seller or one of the many tiny grocery stores hidden on the lanes going north or south. Labyrinthian ways indeed can delight year after year, and sometimes the grape or other vines grow above from one building to the next. Sometimes a *sabeel* with water for the public, or a line of people waiting to buy bread, or a shrine in the Christian Quarter is just enough to frighten motor vehicles away.

Some shops were barely as big as a closet, just a nook between two larger stores. On others, the front and entrance could be deceiving: A few beautiful rugs might be hung outside, but the inside may open up to stacks and stacks of rugs, some new and some very old, woven in Syria or nearby. Usually the merchant knew those high stacks well. Deliveries are always being made to the shops, and teenage boys have carts for the serious shopper to hire until purchases are safely conveyed home.

Straight Street ends not at the old gate on the west side of the walled city but where the western walls would be, except most of the western border is no longer marked by that wall. Some of it is probably a few meters under the present street level, and some of it—like much of the building stones of the Old City century to century—was recycled to build something new. We knew we had left the Old City behind us when we intersected with at least five lanes of southbound vehicles on Revolution Street.

On the west side of that street are a large mosque, a school, and a *hammam* (public bath) built in the sixteenth century when the Damascus population was approaching 100,000. Behind them is Qanawat (Canal) Street; the street makes a slow curve northwest, following the path of a Roman aqueduct that brought water from the Barada River into the southern part of the Old City. It consisted of clusters of mini-souqs: Several adjacent shops sold sewing machines, for example, followed by several that sold chandeliers, soaps, rugs, spices, perfumes. Some sold secondhand clothing, and the items were stacked and displayed on parked vehicles. There was no "cell phone souq," but such newcomers are sprinkled among the shops.

Qanawat Street, where pedestrians seem in control, ends with another busy, broad street to cross, a street rapidly becoming a southbound highway to the town of Dara'a and the border with Jordan about 70 miles away. Most of these many-laned streets were laid out during the French Mandate between 1920 and 1946.

Another city block east and we are on a bridge above what used to be a busy passenger railroad yard. The tracks are gone but the lovely old station stands far to the north. It can be entered from its north side and houses a bookstore and, happily, a counter where one can sometimes buy train tickets to Aleppo. The train boards from the current station a few miles south. We were told that there had been plans some years before to build a shopping mall where the tracks used to be. The station is called Hijaz because it was built for trains going south to the holy cities of Medina and Mecca, 900 mostly desert miles away. By the time this station was built in the early twentieth century, the hajj pilgrims from east and west and north had long gathered in Damascus to form caravans for safety in travel. Trains replaced camels long before the Hijaz station brought the point of departure into downtown Damascus—but it would not be long before trains gave way to planes and buses.

We were then briefly near an area of small bookstores and on to a busy east-west street with the large, open-air bus station called Baramkey (later the bus station was moved far to the west of central Damascus), and to the north small stores of sweets, bakeries, falafel, and shawarma, the fast foods of Damascus. This street then crossed a busy north-south street. In the northwest corner of this intersection is the University of Damascus, the older campus, stretching east and west and including the faculties of science, engineering, education, music, and fine arts. A newer, second campus was a few miles west in Mezza.

Staying Legal

Why did we know and love this walk? In part because we often used Sunday, when we would be in the Old City for the liturgy in the morning, to make our bi-monthly visit to the government building where foreign visitors were to renew their residency. That building was close to Damascus University and, during a seven-year period, we were required to apply every two months for an extension of our residency in Syria. By describing the process, we hope we do not sound impatient with Syria. We are well aware that Syrian nationals who come to the United States for a visit or temporary residency would not undergo as smooth a process as we did as foreigners in Syria.

The immigration office was a four-story building of counters, offices, and stairways. Whenever we went, we would find a line of foreigners like us. The counter for extending residency was on the third floor. A counter ran along three sides of the room, chest height. As usual (whether here or when boarding a bus or coming to a theater or buying bread at the bakery window), lining up and waiting for one's turn was rare. The men (always) on the other side of the counter dealt with stacks of paper. The tools were paper clips, staplers, rubber stamps, and pens. Some of them had amazing skills for coping with the people demanding attention across the counter, dealing with the languages, especially because so many seeking one or two more months of residency had come here to study Arabic but weren't ready for conversation. Like us.

The line for residency permits for non-Arabs was short, but the window labeled for Iraqis often had a large crowd of people, not a line but a large knot of folks with documents in their hands and a sense of urgency. There were not enough clerks to serve them and we could feel their frustration. Most of the folks there had already followed a long path with many such waits and requirements. Many had been given refuge in Syria with hardly a question asked when they crossed the Iraq–Syria border. Now all were in the midst of discovering what they and their children could do in this country.

At the counter for non-Arabs, the first step was showing our passports, then, for less than a dollar, we were given two one-page forms, in Arabic and French (even though the French occupation had ended 59 years before we arrived). Trial and error taught us we were to fill in the required information: father's name, mother's name, their birthplaces, the purpose of our visit to Syria, where we were staying, passport number and expiration date. A photo was necessary and one of the two pages needed a certain stamp. The stamp could be purchased at a nearby store where copies could also be made. So we filled out the forms, then went down to the main floor, out the door, and to our right, every second store was there to sell these stamps or to take the pictures or to copy the forms. When it seemed all was ready, it was back to the same person at the same counter on the third floor, and another effort to reach the front position no later than anyone who arrived after us. But people were patient on both sides of the counter.

The papers and passport were handed back to us with instructions to "see the general" upstairs. Often the general had a friend or two having tea with him, or he might be on the phone, but still would continue to scan whatever papers were placed in front of him. Only occasionally over the years were we asked how it was that we still were "tourists" when we'd been in Syria several years. We answered that Syria had so much to see and we had yet to visit Palmyra. We regret that we never did visit Palmyra.

We were sent back to the counter and the one fixed piece in the routine. After making sure the general had signed the form, the clerk at the counter sent us to a side room that held paper records, probably of our previous visits. Once we were found in the books, the clerk signed our forms again and waved us on to the computer man whose large, old computer always found us. One clerk then initialed our forms, and another would remove some of the papers, give the rest back to us, and then send us back to the general, who just initialed the form without looking at it. Then we'd return to the first person in this chain, who either finished the process or gave us a receipt of sorts—a number scribbled on a scrap of paper—and told us to come back the next day for our passports.

Paper stacked up. On one of the first year's visits we saw, first from inside then from the street below, that the little balconies outside these third-floor rooms were the long-term storage places for all that paper. We saw fat manila folders stacked six feet high, one stack leaning on another. Not the most elegant system, but on the other hand, no one could hack into these files.

This might sound like something out of Kafka, but in fact it wasn't. It didn't take all that long once you learned the routine. We were soon recognized by many of these employees, and we were always treated politely, though these men had hard, long, boring jobs. They did this in crowded rooms with no air conditioning and rarely any fans. We understood why they sometimes sat smoking cigarette after cigarette just under the "No Smoking" signs. Whoever had been the main person we dealt with that day would be pleased to hear Theresa say, as we finished, the Arabic phrase *Allah yissalim hal-idayn. God bless your hands.* This might be said to anyone who is doing a service for a person. Invariably this common expression was acknowledged with a bow of his head to us. What seems like a cliché is all of a sudden a true blessing to giver and receiver. Why did ritual words like these seem more than routine, seem instead a staple of life for Damascenes—so much more than "Have a nice day"?

We cannot deny that this Syrian system had its absurd moments. Many times we felt like snapping, "We have seen the general twice! Why should we go back?" Or, "You left your cigarette burning on the file cabinet when you came back to the counter." But it was basically human beings dealing with other human beings. The people we dealt with here probably went back home at night to say, "Honey, that crazy American couple? They're still here! They're still not sounding too good in Arabic, but the wife is absolutely fearless about trying."

When all was said and done, we had to admit that the process was predictable, human, and generous. We were always aware that non-Europeans who obtain visas for the United States have a hard-to-impossible time extending them and will probably have to pay hefty fees, including lawyer fees, to do so.

And when it was finished, we rewarded ourselves with kenafeh from the bakery across the street. Kenafeh is white cheese baked in shredded phyllo dough and covered with syrup and chopped pistachios. At this particular kenafeh shop, the round trays emptied quickly but new ones were always coming from above, handed down to the ground-floor workers. The shop was a sort of extension from a mosque and adjacent to a bus stop, so if we happened to celebrate our two more months of residency just before or after prayer time, the kenafeh stand would be especially busy. And its employees were as patient and human as those in the residency permit office across the street and up the stairs. May they all and their families come through these times.

2

The Mosque:
Most Democratic of Spaces

Ameen Rihani, a Lebanese-American literary figure and early theorist of Arab nationalism who died in 1940, described what might be the essence of a mosque:

> Of all the places of worship I know—and I have lugged my unshrived soul and my weary limbs into many a foreign temple—the mosque has always impressed me as being by far the most democratic and the most unstinted in its varied hospitalities. There is nothing in it or in its economy to flatter the rich, or offend the poor, to repel the weary, or distract the devout...[It is] a clear open space, unencumbered and un-taxed, where you can come and stay when you please and as long as you please. (*The Path of Vision: Pocket Essays of East and West*, page 144)

What a wonderful insight not only into the spaces called mosques, but into Islam itself. That was certainly our experience even and especially in the great Umayyad Mosque in the Old City, built in the early eighth century during the Umayyad dynasty whose leaders chose Damascus as the administrative capital of the Islamic Caliphate.

Children play, families eat their lunch, and people sleep, pray, recite the Qur'an softly from memory or read the text, or just wander about. When the call to prayer is given, hundreds of men and women come in to pray together, a prayer of sound and posture and gesture that takes only five to ten minutes.

Christians (Quakers and a few others excepted) are not so familiar with their own gathering places being "democratic." Church architecture in Europe and beyond literally built into these spaces the familiar setting for performer and audience. Churches seem to be places where the people assembled are expected mainly to watch or listen. There is much to learn from the architecture and activity of the mosque.

THE UMAYYADS WERE THE LINK between Damascus and the Hijaz, where Islam had begun in the life of Mohammed and his followers and in the words revealed to him, the Qur'an. We always find it important that the meaning of the Arabic word *Qur'an* has to do with "Recite!" Qur'an is a command to speak out these words. These texts were spoken words first, memorized words. For all the artistry and beauty of Arabic calligraphy, the Qur'an was more to be proclaimed and known by heart than to be ink on paper.

The desert cities of Mecca and Medina would remain central to Islam, but the thrust of the early Muslim leaders was to bring Islam from the desert to the cities and the peoples beyond. Damascus, then a weakened part of the Roman/Byzantine Empire, was ripe for the new religion, so much so that 29 years after the prophet's death in 632 CE, the caliph Mu'awiya, himself from the Syrian area north of Arabia, moved the administrative seat of the caliphate to Damascus. Damascus was again, but for less than a century, the center of an empire. This empire, though, would extend east beyond Persia and west across North Africa and then north to the Iberian peninsula. It is from Caliph Mu'awiya that we have "Umayyad" as the name for the Great Mosque of Damascus as well as the dynasty that ruled from Damascus for nine decades before the Abbasid revolt and the founding of the new Muslim capital city of Baghdad.

As in Jerusalem, where the al-Aqsa Mosque had been completed in 705 CE, a great mosque was needed in Damascus. Its location must have seemed obvious to the Muslim community. By that time, already for more than a thousand years, the place of the highest temple and then the highest church was constant even if the god honored there changed. Since the temple of the Aramaean god Hadad had been built, probably in the ninth century BCE, the residents and/or occupiers of Damascus had not changed the place of their religious center. When the Christians arrived, this area was marked already by the Roman *temenos*, a sacred, walled area. The city's largest Christian church was built within these walls, no doubt recycling the stones of the old temples, and for a period in the late seventh century, both Christians and Muslims worshiped inside the walls—the former in their church, the latter east of the church facing the south wall. All used a common entrance in that wall. It can still be seen but has long become part of the wall itself.

Apparently, neither the Muslim community then nor since then thought it inappropriate that the Greek text carved around this southern entrance by the Christians remained and is to be seen today. Based on Psalm 145:13 it translates: "Your dominion lasts for ever, O Christ, and your rule for all generations." Near this rises one of the mosque's three minarets. Built in the thirteenth century, it came to be known as the minaret of the Prophet Isa (Jesus). This surprises many Christians who have never understood the importance Islam gives to Jesus, Mary, John the Baptist, and others we know from Hebrew and Christian scriptures and Muslims know from the Qur'an. On our first visit to the mosque, we learned that this minaret is thought by some of the Muslim community to mark the place where the Prophet Jesus will appear in the end time.

Caliph al-Walid and the Christians seem to have agreed around the year 700 that a central church would be built elsewhere and the entire enclosed space would become courtyard and mosque. Gradually Islam came to prominence with its rituals and scriptures; the Christian community remained in Damascus even as the ground that had been central to rituals long before there were Christians now passed to another people of the book.

The Courtyard

Like all non-Muslim visitors, we entered the Umayyad Mosque through the gate in the middle of the north wall after first removing our shoes outside the gate. This is the way of every mosque: shoes outside. And it is the way of many Arab homes, Muslim or not. What makes for cleanliness makes also for hospitality and something like equality.

Inside the walls, we stood amazed—and not only when we entered the first time. Our walk around the outside walls of the mosque gave no hint of the beauty inside, no sense of how, inside, architecture and art and the people present at any given moment, the play of all three together, become simply a blessing, an embrace. The courtyard's breadth of open space and the sun reflected in its vast floor made that floor seem to be made not so much with white marble slabs as with light.

On our first visit, we paused about 250 feet from the west wall to our right and an equal distance from the east wall to our left. In front of us, 300 feet from the gate we had entered, was the wall that divided the ancient *temenos* (sacred and walled) space, built on the directions of Caliph al-Walid. In this wall are the entrances to the prayer hall.

This was the way the caliph, 13 centuries ago, had transformed the enclosed sacred space. This courtyard is perhaps 60 percent of the area within the ancient walls. Al-Walid left this much open to the Damascus skies and wrapped in high walls. The lower part of these walls now surrounding us were covered in marble that caught the bright Damascus sun so that both walls and white marble floor made us feel a sun that is so constant and warm in this oasis city. Like most first-time visitors, we began to wander in the courtyard and only after that noticed how the higher portions of the walls were covered with mosaic images. Mosaic until then had been a part of the Roman and Byzantine culture. Now the Muslim caliph, still in the first century of Islam, embraced this art.

The creators of the mosaic said they were making pictures of Paradise, but it was Damascus, this fertile oasis between the mountains to the west and north and the desert to the east. So we thought that first visit. Yes, with those tiny pieces of colored glass and stone, those who lived in Damascus with eyes wide open knew how to make images of Paradise. From the early eighth century until the late nineteenth century, these mosaics surrounded the courtyard, catching the sun rising and setting, dazzling pilgrims from far away. The internet provides many websites where the mosaics that survived or were reconstructed after the fire of 1893 can be seen. One must now imagine how they appeared during those twelve centuries before the fire.

All our visits to the mosque, inside and outside, were as stimulating yet restful as that first one. Sometimes we brought friends who were visiting from the United States or elsewhere, but often we just came and found somewhere to sit on the floor of the courtyard for a while before entering the mosque. At the center of the courtyard is an ablution fountain for washing before prayer, but very little else is placed within this space—except the people themselves. Families or other groupings sat in circles sharing the food they had brought. We would note the varied dress of Muslims on pilgrimage whether from nearby Jordan or from Iran or Pakistan or Indonesia or Malaysia, from Africa and Europe and the Americas. And we saw tourists in groups with the leader holding high a sign. Always there were many non-Muslim tourists, the women usually wearing the very dull garment the mosque provides to cover their hair and clothing. We told all guests they would be leaving their shoes outside the courtyard. For us Westerners, this is strange—until you do it.

On every visit we made, we noticed how children were somehow freed to delight in this space and make it their own. They would run and play games they made up. The gleaming floor, the walls so far apart, everything in the courtyard itself freed them and delighted them. It became theirs. We saw children doing cartwheels. Once we saw a child running with a kite high in the air. Parents always seemed relaxed and calm. In the winter months, if it had rained a bit, the children would run and slide on the damp tiles. Of course some tourists would seem more interested in taking pictures than in really seeing. There would always be groups or large families sitting in circles on the marble floor. We never saw anyone selling anything once we entered the courtyard.

From *Damascus, A History*

For much of our education on the history of Damascus, we relied on *Damascus, A History* by Ross Burns. His description of the mosaics is worth quoting:

The Caliph assembled a team of local and imported craftsmen clearly schooled in the classical tradition and its local variations. The synthesis was very much the Umayyads' own though it borrowed elements long familiar in the local repertoires. Some 40 tonnes [80,000 pounds] of glass and stone cubes (of which twelve tonnes in green alone) were set so that the whole space shone and glimmered like a fantastic garden, each cube carefully angled to catch the light when seen from below. What we see now is a compromised version of the original but it is still enough to give a sense of its overpowered impact….

The surfaces abound with life yet there are no signs of human or animal representation in accordance with the norms of the new faith. Instead, on a shimmering gold background was spread a prolific carpet of vegetation and streams interspersed with orchards, palaces, rotundas and houses piled up in a style that seems to borrow elements from many traditions, from oriental to classical, though the predominant idiom was Byzantine seen through a Syrian prism…. [H]ere was depicted an accessible Paradise that must have drawn gasps from all who ventured into this fantastic garden. This, particularly to an Arab audience, bore out the many descriptions of Damascus as the point on earth that provided a foretaste of the Paradise Islam offered to the faithful. Nothing to rival it had been seen in the world until then; and nothing since. (pages 116–18)

THEY COME AS THEY ARE. On one visit to the Umayyad Mosque, perhaps two years or more into our Damascus time, we were there as the afternoon prayer began. Then near us, something amazing. Two boys, perhaps brothers and maybe eight and ten years old, came hurrying up toward the lines of men making the prayer together. No adult seemed to be with them. They stood close to each other, facing Mecca, and joined in the postures of those already at prayer. They seemed to know every word and movement and silence of the prayer, and so they prayed with the others to the end of the prayer, their lips moving, performing the kneeling and bowing and touching their heads to the ground, totally wrapped in their prayer. All of this is not unusual, not what caught our eye.

What caught our eye was this: The two boys were dressed in complete Superman outfits: blue tops with the giant red "S" on a yellow diamond, blue leggings, and long red capes. They had no self-consciousness about this at all. All their attention seemed on their prayer, just like those around them.

The Gates of Mercy

One traditional prayer on entering the mosque is "O Allah, open to me the gates of your mercy." From the courtyard of the Umayyad Mosque, we came within the mosque itself. From the bright Damascus sun and all the light it creates in the walls and floor of the courtyard, we entered the dim interior.

We were dazzled by the sheer volume. The roof must have been up there somewhere, for here on the ground with us were the great pillars that line up west to east to make those three equal aisles. Each pillar seemed so high and mighty close-up. As they make this procession from west to east, they nearly disappear. Standing just inside the doors, we could not tell whether there was an east wall and even the south wall, the wall facing Mecca, seemed a city block away—because it is!

Our feet told us we were moving from stone to fabric at the threshold between courtyard and prayer hall. In 2005, the floor had who-knows-how-many rugs overlapping one another, many designs and colors and sizes—a hodgepodge of patterns and colors. During our years there, the rugs went away (we missed them) and instead the floor was covered by a carpet as large as the entire prayer hall (150 × 40 yards).

How did this enclosed and covered space along the inner south wall of the ancient *temenos* come to be? Between the years 705 and 715, workers and craftspeople, Muslims and Christians and Jews, built a high wall stretching from the east wall to the west wall of this enclosed area. This high wall separated the uncovered area, the courtyard, from what would become an immense, covered room whose east and west walls were built parallel to but slightly inside the east and west walls of the *temenos*. The original south wall, 175 yards from east to west, faced toward Mecca and became the focus of the prayer hall created within the enclosed space. Thus, the whole area became the place of prayer for the Muslim community. This enormous space was then covered with a pitched roof and central dome.

We sensed no rules about where we could wander in this space. The coming and going through this northwest door and through another entrance/exit in the south wall was constant, as it seemed to be on every visit we made.

Intricate glass mosaics glisten in the sunlight on the façade of the Umayyad Mosque. Vast archways beyond human scale border the open courtyard. Photo by Viktor Hegyi.

Months after we moved to Damascus, Theresa's sister Julie, a Daughter of Charity, came from California for a 10-day visit, our first American guest in Damascus. One evening, we three went with our good friend Abdullah to the Umayyad Mosque. Abdullah, whose home was Aleppo, was then just finishing undergraduate studies in English literature at Damascus University. He had become a bright part of our time since the day he saw us standing befuddled on the street beside the university and had, in fine English, offered to help us.

That evening the four of us stayed in the mosque quite a while. We slowly walked the full length of the room and back. As always, we saw how this immense enclosed space made people feel at home or perhaps better. Some are praying, some resting, some sleeping. Some read from the Qur'an. Children play on the soft carpets. Parents have brought food and drink for their children. Always a dozen or more people are standing in prayer at the shrine of John the Baptist. While tourists are welcome, something in the space quietly convinces that this is a place to be respectful of all. It is not a "sight" to see, not a museum.

THE MOSQUE IS PREPARED in a way that feels like home. The floor is covered with soft carpets and there is a calm, peaceful light. The prayer in its essence elicits peace and harmony. A literal connection between us is found during the prayer. We stand in lines and we stand so close together that the shoulders and the feet (without shoes) of each one willingly touch the ones on either side, not only in the standing position, but also in the postures of bending over, kneeling and the movements of the hands. The inspiring recitations of the Qur'an, the emotive speech of the Imam, the neighborhood gathering, the congruent and harmonious movement of the prayer and the precise connection of shoulders are all the wonders of the congregational Friday noon prayer. It elicits a sense of devotion and belonging, a feeling of unity and shelter. It's a religious duty yet a personal need. Without the zeal of experiencing it, one feels loneliness and a sense of something missing. It's one great migration to peace.

—Ziad Al-Shamsie
Iraqi Student Project

Call to Prayer

We knew that when the call to prayer is given, its amplified sound outside is that of many voices, while from other mosques in the city, one hears a single voice. But that day we saw that when the time comes to call to pray, a number of men enter a room against the west wall, face toward Mecca, and chant together. We could hear their unamplified voices as we watched from outside the door to this room, at the same time hearing just barely the amplified sound from outside. We were awestruck. Always after that, we tried to time any visit to the Umayyad Mosque with the time of a call to prayer.

During the next few minutes, men already in the mosque began to form a line close to the south wall. They stood one very close to another, up and down as the line grew. Our friend Abdullah joined those preparing to pray. Then a second line began behind the first. Sometimes we saw these lines reach the east and west walls. So many were here with us and we never realized! But also, through the two entrances, a stream of men and women were entering. Those coming through the south doors, that open to the souq, were leaving their shoes outside the wide entrance. Those entering the north doors, as we did, had been barefoot or in socks since entering the courtyard.

The women form their lines about midway between north and south walls. Even very young children take their places beside father or mother and often have already learned the rhythm of the prayer. Adults and children who cannot stand or who cannot kneel and bow are there also.

Maybe ten minutes pass after the call to prayer before the prayer itself begins. The leader, like everyone, faces Mecca but takes a position facing one of the four mihrabs or deep niches in the south wall that mark the direction of Mecca. The prayer is not hurried, but the slow movement of so many from standing straight to kneeling and bowing until one's forehead touches the ground, then sitting back, then rising. Those praying have the rhythms in their bones, the words in their hearts.

Courtyard arches of the Umayyad Mosque with glass mosaics. Photo by Bachar Azmeh.

The silent moments are truly still and seem clearly as important as the chanted moments. The texts are simple and known by heart from an early age; so too is the rhythm of sound and silence, movement and stillness.

Those who come late join in but often continue on their own when the assembly is concluded and most are returning to their work in the nearby markets, workshops, and offices. Five times each day, people pray in this way in this Great Mosque of Damascus, as in every other mosque.

Always we tried to join the prayer by facing the south wall and simply standing still in a place near one of the pillars. We could imagine how different this prayer seemed to the Christians of Damascus in that first century of Islam. But also how attractive. There is an absence of hierarchy, an absence of "those who know and those who don't," and perhaps some Christians were just tired of generations of disputes among their hierarchies about what was to be believed by all. At any rate, little by little over the first 300 years of Islam, Damascus was slowly becoming a city where Muslims were the majority.

The Pope's Visit

There was a small post office near our apartment and we went occasionally to purchase stamps, especially ones we hoped our friends outside Syria would find beautiful or interesting. We often sent postcards to family and friends, and we liked to use different sorts of stamps for the cards, even in these days of email. At one point, we bought a quantity of the "pope stamp," maybe not what one expects on letters sent from Syria. It shows John Paul II and the Umayyad Mosque in the background. On May 6, 2001, the pope removed his shoes, and as *LA Times* reporter Richard Boudreaux wrote, "...shuffled slowly into the Great Omayyad Mosque here Sunday evening to become the first pontiff to visit and pray in a Muslim house of worship." John Paul II kissed the Holy Qur'an and in his address said:

> I am deeply moved to be your guest here in the great Umayyad Mosque, so rich in religious history. Your land is dear to Christians: here our religion has known vital moments of its growth and doctrinal development, and here are found Christian communities which have lived in peace and harmony with their Muslim neighbors for many centuries...
>
> It is important that Muslims and Christians continue to explore philosophical and theological questions together, in order to come to a more objective and comprehensive knowledge of each others' religious beliefs. Better mutual understanding will surely lead, at the practical level, to a new way of presenting our two religions not in opposition, as

has happened too often in the past, but in partnership for the good of the human family....

In Syria, Christians and Muslims have lived side by side for centuries, and a rich dialogue of life has gone on unceasingly.... For all the times that Muslims and Christians have offended one another, we need to seek forgiveness from the Almighty and to offer each other forgiveness.

WHEN WE MOVED TO DAMASCUS, we held only vague notions of its history. How have we understood the arrival of Muslims 1,400 years ago in lands where Jews and Christians and various other folks had been living together for centuries and not all of them stormy? Most of us have imagined violence, imposed conversion, martyrs. The facts do not support this view.

We were in Damascus when the Metropolitan Museum of Art in New York City opened its expanded and much-praised Islamic Galleries in November 2011. The Met also organized a temporary exhibit (March to July 2012), *Byzantium and Islam: Age of Transition (7th–9th Century)*. The museum published a beautiful volume of essays and photographs. Peter Brown, the foremost scholar of Late Antiquity (third to eighth centuries) in the lands of the Roman Empire, reviewed both the book and the exhibit. In the May 10, 2012 *New York Review of Books*, he emphasized the amazing continuity as Byzantium gradually became Islamic:

> The few clear signs that Islam had, indeed, become politically dominant in the Middle East by the end of the seventh century strike us with almost ominous intensity. For there are so few of them.
>
> ...In the last room, we come on pages of the Koran that look as ornate and magnificent as any Christian gospels of their time. They are covered with a Kufic script, whose bold foursquare lines have an ancient grandeur, strangely unlike the fluid scripts that we now associate with medieval and modern Arabic.
>
> Most surprising of all, we can now suggest that the spread of Islam did not happen overnight. It was not imposed by force on the conquered peoples. Although their position as the rulers of a successful empire doubtless weighed heavily in their favor, Muslims talked their way into the Middle East quite as much as they fought their way across it....
>
> Islamic civilization in its first centuries owed much of its richness to continued religious conversations among Muslims, Jews, and Christians. These conversations slowly changed the religious texture of the Middle East to the advantage of Islam. But until the year 1000, at least, it was the Muslims, and not the Jews and Christians, who were the minority religion. What we are looking at is not the Islam of the modern imagination. It is a very new Islam that was still trying to find a place for itself in a very old world.

"What Drives People to Prayer?"

Five years after we first entered the Umayyad Mosque, we had an encounter that has helped us better understand that space. In spring 2010, Damascus had a film festival called Dox Box. It featured documentaries by Syrian filmmakers but also new and old documentaries from other places. Three American documentary filmmakers were in attendance, including D.A. Pennebaker, who was there with the documentary he made 45 years earlier about Bob Dylan's 1965 concert tour in England; *Don't Look Back* was the film and the approach to documentary that brought Pennebaker a wide audience and many imitators. Watching it in 2010 in Damascus with the now-85-year-old filmmaker present was like entering a time machine: Whole cartons of cigarettes are smoked as Dylan, alone or in a crowded hotel room, writes at his portable typewriter.

Another of the U.S. filmmakers at the festival was Jehane Noujaim, an Egyptian American known then for her film *Control Room* about the way the invasion and occupation of Iraq were covered by the media. A week before the festival, a friend involved in the planning told us that Jehane Noujaim was coming. We invited her to talk to some Iraqi students who had heard her TED talk, and she agreed, bringing with her Pennebaker and another filmmaker, Chris Hegedus. About an hour into the conversation, Pennebaker described his visit the preceding day (a Friday) to the Umayyad Mosque at noon. He said he had never seen hundreds, maybe thousands, of men and women doing the prayer, together standing, bowing, kneeling with head bent to the ground, all as one in both the silence and the chanted words. This had amazed him and he wanted to know what could bring this about. What did these people feel? Why were they there?

Nearly every Iraqi in the room wanted to speak urgently to Pennebaker's question. And so they did. They spoke, sometimes with difficulty because of their emotions, of their own experience of prayer. We later asked them to expand on their responses in writing; the following extracts provide a sample.

"What drives people?" When I started answering, my imagination took me back to the mosques I've been to in my life and the feelings of humility and security I experienced there. Tears flowed from my eyes. No words I spoke were enough to answer a question of that scope or magnitude. The word that comes closest to describing what we feel inside a mosque is probably "nexus." There people share a common purpose, they discard all the worries of life and just experience tranquility, a nexus of positive will. Being a Muslim is my pillar of strength. It is my sustenance in life, which helps me face its difficulties. It is my light in the darkness, my ethos by which I live and my creed which I will pass on to my children afterwards. (Zaid)

When you start praying, stand with respect and attention. Forget the world and everything behind you with the call of the most magnificent words: *Allahu akbar*, Allah is the Almighty. This amazing call makes you feel the greatness and majesty of God and fills you with love, respect and solemnity. (Alaa)

When I am in bed every night, thinking about my problems, and when I feel that I am about to cry, I remember that God is there for me to help me overcome my hardships. As long as I believe in God, I will never lose my way. I always think of God's glory and I believe that I am an extremely tiny creature in this huge world, and I say to myself that my problems are nothing according to the whole wide world. In these moments, I go to my small rug that I use to say my prayers on and sit myself on it and just pray to God and forget about every crisis. I ask God to remove the hurt from the Iraqi people and bless them with freedom one day. Islam is the power of love, hope, optimism, passion, generosity, giving glory to God. This is the power that makes Muslims bow and I am proud of being one of them. I say, "God, I thank you. I am delighted to honor you. I love you and will pray and bend down for you to the last breath." (Tamara)

For me, praying is in my house, in my own room, and solitude gives me this significant feeling that I'm not seen, not heard and not judged by any being but my God. Allah can understand the deepest secrets without having me prove anything. How comforting it feels those few moments away from the world of appearances and judgments. When the inside is all that matters, I feel peace with myself: knowing when I'm heard even when I'm speechless, and that I'm seen where nobody can see is, to me, the absolute serenity in praying. (Sundus)

The kneeling concept in many cultures is a humiliation to the one kneeling. However, with Islam, it is so different. While you are kneeling, a strange feeling starts from your forehead, which touches the ground first. You become very calm and the environment extremely silent around you. Each one who does prayer wants to enjoy these moments of dignity. This feeling starts in your chest and it expands to your arms and legs. Then it turns to tremendous power and you feel how you are respected by God. This is completely bizarre. You are in the lowest position you can reach, but you mention your Creator who is in the highest place in the whole universe and who gives you safety. And you become sure that you are neither weak nor alone. You are related to the strongest power and to the most miraculous energy. (Mustafa)

Both in our visits to Iraq and then the years in Syria, we became aware that our Western presumptions hadn't prepared us well. Many of us have little experience of Islam and little sense for how Jewish and Christian communities had lived side-by-side with Muslim communities ever since there were Muslims in the seventh century CE. Sometimes it seemed we lacked not only an honest telling of the history, but an insight into the sort of community built by people who could both take their own religious tradition to heart and love it, but at the same time have only respect for those who live by different religious traditions. Communities at peace don't make the evening news or the history books. One has to search it out to learn about the centuries of Islam and Judaism and Christianity living together in mutual respect, each evolving, each having its saints and sinners. This is more than just tolerance.

One of our Iraqi students told about the day she and her mother and sister fled from Iraq, taking a bus to Syria by way of Kirkuk and Mosul. The bus broke down; they and the 40-plus other passengers (these were the days when thousands of Iraqis were leaving for Syria every day) had to find shelter for the night. They all entered a mosque in Mosul—still strangers and probably mistrustful given the violence they had all experienced in Baghdad.

It was awfully cold that night and the mosque was not any warmer. Every family took a spot to sit in and sleep. But it was too cold to fall asleep. Back then, no one knew anyone other than their families. But somehow people started to get closer to each other and talk. I don't know how we ended up in a big circle so close. I thought it was the cold that made us approach each other for warmth. Everyone was talking about their stories and soon we knew each other. There was a lot of laughter and tears as well.

After hearing everyone's story, I realized something that shocked me and I was wondering if I was the only or the first one who could see it. What I realized was that we were Shiite, Sunni, and Christians, all together in a mosque. And no one really cared about that but instead we were just a big family trying to make it through together. You could hear our talks and laughter from a distance. I felt I wanted to get up

Many respond to the call to prayer while others walk the length of the prayer hall or sit and rest along the sides. A simple grandeur seems to equalize us all.
Photo by Robert Rosser.

and tell everyone to notice that. "What are the odds?" I said to myself. "Could it be the thing that set us apart once is reuniting us again?"

Later, the soldiers brought us heaters and blankets but it was too late; we already found our way to get warm. I thought everything happened for a reason. If the soldiers brought us the blankets and the heaters earlier, this would not have happened. This made me realize such a vivid truth about my people: We don't hate each other! It could be all a misunderstanding. It gave me hope in my life that Iraq will one day rise up again and reunite when all people see one truth and one destiny. And not just Iraq, but the whole world.

3
Arabic:
The Language and Our Teachers

We had been told by people who know about such things that if we wanted to learn Arabic, we should go to Damascus because it is less Western than other Arab cities and isn't full of English speakers like Beirut and Amman.

No one told us, however, that in Damascus the spoken Arabic is full of music; we discovered that for ourselves. We listened to women chatting on the minibuses. We listened to men having tea in front of their shops. We listened to children singing their way home from school. We listened to cab drivers (to our ears, the most musical of all) talking to their passengers or in conversation with one another. We listened to customers and bakers talking. Later we listened to young Iraqis mimicking the "*Shammi* Arabic" they heard in Damascus; they too found it musical.

The Palestinian poet Mahmoud Darwish wrote "The Damascene Collar of the Dove," a poem of 22 stanzas, each stanza beginning with the phrase "In Damascus" ("*Fi Dimashq*"). In the ninth stanza, perhaps he is thinking about the sounds of everyday Arabic in Damascus:

> In Damascus:
>   speech returns to its origin,
>   water:
>   poetry isn't poetry
>   and prose isn't prose
>   and you say: I won't leave you
>   so take me to you
>   and take me with you!

Gabe's experience with languages other than English had been much Latin and a very small smattering of several other languages. Theresa's second language was Spanish and she had a love of Slovak, the language of her grand-parents. For both of us, this experience of Arabic broadened our sense for what a language is and does, and for how translation is never merely a mechanical process. Our teachers and our own study gave us a great gift: love of Arabic's music—from the call to prayer to the everyday buying and selling in the souq—and some inkling of Arabic's own genius.

Hussein

We began daily lessons with our first teacher, Hussein Maxos, two weeks after our September 2005 arrival in Syria. We were introduced to him by a friend from Pennsylvania who arrived in Damascus with excellent formal Arabic and who wanted Hussein to teach him spoken Arabic, especially the way it had evolved in Damascus.

Hussein lived with his wife and their child in a very small apartment near Souq al-Jouma'a, the mile-long market of all good things on the lower slope of Mount Qassiun (see the maps on pages 34 and 35). This market street follows the now-underground Yazid Canal, dug in the late seventh century and the last of the canals built to spread the Barada's waters broadly and so meet the needs of the expanding population.

Hussein's approach to teaching foreigners how to speak Arabic was through immersion in the spoken language. Working with Hussein for two hours each day, we spent months learning letters and sounds by practicing simple street dialogues. He had developed scripts that included expressions that establish conversational bonds for greeting, parting from, asking questions of, and responding to questions that typically arise in conversations with Damascenes.

We moved slowly, but eventually we were reading transcriptions as we listened to two characters on a comical radio soap opera that had long been very popular in Damascus. We used to think of the two characters, Hadiyeh and her husband, Abdul Rahman, as the Syrian Fibber McGee and Molly, or the Arabic-speaking George Burns and Gracie Allen. Usually we found it was enough to sing a few measures from the program's theme song—a duet back-and-forth between the couple—and any Damascus resident would smile, laugh, and start singing with us.

We would eventually meet several students from the United States and Europe who had studied with Hussein. Many had studied classical Arabic in college and wanted to learn the spoken Arabic. That's where the soap opera and the dialogues Hussein created were so helpful to them. These students in their early 20s often amazed Syrian friends who had never heard anyone handle

Hussein's Story

I am a Syrian Arab aged 45, and have been living in Damascus for 23 years. I am a middle son with five brothers and sisters living in Syria, Lebanon, Libya, Saudi Arabia, and the United Arab Emirates. Because of anti-corruption policies for police officers, my dad was moved from one town to another every year or two. We lived with people from every religious, ethnic, and racial group in Syria. This was sometimes uncomfortable, but it was also a rich background for later studies and a career in languages, linguistics, and cultural studies.

After obligatory military service from 1985 to 1988, I decided to settle in Damascus and start a new life. In a conservative society based on family connections, in Damascus I had to be self-made and largely self-taught. I had been best in my class in Arabic and English all through elementary and high school, so I chose to study languages: English in the American Language Center (ALC), German in Goethe Institute, Arabic morphology and advanced grammar at the Syrian Asia Institute, and Persian at the Iranian Cultural Center for one year. I began in short-term work and private lessons to prepare for a career in tourist guiding and in teaching Arabic to non-Arabs.

Soon I focused on understanding why so many of those who begin the study of Arabic drop out before they achieve fluency. I studied all available materials for teaching Arabic as a second language: from Syria, Lebanon, Jordan, Egypt, Switzerland, Austria, Germany, Sweden, UK, and U.S. Most of my students contributed their previous study materials and/or sent them to me from abroad. I also studied Arab culture written by non-Arabs, including orientalists and Middle East scholars. I became devoted to this career and established Arabic teaching programs at European and North American cultural centers.

From the blog of Hussein Maxos, http://hmaxos.blogspot.com.

Arabic so well in conversation. Hussein's approach was to train the ear to hear and then to mimic.

Each day we huddled into a tiny space perched on two folding chairs across from Hussein in his wooden chair near his computer, our knees almost touching. A teeny window above a map brought the sound of the call to prayer to our ears. Above us was a shelf full of notebooks, mostly writing Hussein was working on.

We enjoyed being with Hussein as a friend and we loved having his infant son sit on our laps while we struggled with playing the roles of Hadiyeh and Abdul Rahman. We also loved discussing (in English) Hussein's projects with the Arabic language, which involved collecting Arabic idioms and proverbs as well as religious and other expressions.

As always, the expressions used in another language gave us insight into those of our first language. Especially at the internet cafés, we would hear patrons speaking in Arabic to their parents and family and friends with the formulas of initial greetings followed by questions about health. The conclusion of a phone conversation with a relative or friend would be longer and more elaborate and follow expected patterns. Nothing quite as breezy as "see you around!"

Hussein's sense for the role of the everyday expressions and the expressions used in special circumstances was wonderful, as was his ability to find the right English word to help us appreciate the meaning. As with "God bless you" or "Thank God!" or even "Goodbye" ("God be with you") in English, Arabic abounds in ways of asking God to bless, to protect, to comfort, to grant patience. We learned by listening to people on the streets how to use

During the time of the sanctions in Iraq, we visited the shop of a calligrapher in Baghdad in 1999. He painted this bismillah for us on a piece of cardboard and it has been above the doorway in our home library ever since. Translation: In the Name of God, the Merciful, the Compassionate. Photo by Julian Abelskamp.

mashallah ("Praise God!") in referring to a person advanced in age, "She will be 88 on her birthday, mashallah!" Or in speaking of someone's child, "Your child is so charming! Mashallah!"

Soon we were recognizing and then using the expressions of everyday life in the souqs and stores and streets of Damascus: *al-hamdu li-llah*, Thanks be to God, and *Allah yissalim hal-idayn*! God give peace in the work of your hands! That last one is used when someone has made or prepared something for you as your host or as a merchant or a craftsperson. Most of these expressions and many others are common to Arabic speakers irrespective of religion.

In walking to Hussein's apartment in the labyrinth of ancient buildings and streets and mosques and cemeteries further up from Souq al-Jouma'a, we found many ways to become lost in the tangle of mountainside streets and their two or three level dwellings, each touching the neighboring buildings. House numbers and street names were seldom used, and in those first years, there

Damascus Dialect: Victim of the War?

When I came to Damascus more than 20 years ago, I didn't have any problem speaking the Damascene dialect. By then I had lived in many areas and could speak and understand many dialects, and in my military service I had many friends from Damascus.

Since the first booming of Syrian TV dramas and soap operas in the 1980s, these programs have used the Damascus dialect and now it is familiar all over the Arab world. The Syrian programs reflected real life much more than the competition from Egypt. Syrian drama was also more daring, more diverse, and to make the combination even more attractive, came linguistically closer to the shared Arabic that is the lingua franca of the inter-Arab communications.

Historically, the Damascene way of speaking Arabic was heard as polite, conservative, and urban. Until the present violence, Damascus had the reputation of being stable and relatively more educated. As anywhere, arrogance led to jealousy from the rest of the Syrian population, and a flood of biased jokes. Now that I have lived most of my years in Damascus, my tongue has absorbed the accent completely in a place where a slip of the tongue can cause an embarrassment and consequential suspicion.

The Damascus dialect is more an accent than a dialect because the vocabulary distinction is small. The accent is soft and melodic, and the ends of the words especially in the end of the sentence are stretched, particularly the more meaningful phrases that the speaker needs to stress. There are a few minor grammar and vocabulary abbreviations and flipping, but the situation now has changed as thousands of displaced people took refuge temporarily or permanently in this city.

Dialects and accents are now combining, tangling, changing. Hearing a strange accent is no longer strange. The demographic change has caused population redistribution, and some quiet areas became uncomfortably crowded. Many locals have left and many people from the country moved to the city. Their class or economic status determined where and how long they can stay but all seem to run out of cash sooner than they expect. So many now think of themselves as harmed by all sides and from inside and outside Syria. In Damascus the various local and newly come accents may merge and our old dialect prejudices will disappeared. But so will some of the wonderful ways of speaking our language.

From the blog of Hussein Maxos, http://hmaxos.blogspot.com

were few mobile phones. This is where we discovered we might be able to do the everyday talk with Damascenes, as well as the *hakki fahdi* (literally "empty talk") of ordinary life anywhere, but we wouldn't go beyond that without more of a background in the language itself.

Most of this time we were living in the Old City and the journey to and from Hussein's each day was our introduction to the ways, routes, and drivers of the *serveeces* (minivans) that are for most of the population, even in the villages at the edge of the city, the everyday means of transportation. Automobiles may seem to fill the streets and there are some large buses that need wide streets, but these 10-lira *serveeces* were our transportation to Hussein's and, when we changed teachers, to Yarmouk and Mazen.

Both teachers have contributed to this book. Hussein allowed us to reprint what he has been sending from Damascus during these difficult years; his blog posts (slightly edited) appear in the sidebars in this and other chapters. And Mazen gave us permission to publish a transcript of his conversation with Theresa in January 2015 in Istanbul, where he has established a center for Syrian refugees and is teaching Arabic at a university; it appears in Chapter 17.

Mazen

We began studying with Mazen in spring 2006 and continued until fall 2007. We had heard about Mazen from his students and wanted to meet him before deciding whether to be his students. He was as difficult to find in Yarmouk Camp as Hussein had been to find amid the lanes climbing Mount Qassiun. The two neighborhoods and the two teachers were very different, but they had in common what to us was essential: a love for the Arabic language and a host of former students who kept in touch because they so valued these teachers. For six days most weeks and two hours most days, we had Arabic lessons with Mazen, and we maintained this schedule for a little more than a year.

On warm days, we sat under Mazen's fig tree in the tiny courtyard off his room in the family home that housed his father and some of his siblings, and some of his nieces and nephews. One of the most captivating characteristics of Mazen's garden was a old, large brass key that he had placed on a small branch of the fig tree. For Palestinians, keys remain the symbol of the Right of Return. As time passed, the tree grew and the branch thickened and enshrined the key.

On cooler days, we went inside his large one-room apartment and sat surrounded by his library. In or out, we, like all Mazen's students, came to know Mazen's father and other family members. One sister, a dentist, had her clinic in the building with access from around the corner. She taught dental students at Damascus University. Neighborhood children would come by, and we got to know them, too.

During our class time, we did one or more of the following: telling a story each of us prepared from daily happenings or some part of our lives; going over the sentences we had written; taking dictation, during which Mazen would summarize some news item and we would write down what we could with ears straining to distinguish spoken sounds; and reading a few paragraphs from poetry, a novel, or short stories as we tried for correct pronunciation and quick word recognition. All of these generated vocabulary beyond our retention abilities. Sometimes, too, we would listen to Arabic songs; like all visitors to Damascus, we knew the voice of the Lebanese singer Fairuz, whose songs could be heard especially in the mornings from radios in homes, vehicles, stores. In all these sorts of activities, one thing so easily led to another because we shared many interests.

For the storytelling each day, we each prepared some notes, then we would launch into telling the daily story in Arabic with new words and corrections coming here and there from Mazen. We might tell about some incident from our lives, or about our friends, about the refugee situation, about news we had read on the internet. Sometimes we told our stories from reading we were doing at the time or from literature that we love, novels or poetry especially. At one point, we realized that these stories were becoming piece by piece autobiographies. Examples of this from Theresa's Arabic stories: how she had trouble getting up in the morning and how her mother dealt with that by singing; energy use in the family home beginning in 1940; her first cookbook when she was in fourth grade; how she gradually gathered her library of 3,000 children's books; various adventures in teaching. Examples from Gabe's stories: sleeping in a large dormitory room with 50 other students during high school; memories of the teacher who opened up the world of literature and of writing; spring 1991 spent in Moscow. On Valentine's Day, an occasion even stranger in Damascus than in the United States, Mazen quizzed us on holidays in the United States and was amused and intrigued to hear Theresa explain Halloween in Arabic and Gabe recount his mother's efforts to give birth to her children on holidays.

In our daily writing of a page or so in Arabic (a medium-sized handwritten page, not a 400-word typed page), we tended more and more to put together a series of stories on the same topic. The writing of these little essays took a long time each day because we struggled with vocabulary and word order and grammar. We also had to learn the various forms of each of the 28 alphabet letters depending on whether the letter appeared in the beginning, end, or middle of the word. When we look now at our handwritten Arabic from those days, we are amazed at the beauty of the letters and astonished that our hands wrote them.

Working with Mazen, we began to explore the formal or classical Arabic of public speaking, of what is written for publications and used in plays and music. Compared to spoken Arabic, classical Arabic has a more complex grammar and differs in pronunciation. But this Arabic, the language of the Qur'an, constitutes a bond among all Arabic speakers.

Later, we were told by college-age Iraqi refugees we knew that they disliked the study of Arabic, but it was clear to us that they loved the language itself and were proud of it. They treasured Arabic poems and knew that the roots of Arabic as distinct from other Semitic languages (Hebrew, Aramaic, and others) lay in the oral poetry of the desert tribes. Had their Arabic classes been about poetry and literature? It seemed not. Rather, school instruction in Arabic focused on the fine points of classical Arabic, the written Arabic, the Arabic of the public speech, of the magazines and newspapers, and of course of the Qur'an. We had the impression that they had come to think of this as a language of rules about writing and grammar and pronunciation. For us, Arabic was fascinating even when we couldn't understand, remember, or pronounce the words.

Many clusters of words in Arabic are derived from a common (and generally three-letter) root. For example, the Arabic words for *paradise, jin, fetus, garden, madness, to drive someone insane,* and *beautiful* all have a shared root form. So do *Friday, university, association, assembly,* and *mosque.* We were challenged to find the common denominators among pairs of words (e.g., baby and garden, which share a root, both denote things that grow; a mosque is a communal space, just as university, association, and assembly involve groups of people). Pronouncing the Arabic letter *'ein,* which has no equivalent in English, was difficult for us, which made it hard to buy honey (*'asal*).

Theresa is fearless, unafraid to make mistakes in Arabic. She will chatter in the shared cab, in the market, even on the phone. Children loved to speak with her; often, if she was trying to buy something and the merchant clearly did not understand her, a young child who had been listening to the unsuccessful exchange piped in to try to "translate" for her. Theresa's errors sometimes were accompanied by a roar of laughter. On one occasion, she tried to tell a man we knew, "Your wife must be busy," (*mashghooleh*) but said instead, "Your wife must be crazy!" (*majnooneh*). His laughter seemed to say, "I know what you wanted to say, but instead your mistake in Arabic told another truth."

4

Souqs and Seasons

We often hear, "Eat local; eat what's in season," but we notice blueberries and raspberries available all year round in most U.S. supermarkets, greens abound in vegetable markets all winter, and bright oranges from who-knows-where are stacked up in every produce mart regardless of the season. In Damascus, we became very attuned to what fruits and vegetables were in season. We also watched how families made the most of each season by canning, pickling, and drying fruits and vegetables.

Sold Only in Their Seasons

During August our first year in the Old City, we were delighted to see street sellers offering glasses of fresh mulberry juice! The dark purple beverage was up to the brim in small glasses we shared with all the people of Damascus, the seller sloshing them out in a bucket of water quickly for the next patron to use. Truthfully, we never drank mulberry juice before and in fact remember mulberry trees littering the sidewalks of our hometowns with their fruit. Why didn't people in the United States know about mulberry juice? Our favorite mulberry juice stands were near the perfume shop by the Azem Palace, near the baskets of nuts at the exit of the Umayyad Mosque near Papa Joseph's shop, and under the tree at the Ruqayya Mosque near Bab al-Faradis. (See the Old City map on page 32.)

During our first year we learned a lot about local foods in season by just looking out our room window down into the courtyard below at Umm Karam's. One morning, Umm Karam and her daughter and mother were preparing a mountain of fresh baby eggplants to make a Syrian delicacy: *makdous*. All other housework came to a halt because this was the week to pickle eggplants. Each eggplant was stuffed with a mixture of ground walnuts, red pepper pulp, garlic, and pomegranate syrup. Teamwork was essential because they had hundreds of baby eggplants. The completed stuffed eggplants, now on their way to becoming *makdous*, were placed in jars and olive oil was poured all over them. Carefully preserved, makdous was a household pantry item to be enjoyed as part of a Syrian breakfast.

One week a giant, rotund vegetable appeared on street corners where local peddlers sell the freshest produce. Larger than a softball with a grayish-green, somewhat prickly exterior, it had several scraggly leaves draped down a thick stem about a foot long. We had seen such as these growing near Watsonville in California and knew that they are considered a delicacy. We asked what they are called in Arabic, and were surprised to hear "*ardishokey.*" Yes, these more-than-beautiful creations are called "shokey" (thorns) from the "ard" (earth). Not only were they available as described above, but we bought some already prepared into what we would call artichoke hearts in the United States. But these were giant, about three to four inches across.

Prickly Pears

Our first month in Syria, we were fortunate to meet Hala and Bachar, parents of a young musician who was working on his PhD in New York City and living in our apartment. It was good to have Syrian friends right away, and Hala and Bachar exposed us to the many joys of their beloved Damascus. One evening after dinner, Bachar suggested we go to one of the traffic circles where lighted booths were set up outside for people to gather and sit at little tables and eat cold prickly pears. These *sabara* were picked that day from cacti that grew just outside of town, the prickly spikes scraped off and the fruit plunged whole under ice water or stacked on shaved ice. We had never eaten this fruit before, but it seemed the entire city was enjoying this delicacy and sabara stands were everywhere around Damascus.

Ice cold and refreshing, the prickly pears had a delicate taste with dozens of seeds in every bite. The feeling was like swallowing watermelon seeds and the flesh of the fruit brought relief from the summer heat. Small outdoor lights in many colors dangled above us in long strings as we listened to laughter and chattering in the lilting Damascene accent.

When artichokes appear in Damascus each spring, the sellers and buyers gather in one of the city's traffic circles, Tahrir Square, outside the walls of the Old City. Sellers drove pickup trucks and parked on the outer edge of the traffic circle. The truck beds were filled with tall blue plastic bins where prepared artichoke hearts floated in water. At 10 cents apiece, we ate more artichokes in Damascus than we had ever eaten in our entire lives! We steamed them and served them drizzled with olive oil and lemon juice, sautéed them in olive oil and garlic, mashed them into dips, chunked them to add to salads, added them to pasta dishes. Artichokes were abundant, affordable, and a sure sign of spring.

The apricot (*mishmish*) harvest began with the tiny sour ones that are picked prematurely to thin out the fruit. Later, ripe apricots dominated the souq, blushing in sunset colors. We love the word *mishmish* and have used it ever since, teaching our friends and family to say it instead of the three-syllable English word.

Honey and Hajj

Early in January, a friend told us where a caravan of pilgrims from Dagestan to Mecca were staying. We found the spot (southwest of the Old City, an area called al-Midan, long the staging area for the long overland pilgrimage called the hajj). Here were various old buses, some brightly painted, each of them the bedroom/storage rooms/traveling rooms for these pilgrims. All along the sidewalks, they had set up the things they had to sell. They were on the way home now, a long trip even motorized. Many were selling honey from huge 20- or 30-gallon containers. We bought two large jars, one dark and thick enough to be that "slow as molasses in January" that our grandparents used to describe us sometimes, the other lighter and so delicious that we consumed it quickly. We thought of these pilgrims now heading home into a Russian winter after this holy adventure.

Then mountains of ripe cherries suddenly appeared. Neat stacks of leaves from grapevines were ready to be stuffed and folded around rice and other good things making the wonderful *dolma* (the most common name for stuffed grape leaves, but like so many dishes over this whole region, *dolma* has many regional variations in name and ingredients). And every day the souq tables had the reddest and most tasty small to medium tomatoes we've ever eaten—and we eat lots of them. As the drought worsened with each successive year, the price of tomatoes increased, as did the price of most produce.

Also in spring, garlic was everywhere. Bundles of garlic, the whole plant from roots to greens, four-to-five feet high, were bundled in tens or twenties and made into stacks, or made into walls, or filled wagons pulled by horses or little trucks coming right down the narrow lanes. In some areas of the souq, the garlic walls were taller than a grown person. The souq in Yarmouk Camp (see the map on page 33) had several vegetable stalls filled with mountains of fragrant fresh garlic and when riding on the *serveece*, we would crane our necks looking back at the walls and walls of garlic we were passing. We began using so much crushed garlic to make our hummus and sautéing sliced garlic to go in soups and pasta sauces that Dan, a student of Arabic from Wisconsin who was living with us, remarked, "You're the only people I know who serve garlic as a main dish!"

Garlic even led us to the first political rally we attended in Damascus. We had purchased garlic from a middle-aged man who was usually sitting in front of a butcher's little shop in Souq al-Jouma'a (see the map of Souq al-Jouma'a on page 35) and always he was peeling large cloves of garlic. We were new then and he had no English, but we came to purchase garlic from him often and he would shout greetings to us if he saw us approaching. One day, with some translation help from another shopper, he invited us to come to a protest rally against the U.S. occupation of Iraq. This was late in 2005. So we went with him to a march, and then listened to speakers (just like home). He was a communist and proud of it even though the party in Syria had been treated much like it was in the United States.

Each day we asked, "What's new in the souq?" It could be red beets, turnips, chestnuts, or some different varieties of olives. Or the luscious pomegranates of autumn still piled up months later, giving us excellent juice in the morning or providing rich seeds to toss over salads or munch on after meals. Many times we took our cloth shopping bags up to the souq without planning what we would make for dinner, waiting to see what the souq had in store for us. A huge fluffy cauliflower could become our dinner, steamed and then sautéed in olive oil. Or humongous *silliq* (chard-like leaves) would inspire us to sauté them with garlic and raisins as a main dish.

We discovered another leaf, not giant like *silliq* but equally dramatic. During the first few months of our life in Damascus, a friend who is a doctor came to visit. We went to one of the restaurants in the Old City that had formerly been a home with a lovely courtyard in the middle. When the waiter placed the *fattoush* on the table, Dr. Tom Fasy reached his hand into this traditional salad and pulled out a heart-shaped leaf saying, "Do you see this? This little leaf can save your life!" That little leaf was purslane, and it turns out purslane is helpful in reducing cholesterol. Thanks to our friend's advice, we ate *fattoush* frequently, always adding purslane in generous amounts to this and other salads. We were pleased to always find it at the souq, fresh and lush, with often-muddy roots and leaves still damp from the farm. This vegetable exemplifies the health benefits of the Mediterranean diet.

> ### Stacking
>
> One of the arts of the souq is the art of stacking, not practiced by everybody, but we saw it often and in unexpected places. Sometimes it is amazing. A person builds from some surface a foot to a yard square, and creates the most amazing tower of pomegranates or oranges, melons or onions. The bakeries where sweet pastries are sold do the same thing: Towers rise three to five feet in the windows and on the counters, each building block a delicious creation from pistachios and cheese and honey and dough.
>
> What a natural thing to do, this stacking and building of towers! What happens when you place a container of wooden blocks in front of a toddler? A tower is built until it falls and the next attempt goes higher. So with the bakers of Damascus, especially in the row of shops on the south side of Martyrs Square or those in al-Midan. This architecture from fruit or from pastry makes any advertising unnecessary. The thing itself, and not some big sign about it, attracts.

The Friday Souq

No one seemed to know for sure when or why the Friday Souq (Souq al-Jouma'a) received its name. This frantically busy outdoor market (open every day, and not just on Fridays) has loads of colorful vegetables for sale, piles of mint, salad greens and cilantro, tiny hardware shops, cheese stores, nut shops, bustling bakeries, hummus counters, sewing and notions shops, clothing, and more. The narrow street has tiny shops or tables or counters along both sides. Objects

Silk Road and Agriculture

How did all these good things come to be grown in this small patch between the mountains and the desert? Part of the answer we found in William Cleveland's excellent *A History of the Modern Middle East*. This is mainly a political and social history, but Cleveland wisely pays attention to what's on the dinner table:

Following the Arab conquest of Sind (Pakistan) in the early eighth century, crops from the subtropical climate of India were transported to the Fertile Crescent, Egypt, Africa, and Islamic Spain. In all of these regions, the newly introduced crops became such staples that we tend to think of them as having been part of the cultivated landscape since classical antiquity. But such food crops as rice, sugarcane, lemons, limes, bananas, date palms, spinach, and eggplant as well as the industrial crop cotton were all brought by the Arabs from India to Iraq and then disseminated across North Africa to Spain and to other parts of Europe.... Through their conquests and settlement of diverse climatic regions and the establishment of a trading network connecting those regions, the Arabs, a people whose immediate pre-Islamic existence was not primarily associated with sedentary agriculture, acted as the catalysts for an agricultural revolution that had an impact on the clothes people wore, the foods they consumed, and the ways in which the majority of them organized their working lives.

While we were living in Damascus, a Syrian friend researched and wrote a small book on how the mulberry trees came to Syria and brought not only the wonderful juice to drink fresh in the early summer, but with mulberries came the silk worms, which perhaps are the true founders of the Silk Road.

hang from above. The cobblestones are uneven. Young boys are ready to earn something for their families by stacking a customer's groceries on their handcarts and pushing the cart up the mountainside or holding it firm going down, depending on where the customer lives. As we would weave our way, we often had to move with the crowd single-file past small vehicles unloading fruit and vegetables, or we would squeeze past young children with their mothers, all of us trying to evaluate some bright tomatoes.

One day amidst all this activity, we noticed some people moving aside, glancing back into the narrowest part of the souq, taking on a respectful quietness. We looked back also and saw a satin-draped wooden coffin being carried by several men above their shoulders, followed by a large group of mourners. This was right in the middle of the thickest afternoon shopping, yet the procession moved through the throng, reciting prayers as they walked to the cemetery further up the mountain, just one more part of the daily life of the souq.

On Fridays in the early morning, very few merchants would be found selling anywhere, even in Souq al-Jouma'a. Every part of Damascus we knew was so quiet Friday mornings, like New York City at 8 a.m. on Sundays. After prayer, the souq filled, but for once in each week, it seemed men were a majority of those buying food, often with their young children eager for some treat. By then, many of the merchants were open and ready.

Oven to Hand to Mouth

How many different ways are there to carry bread? We would see people carrying the round, flat Damascene bread, about the size of a large pizza, in stacks on their heads. The stacks of this bread resemble giant pancakes and are most often sold without a bag. Old men with bread on their heads, middle-aged men in suits with bread on their heads, cool-looking teenagers, small kids and grandmothers—all can be spotted walking home, all of them having visited one of the many little bakeries scattered through every neighborhood. Sometimes the bread stack was balanced on a hat or kaffiyeh, other times on the hair. We saw motorcycles whiz by with a stack of bread on the back and bicycles with the front basket full of bread.

When we say "bakery" we mean a bread-baking oven (*furrun* in Arabic) where workers are all day making traditional Middle Eastern flat bread. Customers usually are not inside but lined up on the lane at a window. We

> ### An Oven for All
>
> We often saw teenagers running a dinner errand for their families. Here was one carrying a baking pan filled with fresh eggplant or stuffed green peppers on their way to the neighborhood *furrun*. The ovens that bake the daily bread in any Damascus neighborhood were usually willing to put a family dinner in the hot ovens that baked the bread. The flat round bread came in and out of the oven quickly. Putting a few dinners to cook along the huge oven's edges was easy, and often made the aroma in the *furrun* even finer. The stoves in the home kitchen required buying heavy canisters of cooking gas to be carried up flights of stairs. That made the communal oven even more sensible. Many families had no oven but did well with flat stove-top burners and the baking done by the baker. On summer days, it was a relief not to heat up the whole house when local bread bakers could slide the home-prepared food into their giant ovens.

had a few favorite bakeries that sprinkled black sesame seeds over the bread. Some made whole-wheat flat bread once or twice a week and on those days the lines were particularly long. These bread bakeries were also places where people from the neighborhood could bring dishes they prepared at home that required heat, like eggplants to be roasted, potatoes to bake, tomato-based casseroles, or holiday cookies.

Spice Souq

One of the most magical outdoor markets is the Spice Souq near the Khan Pasha (see the Old City map on page 32). Even the narrowest of lanes where the textiles and quilted fabrics and carpets hang on the walls outside make an ordinary walk seem like a festive parade. Somehow the golden raisins are bigger and better than any we've met elsewhere, the dried apricots and figs look luscious, and the scent of dried lavender, rose petals, and olive oil soap fills the air. Perfumes were being mixed to the buyer's specifications and there was incense too, and dried lemons we used to make our favorite hot drink. Paintings and

In the souqs of Damascus, Syrians and visitors to Syria shop for their food, spices and herbs, and almost all household needs. Photo by Viktor Hegyi.

engraved brass pieces made by local artists are readily available. And there are things from far away, tea and coffee, herbs of every kind and traditional medicines. And of course, whole shops of things made in China, Syrian-made clothing, and products from neighboring Turkey. What is the difference between the souq and the mall? We wish you could have come to discover it for yourself! In addition to local shoppers, there were tourists from other Arab countries, but also Europeans and Asians. It would have been so good if more Americans had come here to experience the people and the architecture and the history.

Merchants heavily dependent on selling to tourists and other visitors (and visitors had been coming in record numbers) felt the effects of Syria's troubles immediately in the spring of 2011. But as the economy itself collapsed, it affected everyone.

A maker and seller of wooden shoes toils in his Old City workshop.
Photo by Bachar Azmeh.

Part 2

Yarmouk Camp (2006–2008)

So many varieties of olives delight everyone on the busy streets of Yarmouk, where tables of foods stretch out onto the sidewalks. Photo by Viktor Hegyi.

5
Life in Yarmouk Camp

Why write about the Yarmouk that no longer exists? For two years, Yarmouk, not just the geography but the community and the stories it held, was home to us. In spring 2006, we were traveling by *serveece* to the southwest corner of Yarmouk almost every day for our Arabic lesson with Mazen, and by the end of the summer we were renting rooms on the third floor of a family house near Palestine Street and the vegetable market.

On the map (see page 33) you will see Yarmouk's borders make a sort of right triangle, with Palestine Street being the hypotenuse as well as the east border, and the 90-degree angle is where 30 Street turns east and passes Mazen's home. All three of Yarmouk's major streets begin at the top of a triangle in a large square called Sahat Batikh (Watermelon Square, because of a fountain in that shape). From there the cars, trucks, and *serveeces* go south on 30 Street or Palestine Street or the street that bisects the triangle, Yarmouk Street.

From first day to last, our every sense would tell us how different Yarmouk was from the other communities in which we lived in Damascus. We write here about Yarmouk as we knew it, before its destruction in early 2014 in the fighting between the Syrian army and opposition militias. During our stay in the camp, it seemed to embody so well the welcome that Syria was accustomed to extending to people fleeing for their lives, whether from ethnic cleansing in Palestine or from the destruction of Iraq that accompanied its "liberation" by the Western coalition. We pay tribute to Yarmouk Camp as we knew it and we grieve for the suffering of its few thousand remaining residents, who have faced starvation and bitterly cold winters with little protection.

YARMOUK CAMP is five miles from the center of Damascus. Formalized in 1957, it is one of 13 camps the UN began establishing in Syria beginning in 1948. Most of the Palestinian refugee camps in Syria, as in Jordan and Lebanon, are associated with the Palestinian Nakba (usually translated as "catastrophe") of 1948–49, when more than 700,000 Palestinians were driven out of Palestine (and into neighboring Syria, Jordan, or Lebanon) by Zionist militias (and later, the Israeli army). The term "ethnic cleansing" had not come into use then, but is now commonly accepted as a description of what was happening.

The number of Palestinians who received refuge is all the more amazing given that these countries themselves had populations and economies nowhere near adequate to absorb so many refugees. But they did. In Syria's case, the nation had only two years before seen France depart as a colonial power. (The French had arrived to run the new country after the Ottoman Empire fell in World War I.)

Syria had no plan for how to receive tens of thousands of homeless people, how to educate the children, find jobs for the adults, provide access to health care for all. In later years, Syria would show much the same spirit to Palestinians again in 1967, to Iraqis beginning in 2003, and to Lebanese fleeing to Syria in summer 2006 when Israel invaded southern Lebanon.

Palestinians in Syria, whether born in Palestine or in Syria, are not Syrian citizens. All have the right to be registered as Palestinian refugees with United Nations Relief and Works Agency (UNRWA). But Palestinians in Syria have, in most ways, the rights and responsibilities of Syrian citizens (for example, free study at the universities if qualified). They do not have Syrian passports but can obtain comparable travel documents from the Palestinian Authority in Ramallah. Most Palestinians will say they want it this way; Palestine is their country and they will return there.

Who could have known that the refugees' return to Palestine, then seen as certain, would still be withheld more than 65 years later? But the right of Palestinians to return to their homes and villages was upheld by UN Resolution 194 in December 1948. Why is such a return considered a fantasy to so many of us? It is still a right Palestinians claim. Perhaps we were slow to understand this because, as Americans, we seem less and less to be attached to the communities where our parents and ancestors lived. The sense of a home place, let alone a desire to return there, seems something of the past. Yet no one denies the centrality of the refugees' claims to any permanent resolution of the Israeli-Palestinian impasse.

And the truth is, the desire to return is very much alive, as we learned when we stopped by a copy/print shop near us to copy some poetry by the Palestinian poet Mahmoud Darwish. While the copying was being done, Gabe had a conversation with the shop's manager about his roots here. As always, he was very welcoming and we began to talk about our countries of origin. Soon he began to tell his own story of 1948, how Israeli soldiers killed his father and his sister in front of him when he was barely six years old. He began to cry as he described that day. He ended his tale and asked, "Why is it that you can go to Palestine and I cannot? Why is it that people from your country or any country in Europe can go to Palestine but I cannot?" Why indeed.

Our Yarmouk

Yarmouk Camp took its name from the Yarmouk River and evolved as Palestinians built temporary and then more permanent places to live along with stores and workshops.

Yarmouk's three busy streets diverge as they move south and seem to widen enough to hold all the living rooms and schools and souqs and mosques of Yarmouk. One more wide street, famous in all Damascus, is Lubya Street, which has one clothing store after another. The street takes its name from the village close to Nazareth that was depopulated in 1948, some of whose residents made their way to Yarmouk. Israel planted a pine forest on the ruins of the village of Lubya as though to erase its past.

> [P]ine trees...cover many of the destroyed Palestinian villages, hiding their remains under vast "green lungs" planted by the Jewish National Fund for the purpose of "recreation and tourism." Such a forest of pine trees was planted over the destroyed village of Lubya. Only the diligent and meticulous work of later generations, spearheaded by historian Mahmoud Issa...has enabled visitors today to trace the vestiges of the village and join in the commemorations of the sixty people who lost their lives there. (Ilan Pappé, *The Ethnic Cleansing of Palestine*, pages 154–55)

When we knew Yarmouk Camp, it was an area of cinderblock buildings, with very few trees and very narrow lanes. We came to appreciate and admire the effort people made to tend plants and vines on their balconies and roofs; a few had spectacular bougainvillea that climbed as high as three stories. The lanes were too narrow to accommodate traditional garbage trucks; instead, tractors pulled carts on which residents piled their trash bags.

The lanes are the playgrounds of children and the hangout places for their older brothers and sometimes sisters. They are the place of mourning the dead, celebrating weddings with music and dance, marking someone's return from the hajj. At sunset during Ramadan, the streets would grow so quiet! We were the only people out walking, and in that quiet, we could hear the clinks of spoons and forks against plates inside the apartments.

These narrow lanes are also the marketplace of street sellers. And the tangles of electric wires above defied understanding but somehow brought electricity to the residents.

Living at Beit Abu Ali

"For rent" signs were rare in crowded Yarmouk, perhaps because word of mouth was far more efficient than signs. A friend took us to a store-front office, which had information about neighborhood rooms for rent. (We had seen many such offices in Damascus and wondered what happens in them because the only activity we could see from the outside was tea drinking by groups of men.) Here we met Abu Ali, who showed us several possible apartment spaces before suggesting that we might want to look at the third-floor rooms in his own family's home. This third floor was intended for his oldest son, Ali, to move into when he married. He would rent it to us if we wanted it; we did, and we moved in the same day.

In the Old City, we had lived in one room; now we had three rooms plus our own kitchen and bathroom for about the same monthly rent, and each of the three rooms was larger than our single room the year before. We now had a guest bedroom that was seldom empty. Two activists with Voices in the Wilderness, Michael Birmingham and Dan Pierson, moved in with us. Both were passionate about gaining fluency in Arabic and volunteered their time for the project that later become our full-time focus.

The guest who stayed the longest, much to our delight, was Rana, an Iraqi journalist. She had been a major contributor in the creation and on-site filming and interviews for *Road to Fallujah,* a documentary that showed the reality of life for residents of a city that was destroyed by U.S. forces in 2004. She had worked with other journalists as a translator and cameraperson, and was active in issues affecting Iraqi refugees in Damascus. She taught us how to make strong Iraqi tea with cardamom and was always cheerful except when she exhibited her righteous anger about the way the United States had ruined her beloved Iraq.

Rana's Iraqi Tea with Cardamom

Ten years later, we still prepare it every morning. The Swan tea that Rana found in Damascus is a black tea that she and many Iraqis preferred when available; it is sold in several stores in Brooklyn in 500-gram bags. And cardamom pods in bulk are usually available in Middle Eastern or Asian food stores.

We follow closely Rana's tea-making process. We fill a large tea kettle with cold water and then measure three heaping tablespoons of the crushed tea leaves in the water. Then we take about 20 cardamom pods of various sizes and crack open each pod, one at a time, with something like a sturdy tablespoon, pressing a pod down just until it cracks. Some of the tiny seeds inside will jump out of the pod, some won't. When all the pods are cracked open, we put the pods and any loose seeds in the kettle on top of the tea, put the top on the kettle, turn on the burner, and bring the water to a boil. We keep it boiling for five minutes or so, then turn off the burner and let it sit for a few minutes.

In small glass cups commonly used in Iraq for tea, we measure the sugar, one or two or more tiny spoons of sugar in the cup before pouring the hot tea.

Mimoon, an Iraqi student we worked with who went on to enroll in a master's program in engineering at Worcester Polytechnic Institute, wrote this haiku inspired by tea as prepared by Iraqis:

Tea with cardamom
Flies me back into Iraq:
Smell of home and hope.

We also had access to the roof above the second floor. Our apartment on the third floor was smaller than the family's rooms on the second floor, where Abu Ali and Umm Ali lived with their three sons. At times, our outdoor-on-their-roof space became our real living room and study room. We would often throw a sheet over the clothesline to create a shady covering and enjoy our breakfast or lunch there. The roof had an area that was suitable for a raised garden: a cement wall about waist-high that separated a once and future flower and vegetable bed from the open roof. We filled the space with tall plants of jasmine, bougainvillea, colonia, and something called Melissa that had leaves with a scent like lemon balm, but more of a shrub. The long, thin leaves are used for tea and in cooking, and are sold dried in the fragrant but mysterious little stores full of colorful spices, herbs, dried flowers, and leaves.

We planted morning glories, and they were true to their name. They became vines, no longer contained by the string web we established around and above our garden. One morning Theresa called out to our neighbor across the narrow street: Shall we make a way for these vines from our balcony toward their house? She loved the idea, and we started to make plans. The next morning when Gabe went out to water the plants, green cord had been mysteriously tossed over to our garden. It came from the neighbors' balcony, where it was tied tightly. He tied it to a pole and tossed it back to their side. For the next half hour we created many lines for the morning glories to cross, throwing the ball of cord back and forth. After that, we tried to train the vines to cross over the lane far below. This is exactly what Damascenes have done with grapevines for centuries, making shady summer lanes on the hottest days. So these green leaves and deep purple flowers with dark violet centers set off on their journey. The vines never quite made it all the way, perhaps because it was too horizontal and they wanted always to ascend. But in the mornings especially, they were lovely to see.

In some ways the flat roofs in Yarmouk served the way closets (seldom part of the picture here), basements, and garages serve homeowners in the United States: as storage for things seldom needed and long forgotten. The roofs were also home to the city's doves. Wherever we lived in Damascus, whatever time of day we were out walking, we could stand still and watch any part of the sky, and witness flocks of doves soaring and circling so that they seemed silver until the sunlight made them a pewter color again. It took us a few months to learn that these flocks lived together on the roofs in every neighborhood of Damascus. We didn't know that caring for them, releasing them, calling them home was an art handed down within families. But eventually we would see from our roof that on some other roof the keeper of some flock—for many circling flocks could be seen at one time—holding a pole with a colorful fabric at the one end. The keeper waved this flag to signal: Come back now.

The roof provided a panoramic view of crowded Yarmouk. We had unobstructed views of the mountains to the south (Jabal al-Shaikh, Mount Hermon in the Bible) and to the northwest (Mount Qassiun). Whenever we went to the roof, we would see others on their roofs.

Water from the mountains to the west made the oasis that became Damascus. Water from those mountains was now in those huge round tanks, often bright red, on the flat roofs of Damascus. Anywhere we lived in Damascus, we learned how to heat water for bathing. No one we knew ever expected hot water to come from the tap all day, seven days a week. In multiple-unit buildings, the water heating equipment was usually located overhead in the bathroom, a false ceiling concealing the water tank (filled from a larger water tank that might be on the roof) and, usually, an electric heater. Depending on the size of the tank, one knew when to begin heating water before the hot water was wanted for a bath or shower. For doing dishes, it was easier and quicker to heat water on the stove, then fill the dishpan. Every stove we encountered needed to have its fuel tank replaced when empty with a full one. One traded in the empty tank for a full and heavier tank at some nearby shop where the empty was accepted and a small price paid for a refilled tank.

Soon after we moved to Damascus, we realized that we had to relearn how to use water. Drinking water was made available for an hour or so, and we filled two very large jars. This took a few minutes only but so often made us conscious of people who have no such access to drinking water, people who travel long distances to wells, women who carry heavy vessels of water.

At Umm Ali's, water was heated not in our apartment but rather on the roof, and the heat source was not electricity but a fuel called *mazote,* which could be purchased from a man whose donkey pulled a large tank of fuel right by the door once or twice a week. The man would announce himself with a deep and musical call: "*MAZOTE! MAZOTE!*" When customers emerged from their homes, large cans in tow, he stopped his cart, filled up the cans, took payment, and continued to the next neighborhood.

We had no south windows to bring in the sun during the winter months, but the roof just outside could be comfortable even in February without a sweater. Our apartment's cinderblock walls seemed to conduct the cold air from the outside and trap it inside.

Life on Yarmouk's Streets

During our first year at Yarmouk, we would sometimes leave the camp (which covered an area less than one square mile) only once a week; some people rarely left. It was its own city.

Our apartment was a short walk to a wonderful vegetable market, with seller after seller displaying vegetables, fruits, olives, nuts, seeds, grains, flours, sugar, cheeses, meats, sweets, and what can only be called "notions." Sprinkled here and there were stands selling hot falafel or hummus or shawarma (grilled meat) turning on the vertical spit next to gas-fed flames making a kind of open oven. Nearby bakeries sold flatbread and pastries.

We learned the numbers and weight measures in Arabic by shopping in markets like this throughout Damascus. The transactions were in cash and never included sales tax. And we learned the amazing honesty of sellers who keep adding to the scales until they give you precisely what you're paying for. A person selling nuts will add a single nut to make it exact. A zucchini seller might add another small zucchini to those we picked out to put the scale slightly above what we wanted. Here as elsewhere, what was available in fruits and vegetables came and went with the season, except bananas—always bananas, usually from Lebanon but, according to the stickers, sometimes from Ecuador.

In Yarmouk, we saw the garlic season arrive twice: sheaves of garlic tall as a person, bound for stacking or standing, looking like a harvest home. Of course one could buy garlic on short stems or garlic cloves peeled and filling large tubs, but nothing was as beautiful as these harvest booths that seemed to be built from the garlic they were selling.

That first week in Yarmouk we stopped for fresh-squeezed orange juice at a corner stand. A young man ran around the corner and came back with two chairs for us to sit in as we drank the juice. Two of his friends came to meet us because they couldn't believe that two fairly old Americans had chosen to live in Yarmouk and to study Arabic with a Palestinian teacher in their neighborhood.

One of the joys of our Yarmouk streets was the songs or cries or chants of peddlers as they travel through the narrow lanes with their wares. How did "peddler" acquire a negative meaning in English? One morning around 8 a.m., we heard a delightful seven-note song coming from the street below that came from a young boy with a tray balanced on his head full of rectangular pieces of cake iced in pink and white.

A less pleasant sound that was familiar in 2006 was that of old bulldozers knocking down buildings, including a mosque near the copy shop we often visited. Clearly the cinderblock buildings were quickly built and never meant to last. One month later, we saw that the debris had been cleared and a deep basement had been dug. Builders had reinforced the basement walls and tall, skinny logs were in place to support the pouring of the ground floor. We could see workers in the basement slinging wet cement onto the bottom of the first floor, but above them, standing on that as yet unwalled first floor, we saw a row of about 18 men at prayer, all rising from a bow simultaneously. Most were clad in light-colored cotton *dishdashas* (the traditional loose-fitting, shoulder-to-ankle garment). We were seeing two kinds of human movement, each involving a similar number of participants: those above doing the unison movements of prayer and three or four meters directly below them, the commotion of the workers in the basement. We paused and felt the blessing that their presence was already bringing to the neighborhood.

The bulldozers had an easy job. We were reminded of this when we read in 2013 and 2014 that bulldozers were again busy at work demolishing the neighborhoods that were so familiar to us. What may rise there in the next few years will likely have no relation to the community that built Yarmouk and lived there for three generations.

Ramadan and the Eid

Each day walking to class, we would pass a small neighborhood mosque, often at the time of midday or afternoon prayer. When Ramadan came, the number of people praying increased. To accommodate them, huge rugs were brought out into the street. More than 30 people were kneeling on the mats praying among the vegetable sellers, the man with fruit drinks for sale, the motorcycle whizzing noisily by, the kids playing, the three-wheeled vehicle loaded with watermelons. So much human commerce in this tiny area, and the prayer now another part of it. What does that say of a community that accepts it as normal?

It is probably well known to all by now that those who keep Ramadan do not eat or drink anything between sunrise and sundown. That's one thing when the four weeks of Ramadan come in the winter, but quite another when it falls in the summer. (Ramadan follows a lunar calendar and so has no fixed date on the Gregorian calendar.) For the month of Ramadan, we were awakened maybe two hours before sunrise by the chant of a man who roamed the streets carrying a tambourine-like instrument, which he struck (loud as he could) while chanting the standard call to wake up and eat before sunrise, "You who are sleeping, say that That who is eternal [God] is One."

Early in Ramadan, we would see the moon waxing each night in the western sky. After breaking their fast, many people would go walking. Some shops opened again but never seemed busy. People were mostly just strolling and talking and creating a time unlike other time. Then the streets would quiet down. For many, the different rhythm of their days and nights in Ramadan means rising before the sun for their second meal of the night.

The rhythm of daily life was altered during Ramadan. School days were shorter, and business hours were adjusted. As sundown approached, the internet café that we used closed so that the two young employees could make it home in time for the evening meal that breaks the fast (*iftar*). The streets would still have a few drivers hurrying home, but we also saw many people pedaling home as fast as they could on bicycles, often with a bag of bread hanging from the bike or clutched by the riders.

What we came to love during Ramadan was the hour before darkness and the first hour of darkness as people rushed to get home before the sun disappeared. Sometimes we saw that a few workers had brought their food and broke their fast together. Or families might drive to an open space near the freeway, unpack their food, and break their fast under the palm trees. During Ramadan, every pastry shop that makes the traditional pastries with nuts and/or cheese would extend into the sidewalks or the streets with tables displaying, during the last few hours of each day, not the normal sweets only but those specifically offered during Ramadan.

Sometimes we walked at sunset to enjoy the silence of the streets. Silence outside, lights and sharing food inside. No traffic to watch for, no children playing soccer in the lanes. Inevitably we saw a few stragglers rushing toward home. As we walked past homes, we could hear the soft sounds of forks touching plates and birds singing in the eucalyptus.

Obviously there are Muslims who do not observe Ramadan, but those who fast seem to accept this and the non-fasters do not flaunt their lack of observance. We took note of the ways these Ramadan days create community and the identity of individuals within the community, something we Westerners have traded in for other promises. In Yarmouk especially, we felt embraced by the observance though we did not observe. But there is care and renewal of spirit and forgiveness perhaps. One could grasp that Islam brought long ago and still maintains a solidarity both in fasting and in dining together, a beauty in daring to wake people at 4 a.m. with a drum and a chant, the good of anticipation and joy, not embarrassment with piety. And also tolerance. The rituals that embody such things are not didactic, and they are not to be reduced to "it means this" or "it means that." They are, at heart and at their best, a way that those "habits of the heart" sustain the community and the individual. It isn't what they *mean* so much as *rehearsing* what *we* mean and what vision we have of our lives and our world.

As the end of Ramadan approached, we saw that Islam has not escaped the eager embrace of buying and selling, and the sidewalks and even the streets of Yarmouk became more filled with merchandise as people shopped to prepare for Eid al-Fitr, the three-day holiday that marks the end of Ramadan. ("Made in

China" was seen as often here as in the United States.) Carts and tables and even blankets spread on the sidewalks were full of merchandise. Clothes, shoes, underwear, hardware, but also the pastry shops and bread bakeries and butchers and cheese shops—everything bursts out of the store's walls and the sidewalks and half the streets become tangles as the crowds inch their way through. This hubbub happens in the afternoons until sunset and then it ends totally, completely, and silence reigns for an hour or two.

Ramadan ends when the next new moon is seen. (This happens only in the evening, which means that the holiday is announced only the night before.) The Eid is a celebration of Ramadan's blessing on the community. For three days, government offices and schools close. Many families in Damascus took advantage of these days to visit their relatives in the family's village; this didn't happen in Yarmouk, obviously, because the villages of the parents or grandparents are in Palestine. Yarmouk stayed full of people for the Eid.

For Eid, swing sets and rides would show up: on side streets, in parks, on tiny cul-de-sacs. The rides came in all sizes, nearly all of them without motors. Children could line up to ride in the swings, or Ferris wheel–like contraptions, or various other very old but very sturdy ways to have some fun. Teenagers and parents provided the locomotion. One of these was a swing where four children sit on a "porch swing" facing four other children on another porch swing. The teenagers help this big swing rock back and forth, higher and higher, just to the point where one can't watch to see if gravity is still in charge.

A red train of six cars, each holding a dozen or more children, appeared on the shopping street near us each night, and some nights its route went right under our windows. This train used a motor. People heard it coming and went

NEW YEAR'S EVE at the end of 2006 coincided with the beginning of the three-day Muslim Eid (festival) called Eid al-Adha. It marks the end of the hajj, the pilgrimage to Mecca. Its central story is the story of Abraham and Ishmael (much like the story Genesis tells about Abraham and Isaac). Both stories end with the sacrifice of a ram and not the child. Sunday, on the minibus ride to church in the Old City, the streets and shops were still holiday quiet, but for a long stretch, the broad sidewalks had become home to one flock of sheep after another. Feeding troughs, sawdust, the works. Sheep are apparently very smart about not stepping off the sidewalk into busy streets.

But they might not be so smart about what lies ahead. One glance at the clothesline-like ropes stretched here and there would tell them that these big, lovely fleeces came from somewhere—maybe from their fellow sheep who stood there munching yesterday.

Later, walking some streets near our apartment, we could see the whole sequence. We saw improvised pens of live sheep. Butchers with carcasses on hooks in front of their shops were cutting, chopping, washing. Pools of blood stood here and there. And piles of the fleeces, clean or being cleaned up. Will most of this fresh meat go to a freezer? Where is it? We were told that those who can afford it, pick out a live sheep, buy it, have it slaughtered and fleeced, and take the carcass to a butcher shop to be cut up. But the buyer keeps very little and distributes the rest to those who could never afford this. During the days of Eid, the fleece is often hung outside the house of the one who purchased the sheep.

to their windows and waved to the children passengers. One evening, we heard galloping only to find we had horses here and on many other little streets. Children lined up to ride them around the neighborhoods.

Watching the children play reminded us of the lack of playgrounds and parks. Children generally played in the streets, but the few wide streets were full of traffic most of the time, and some corners were completely blind. Needless to say, these streets lacked sidewalks.

So many parents with preteen boys, and not only in Yarmouk, seemed to think that a necessary part of Eid was toy guns. They appeared in shops and from street sellers in the last days of Ramadan. Then appeared in the hands of the boys as soon as Eid began. Clearly not everyone appreciated this. Theresa saw a grandmotherly woman, having been "shot at," take the toy gun and crush it in her hand. But each year we also noticed, a week later, no guns to be seen.

In some ways, the neighborhood seemed a world unto itself. It felt as though both Ramadan and the Eid took place in this small space with no reference to any other communities. We were amazed to see that the tables in the little restaurants—inside and at the outside café-like seating—were filled at 1:30 p.m. with children in their holiday clothes behaving themselves well. No adults accompanied them. We were told that this is a tradition (maybe just in Yarmouk?) to use the Eid gift of money this way, having lunch at a restaurant with your friends. Later in the evening, the adults were there, families or couples together, just strolling, watching the children's rides, having sweets or popcorn or other treats.

During our early-morning walks through the neighborhood toward the end of Ramadan, we had noticed that rustic structures made of wood framing, covered with pine and cedar branches, set up at the door of the typical two- or three-story apartment buildings. Strung over and around the branches were strings of small prayer-flags with words written on them. We soon learned that these special arbor-like structures were built to welcome home people returning from the hajj (the pilgrimage to Mecca). Later we had one of these structures at the end of our block. Music was playing and a celebration was happening outside this hajji's house.

About 25 men were holding hands and dancing the *debkeh* in front of the hajj house, live vocalists and musicians singing and playing traditional songs. The lead dancers were older men swinging their prayer beads or white handkerchiefs as they led the line of dancers with quick steps. Little boys from the neighborhood stood behind the row of dancers, imitating their steps, trying to catch up with when to kick, when to step, and when to leap. At one point, men inside the circle put one man on the shoulders of another, then a third on the shoulders of the second, forming a three-man dancing stack!

The next night the celebration continued, this time with about 60 men dancing in this street that was only about 14 feet one side to the other, so now filled with a vibrant rectangle of 60 *debkeh* enthusiasts, and another smaller circle in the middle dancing intensely in triple-time. Then came the third night and this time there was a three-story high flag of Syria suspended at the end of the street as well as a stage for a band. We went outside to listen when the music was most lively.

A Wedding and a Death

Very near our home, several Iraqis opened a tiny bakery, a reminder that Yarmouk also hosted refugees not from Palestine. We would stop and chat with them sometimes, but were still surprised when one of the young men, Zaid, invited us to his wedding. The wedding venue was a five-minute walk from home on busy Falasteen Street. Three minibuses brought guests from other neighborhoods. The hall was upstairs, a large room decorated with artificial flowers. Bride and groom sat on white and gold throne-like chairs placed on a platform. The groom wore a dark brown suit and had a big smile on his face when he saw us. The bride had her hair done up, decorated with glitter and tiny white flowers, curls cascading over one shoulder. The bridal gown was spread out all around her. Her mother stood nearby greeting friends and relatives who approached the platform with blessings and congratulations. Folks came forward with their own cameras and stood with the bride and groom for pictures.

There were two singers in tan suits and two musicians on synthesizers. The music seemed traditional with a pattern of slow beginning with calm singing and gentle strumming, then suddenly switching to an up-tempo beat where all the folks who wanted to dance jumped onto the dance floor. The songs were long and familiar to many, with rhythmic clapping from the people watching. But only men were dancing! Guys in couples, guys in triads, guys by themselves, guys who sometimes raised the groom on their shoulders and held hands as they danced in a circle. Some of their dancing was very suggestive and some of it wild. Men sat at tables around the dance floor while the women sat on another level about five steps up overlooking the dancing. Couples like us sat in the women's section, and we were seated at a table with a couple whose home was Baghdad before taking refuge in Syria. After more than an hour and a half, 40 men joined hands on the dance floor for the traditional *debkeh*, leaders on both ends of the snake-like formation swinging their prayer beads in the air.

After the dancing we were served Iraqi *samoon*, a crocodile-shaped bread, with some chicken inside it and served with a splash of salad greens along with an orange. A server came around with pieces of frosted sponge cake and bottles of soda. When we left, deafened by the volume of the music, we saw the bride and groom make their way to the dance floor, probably for their first ever dance together.

Rites of passage were more public in Yarmouk than we had experienced at home. We would see in Yarmouk the funeral tent set up in some narrow street at least once a week, and sometimes we saw pick-up trucks carrying the coffin from the home to the place of burial. A few or many people would be following on foot while prayers were sung over a loudspeaker, often by someone in the cab of the truck.

On our way to our teacher's house one day, we came upon a silent group of men sitting in four rows of perhaps 25 chairs each, all placed within the slim area between two apartment buildings. Clearly it was a funeral gathering, without the tent we usually see in winter. The men were each holding a portfolio chapter of the Qur'an taken from the unbound holy book on a table nearby.

Each man was silently reading, reflecting, here in the middle of the neighborhood. It was such a contrast to the hustle and bustle of the streets surrounding them. The shade of a massive bougainvillea protected some of them in this silent, prayerful setting. We later learned that on the third day after a death the mourners try to read the entire Qur'an in this collective manner, each selecting chapters from the box and reading. Western Christians, and perhaps others too, do not really understand the relationship between the Qur'an and the Muslim. A first step might be to realize that though the book holding the text is honored, the Qur'an itself is the text recited rather than the text written. It is speaking and sound, not print. No one was doing silent reading that day, but in soft murmurs the words on pages became their own.

Late one morning, we were studying on the roof when we heard music we had come to associate with a funeral. It was close. A little later, as we went down the stairs on our way to Arabic class, we saw many women on the second-floor landing and the door was open to the family's apartment. We could hear women weeping inside. Young men were sitting on the stairs between the landing and the front door that opened off the street. We knew that someone had died in the house.

When we walked back home after class, we saw that the lane between the house where we lived and the house on the south side of the lane now held a long tent that touched our building on one side and, on the other, the building across the street. This little street was thus closed to any vehicle, but pedestrians could walk through the tent if they wished.

Soon we learned that Abu Ali had been taken to the hospital the day before with chest pains and died the next morning. In the seven months we had rented the top floor of the family home, he had been the one to collect our rent, to demonstrate how things worked, and to fix whatever needed fixing. That he did, always, with a single tool: his hammer. And it was all he needed. Now, without any prolonged illness, still in his 50s, Abu Ali had died and been buried that very day, as is the Islamic practice. Then the three days of mourning and condolences began. The tent was full of men and the apartment full of women when we returned from class, and it was this way for much of the next day and again the day after that. So many women came to sit with Umm Ali in the apartment; so many men came to sit outside in the tent. In Yarmouk, the word of someone's death spread on the streets and by phone, brought all the friends from a person's whole life—or so it seems to us. The funeral music has its own quality and each time it is heard, people must want to know who has died. Walking the streets here each day, the funeral tents became very familiar to us.

Theresa joined the women sitting with the widow on Wednesday morning. Some of the women with Umm Ali took turns holding Abu Ali's grandson. At some point, Umm Ali asked her daughter to take the large photo of Abu Ali's off the wall. Holding this framed photo, Umm Ali began to tell Theresa about how long they had been married and lived in this house, and how she would miss him.

Gabe sat with the men that night. In the tent there was silence and the chanting of prayers, but very little conversation among the men. Some prayer beads had been placed on a small table in the center of the mourners to be used by those who did not bring their own; an unbound Qur'an was available for those who wished to select a chapter to read quietly.

In both spaces, we were offered strong coffee in small, handleless cups. Two cups were passed among all the mourners.

People in Abu Ali's generation were the first generation born outside Palestine. His grandchildren are the fourth generation to live their lives outside Palestine.

With Abu Ali's death and the mourning that followed, we began to learn a few of the beautiful Arabic phrases people use at the time of death: May God be merciful to her/him. May God give you strength. May God provide a dwelling place in paradise. There seems to be none of the "I'm sorry" and very much of reliance on God, very much also of a sense that life goes on and the various circles of community continue.

"Get Out of There!"

After her husband's death, Umm Ali began to learn what was required of those who rent rooms in their homes, especially if the renters are foreigners. She was also learning how many variations there were in this advice. But in spring 2008, she asked us to accompany her to a close-by office where taxes and other fees—even utilities—were paid. For most of that morning, we were shuffled back and forth between various desks. Computers were becoming common in Damascus in these years and the internet had been available at least since Bashar al-Assad became president in 2000. He had until then served as president of the Syrian Computer Society. But it was taking time to trickle down.

At some point Umm Ali was convinced that we could make no progress here until we visited a larger municipal office of taxes in downtown Damascus. We went together by taxi to a tall building near Arnous Square (Sahat Arnous), famous for its too-large statue of Bashar al-Assad's father, Hafiz.

This office building seemed to us to be on a different planet than Yarmouk. Even to enter, some document had to be shown. Inside, men in suits hustled from office to office. Elevators were full of those moving from one floor to another in what was always a multistep process to complete any business. Umm Ali had a name from a friend in Yarmouk of someone who would perhaps help us. She asked for him and when he came, met with him while we waited. Language was a problem throughout this adventure. We couldn't pick up the details, but we were clear that this wasn't going to be cheap. Nor quick. It was also clear that neither Umm Ali nor ourselves quite understood what we were paying for or why we needed whatever it was. So, all in all, this was for us the sort of experience common to rich and poor countries alike. Nikolai Gogol would have recognized it at once.

When it seemed that an amount had been set and that we were the ones who were responsible for it and that it was far more than anticipated, we called Mazen. He knew we were going to spend the morning with Umm Ali and asked where we were. Theresa told him. His answer was instant and urgent: "Get out of there! Leave! Right now! Don't pay anyone anything. Leave! Get out of there!" Theresa handed the phone to Umm Ali and he repeated this in Arabic.

None of us asked another question. We quickly descended the staircases, left the building, and took a taxi back to Yarmouk. Umm Ali, with some advice from Mazen, soon found where the necessary papers could be had and fees paid in Yarmouk and our shared adventure smoothed out some rough times of our two years in her home. And we learned that both Syrians and Iraqis who were told they needed to obtain some license or pay some fee there had the same advice as Mazen.

This Old House

During our second year in Yarmouk, just when the weather turned warmer in early March, we learned that Umm Ali had sold the ground floor. We had never seen what was there, and now workers came and tore out every inside wall, bagging the debris; then they knocked apart some of the cinderblocks of the outside wall. New cement pillars went up from big pits that had been dug into the earth after the floor had been hauled away. Dust. Mud. Old plaster, old doors.

Umm Ali and her children packed up and moved out. They told us they would be living in a building about 200 meters away. Then the workers went to work on the second floor, tore out the inside walls and most of the outside walls. Umm Ali promised us that the family would be back in three months living in an entirely new set of rooms. At 7 a.m. each day, the sledge hammers seemed to make everything that was left, ourselves included, vibrate. But other days, no workers came. One morning we heard a horrible, crashing sound as if a bulldozer was breaking up the foundation of the building—no warning! And indeed, a bulldozer was breaking up the foundation of the building. We were the only ones living in the building, perched on top of what looked like two bombed and vandalized floors, almost an image of what was to come.

Work came to a halt and we went on living like squatters on the top (third) story of our building. We would enter the now-skeletal building and climb the stairs that went from no first floor to no second floor and up to our third floor. At night, if we were expecting any visitors, we would set out candles on the steps to our door. All the electricity was gone except in our apartment, which now felt as though it was perched in the sky.

Several neighborhood cats noticed the vacancies on the first two floors and moved in. Eventually some new pillars were poured and new cinderblock walls enclosed the ground floor.

Despite the chaos of our surroundings, Theresa's garden—snapdragons and Sweet William, sunflowers, and morning glories—planted the previous summer in old oil barrels and boxes on the balcony/roof continued to thrive. And we had herbs and jasmine, the Damascus city flower.

Even during drought and strife, the bond between humans and their gardens endures.
Photo by Bachar Azmeh.

6
Border Crossings

Borders arrived recently in the long life of Damascus. Passports, visas, stamps when you enter, stamps when you leave. Some think the current situation in Syria and Iraq and beyond may lead to more borders for more nations. Was Woody Guthrie onto something when he added a verse to "This Land Is Your Land" that seems to deal with borders that say who can go where and who can't?

We stayed put in Damascus, and when we left Damascus, it was usually for somewhere else in Syria by bus or train. But we went to Jordan a few times and to Lebanon a few times over these seven years to visit friends.

Jordan

In the spring of 2006, we took a shared taxi from Damascus to Amman; while we waited for other passengers, we agreed on a price with a taxi driver and convinced him to make a one-hour stop at Ezra'a, a small town just off the Damascus to Amman highway so that we could see two ancient churches still in use. The driver expressed interest in seeing it himself, and two prospective passengers were willing to make this diversion.

We found Saint George church in the town of Ezra'a. Before the year 515 CE, this church was probably a Roman temple, but the Greek inscription above the west door says, "What was once a lodging place of demons has become a house of God." It is a house now for a Greek Orthodox congregation. A woman with her very lively three-year-old son came to unlock the church for us. The inside is a "circle in a square" configuration with the altar to the east side. Plastic chairs, for use when the wooden benches are filled on Sundays, were stacked against the ancient walls. The building itself, its dark stone, font, and altar, has been home to a Sunday assembly with their stories and saints and tribulations for 1,500 years. The patron for whom the church was named is that George known as the dragon-slayer but known also as the patron saint of England and other places. Saint George, said to have been martyred by the occupying power (Rome at that time), is as popular among Syrian Christians as Patrick and Bridget are with Irish Christians. Everyone, driver and passengers, enjoyed the visit and the ice cream bars we bought across the street. A second church was nearby, but not intact: partial walls and arches with yellow mustard seed and red poppies growing everywhere as well as signs that the church was a place visited by animals and humans in need of some shelter.

Amman

In Amman, we visited with Kathy Kelly and Cathy Breen, friends from Voices in the Wilderness who were staying in Amman and were in contact with many Iraqis, some now refugees in Jordan, some still in Iraq. The news from Iraq was grim: An hour a day of electricity in cities of central Iraq. Bad water. Hospitals with nowhere to put the daily flow of dead bodies. Doctors who have to let the armed militias have their way right in the hospitals. Thousands of kidnappings. No economy, few jobs, tremendous fear, corruption at every level, and so many of those who should have become teachers and leaders now murdered or living as refugees in Syria or Jordan. Beyond the violent deaths and the suffering were the victims no one counts now: the children dying from bad water or the cancers caused by depleted uranium. Wars don't end when they end. This was spring 2006; how long would be your list or ours of disasters to come in Iraq? It continues now.

Later that night we visited with our dear friends Ghada and Sameer, who had befriended us when we were passing through Amman on our journeys to Baghdad before the U.S. invasion. In 1999, Ghada had helped us sanction-breakers choose children's books in Arabic to take to Baghdad and gave us medicines to carry. Over our several visits in and out of Iraq, always through Amman, Ghada and Sameer had hosted a welcoming meal with us, but mainly at their home they served laughter and serious discussion, and we always loved time spent with them and their children.

On the way back to Damascus, we had a marvelous four hours in a packed taxi. We were blessed on this occasion. The driver, from Damascus, was right out of the Syrian soap opera we were studying to hear spoken Arabic—happy, loud, gesturing, joking, and knew the good, quick roads. One of the two other riders was a young Syrian man coming home for a month from Moscow, where he opened a restaurant that offered Middle East specialties. He spoke Russian and Arabic, the driver Arabic and about ten good English words. The final passenger was a professor of architecture and design, a Syrian but now on the faculty of a university in Amman. He spoke some English, but was also fluent in Russian and of course Arabic. He was returning from six months at a university in London where he was doing research on Islamic mosaic work.

On another short trip to Amman in 2007, we met a young Iraqi doctor who had finished medical school in Baghdad. He fled to Jordan after three guns were put against his head while he was in the surgery room and he was told never to come back to the hospital. In Jordan, he was able to do a one-year internship at a hospital, but as an Iraqi he was not allowed to do the medical residency required before he could practice. In hopes of finding a residency program that would take him to the United States or Canada, he shared with us a letter he had written:

> In March 2003, after the fall of the Saddam regime, I was in the fourth year of my medical studies. The hospital belonging to my college, where we did our training, witnessed the worst days in its whole history. The electricity was cut off for months, the refrigerators in the hospital morgue ceased to operate, and we had to bury many bodies in the gardens of the hospital to avoid the spread of disease. Virtually no medical materials and no equipment were available for treatment of our many patients or for operations. There was no regular staff of doctors and nurses at all. I and many of my student colleagues became volunteers to work in the hospital, trying to save lives that could be saved. It was illegal for us at this stage to perform minor operations, but we had no other choice.
>
> Later we faced many other obstacles: no beds, no medical materials, no equipment, no oxygen, no intravenous fluids, no IV sets, no syringes, no urine bags, no NG tubes, and no medications. The senior doctors asked for our assistance in major operations and we became a primary assistance in general surgery. We were operating the anesthesia machine on generators and working by the light of candles, especially in emergencies.

This young man had practiced surgery in these difficult years, had lost good friends, had his life threatened, and had somehow kept a strong and cheerful and gracious spirit. But no one wanted him.

We always found it hard to be interested in Amman itself—a sprawling city created largely in the last 100 years, but still, its foundation was the city the Greeks called Philadelphia ("brotherly love") more than 2,000 years ago. We did love the area around the open-air bus stations where the dear Al Monzer Hotel was then, the place where the Voices in the Wilderness delegations to

Iranian-American journalist Farnaz Fassihi covered Baghdad from 2003 to 2005 for the *Wall Street Journal* and wrote *Waiting for an Ordinary Day*; the stories she recounts were similar to those we were hearing from the Iraqi families we were meeting in Damascus. One theme stood out for us: The 2003 war and occupation, all the violence unleashed in Iraq, tore up the lives of people we'll never hear about and did so in ways we Americans, chief enforcers of the sanctions for 13 years and then invaders and occupiers, are never challenged to think about. All this even though Fassihi's story ends before some of the worst of the violence began.

One of the Iraqis whom Ms. Fassihi came to know and whom she wrote about is—to our surprise—our own good friend Amal, whom we had been visiting in Amman each time we were there. Fassihi tells how Amal gave much of her life to encouraging and preserving the arts and the crafts of Iraqis, even through the time of the sanctions. Fassihi quotes Amal from an interview in the early days of the occupation: "Did you see what they did to my gallery? It's all gone. Everything is destroyed. The paintings, the window you liked, the carpets, the tiles.... This is what they call liberation? They are savages, barbarians. They stood aside and watched our city get looted and destroyed."

Iraq would stay a night before the road trip to Baghdad (12 hours at least), and another night after the return to Jordan. Once the owner showed us the guest room that held all the things left behind by guests over the years, all still waiting for someone to come and claim them. The Al Monzer made up in human kindness for so much that it didn't have and didn't need. And from there we could walk down to the remains of a Roman amphitheater and walk past the older streets and restaurants and shops. Or go the other direction to a craft exhibit space. And this area was wonderful for hearing both the Muslim call to prayer and the Christian bells morning and evenings.

Jerash

On one visit to Amman, Ghada took us to see the Roman city of Jerash, only 45 minutes north of Amman, for a quick view of all of its wonderful public places: theaters, fountains, roads, temples, baths, markets. And Jerash didn't disappear when the Romans did. It continued into Byzantine and Islamic times. New to us was the "great oval" at Jerash, a soccer field–sized space, paved with immense stones that are laid in a rounding oval shape, this whole open space surrounded by great pillars. Always we seem to love most the great public open areas: Red Square in Moscow, the Umayyad Mosque courtyard in Damascus, the Great Lawn in Central Park. This oval at Jerash is one such open space.

Amal

Always in Amman we would visit Amal, an older friend from our many visits to Baghdad. There she was helping artists and their arts survive the hardest days of the sanctions. Like so many others, she could not live safely in occupied Iraq. She was eloquent (in several languages) about what had been done to her country. Even in ever-harder days for Iraq, she was thinking of what can be done to bring life and beauty to Iraqis. Amal especially talked about the way Shi'ite and Sunni and Christian and Jew have lived together in Iraq for centuries and still did so in her own lifetime, only to have outsiders set them against each other.

A year later we were visiting Amal again, and she talked about her unforeseen opportunity to go to Mecca. The worlds she moved in are very secular, but she spoke of how traveling to Mecca and being there just for a short time had brought new dimensions to the way she sees both beauty and tragedy. For her, this was completely unexpected. She described what the most familiar words of Islam, "In the name of God, the Merciful, the Compassionate," mean against the horror inflicted on the Iraqi people.

The last time we saw Amal in Amman, she introduced us to a long-time friend of hers. They had done graduate studies together in Europe in the 1960s. Now in their 60s, they remained dear friends; either could finish the other's sentences in any of their languages. They were now refugees and exiles, not even knowing what has become of their homes in Baghdad and, in Amal's case, required to leave Jordan periodically or lose her right to residency there. Even four years into the U.S. occupation, when they spoke of what has happened, they could hardly believe that the United States, for which they had once such great respect, had fallen to such levels of ignorance and brutality. They knew well what had been lost and may never be recovered.

Amal was best at finding and asking, passionately, the right questions: Why would the United States unleash such destruction and chaos in the cradle of civilization? Why would outsiders take an already difficult time and make it so much more wretched? Why is there no electricity, clean water, or employment, after the invasion and occupation? Why don't outsiders know that Iraqis—Christians, Muslims, Jews—lived in peace for more than a thousand years? Why has the United States promoted the present sectarianism? Why have people like her, the educated people who are needed to form the core of any nation, been driven out? And there are no answers to her questions.

Lebanon

In the weeks we were away from Syria in summer 2006, Damascus was receiving refugees from the west (Lebanon) as well as the east (Iraq). Israel had invaded southern Lebanon on July 12 and for a month had—by land, sea, and air—waged war against the Lebanese population and the infrastructure (roads, bridges, energy supplies). That had ended in a UN-brokered ceasefire. The UN High Commissioner for Refugees said that the invasion essentially wiped out 15 years of postwar reconstruction and development in Lebanon. The fighting also took the lives of more than 1,000 Lebanese and 160 Israelis.

Rabi'a of Basra

When we were with Ramzi in Basra, Iraq, he guided our group to the tomb of the Sufi mystic, Rabi'a of Basra (died 801). Islamic scholar Annemarie Schimmel (in *Islam: An Introduction*) says of Rabi'a that she was the first Sufi mystic to move from a sense of holiness and mysticism based on self-denial and asceticism, to one based on love:

> Numerous are the legends that surround this great woman saint of Islam.... She was seen one day in the streets of Basra, carrying a bucket in one hand and a torch in the other one. Asked the meaning of her action, she replied: "I want to pour water into Hell and set fire to Paradise so that these two veils disappear and nobody worships God out of fear of Hell or hope for Paradise, but only for the sake of God's eternal beauty." (pages 104–105)

A worker in the cemetery helped us find her tomb and we stood there silently. So within hours of visiting a Safwan child disabled for life by our military, we were challenged to understand at least one bit of the faith that sustains Muslims.

During the assault, one million Lebanese fled their homes in southern Lebanon and in the southern parts of the city of Beirut. Most found refuge in Lebanese towns north of the violence, but about 250,000 were given ready entrance to Syria, where Damascus provided shelter and meals in schools and homes. The Red Crescent and its many volunteers were crucial to caring for so many refugees.

We returned to Damascus in September, now living in Yarmouk. Mazen, when we saw him for our Arabic lesson, told us to go and see what the Israeli military had done to Lebanon. We did. The first October weekend, more than a month after the Lebanese refugees in Syria had left Syria to begin putting their homes and towns back together, we took a bus from Damascus to Beirut.

The bus would normally take as little as two hours, mostly uphill until the border crossings, then up and down until eventually down to Beirut spreading out along the Mediterranean. As soon as the bus moved west from the Lebanese border and the passport inspection, we saw the highway bridges that Israeli bombs had rendered useless at the time the refugees from south Lebanon were trying to cross into Syria. This made their journey much longer, and it would be years before repairs allowed traffic to use the old routes.

Once in Beirut, we contacted our friend Ramzi, who was living in his grandfather's house near the city. We had traveled with Ramzi to Iraq as members of Voices in the Wilderness. (See sidebar on this page.) Ramzi suggested we see what had happened on the south side of Beirut. We asked our taxi driver to show us what had happened here two months ago. We then saw several areas where one or more of these 8-to-10-story buildings had been left part rubble and part rooms open to the world, the couch still against the far wall six stories up, the floor tilting down, the outside wall gone. Ceiling fans turned in the breeze and chandeliers gently swayed to add to the weirdness of the scene. We walked through one bombed out area the size of several football stadiums. On the edges were high-rise buildings that from one side were crumbled and ready for the wrecking ball, but when we walked round to the other side we found people selling fruit and flowers from the ground floors.

What evils were being concocted in these crowded apartments? Something so terrible that all these homes—and that's all they were: homes—had to be destroyed? We had the rubble at our feet: school books and novels, pieces of clothing, spoons and forks, photographs. Families lived here, and somebody took aim and made rubble of their homes.

Along the Coast

The next day we went south from Beirut, past the Beirut airport (bombed by Israel, now functioning again), then the sea highway with the Mediterranean at our right where Israel's ships kept all commerce out of Lebanon for over a month after Israeli planes bombed fuel storage tanks and created an oil spill larger than that created by the Exxon Valdez along the Alaska coast.

We passed banana trees and citrus orchards and groves of eucalyptus trees. Again, because the main highway had been bombed in so many places, traffic had to use the older, narrower roads that took us to Sidon and Tyre, cities that were trading with Jerusalem 3,000 years ago. These were the Phoenicians we learned about in the sixth grade. Israel's targeting of water and sewage treatment plants, electricity facilities, bridges, and roads, seemed to us a page from the U.S. air attack on Iraq in 1991 that purposely destroyed the life-sustaining infrastructure.

From Tyre we went east and south through many villages in the hills, olives and tobacco growing here and there. Many of these towns had homes destroyed by bombs. The million or so residents of the south had mostly fled from the bombing, many to Syria, some north to Sunni or Christian villages where some interesting bonds must have been forged.

Aita al-Shaʻb

We spent most of that day in the town of Aita al-Shaʻb, maybe a mile from the Lebanon–Israel border. The town had 13,000 residents or so before the war, but most were now homeless and staying elsewhere. We watched as trucks too big and noisy for this rambling place scooped up the walls of houses and all the tattered marks of human community and memory, dumping the debris on a hillside outside the town, a spot where the border with Israel runs along the top of the next hill. We stood overlooking a fertile valley, which the retreating Israelis left peppered with unexploded cluster bombs.

Aita al-Shaʻb had no hospital and only one of its five elementary schools escaped destruction. An organization called Samidoun (Arabic for "steadfast")

The United States and the Bombing of Lebanon

In their account of Israel's 2006 assault on Lebanon ("How Hezbollah Defeated Israel"), Alastair Crooke and Mark Perry described the U.S. response to an Israeli request for precision-guided munitions:

The request was quickly approved and the munitions were shipped to Israel beginning on the morning of July 22. Senior Pentagon officials were dismayed by the shipment, as it meant that Israel had expended most of its munitions in the war's first 10 days—an enormous targeting expenditure that suggested Israel had abandoned tactical bombing of Hezbollah assets and was poised for an onslaught on what remained of Lebanon's infrastructure, a strategy that had not worked during World War II, when the United States and Britain destroyed Germany's 66 major population centers without any discernable impact either on German morale or military capabilities....

"There is a common misperception that the [U.S.] Air Force was thrilled by the Israeli war against Lebanon," one Middle East expert with access to senior Pentagon officials told us. "They were aghast. They well know the limits of their own power and they know how it can be abused.

"It seemed to them [USAF officers] that Israel threw away the book in Lebanon. This wasn't surgical, it wasn't precise, and it certainly wasn't smart."

had now begun some modest projects, including helping children recover from trauma. The staff, mostly volunteers, were helping the whole population learn how to recognize and not to touch those clever little cluster bombs that Israel littered over southern Lebanon in the two days before the ceasefire began. These bombs—meant only to kill and maim people without destroying property—came in many shapes and colors. Some looked like rocks, some like lemons, some like toys. They explode long after wars end.

That afternoon a group of 15 teenage girls had gathered at the school to learn about first aid. They welcomed us with delight, and for an hour we visited and sang songs, in awe of their smiles and inquisitiveness. We sang "We Shall Overcome" with them, English then Arabic, and the "We are not afraid" verse. Looking at these young people, who had just become homeless in the preceding weeks, we had the sense that no amount of bombing could break the spirit here.

Teachers

Back in south Beirut, we again visited areas hit hard by bombing. We saw a woman there who was bending over a small pile of rubbish, her face wisely covered by a dust mask as bulldozers behind her moved the debris that was once a high-rise apartment building where she lived. She snatched up a silk blouse and some pages from a book. As she continued to sift through the remains, I (Theresa) approached her and called out a hello.

Her name was Umm Hassan and we exchanged the traditional kisses of greeting. She asked where I was from and was eager to tell me about her situation. She had lived in that building 30 years and now almost everything she had was gone. She described the heavy bombing and her decision to take her family to Tripoli in the north of Lebanon until the bombing stopped. "Come meet my daughter. She's behind the building." With a big smile and great pride, Umm Hassan introduced Lubna, also a teacher. Lubna and I talked as teachers do: "What grade do you teach? How many kids in your class? How long have you been teaching?" There was joy in Lubna's face as she talked about teaching science and what good students she had.

Lubna introduced her six-year-old daughter, who said, "Even if they try to kill us, we are not afraid." Lubna whispered, "My daughter is full of spirit." It was amazing to be speaking with three generations who, having just lost their homes, did not exhibit anger or bitterness. Umm Hassan kept searching through the debris. Lubna offered, "Hezbollah gives us schools and hospitals that the government doesn't give us. Hezbollah will take care of us." Soon Umm Hassan discovered a rug and yelled at the oncoming bulldozer to watch out as she retrieved it. Later she handed Lubna a heavy green bag. Lubna cried out, "These are my treasures!" and showed the contents: her lesson plans!

Snowy Trip to the Border

In 2012, my (Gabe's) visa was due to expire on February 29, and so Theresa and I went early to the Office of Passports to have our residency extended, as we did every two months. Theresa's visa was still current; when she came back from California in December (where she went for the birth of her grandchild), she legally entered Syria on the visa she was given while in the United States. She had also obtained a new Syrian visa in my passport, which she carried with her to the United States and then back into Syria. But I had not entered Syria on this visa. The officers behind the counter spotted this problem. After much back-and-forth, it became clear that I had two choices: I could stay illegally, or leave Syria at once and re-enter, if the officers at the border allowed, with a new stamp in my passport before midnight. When I asked, "What are my chances?" the best answer was "Inshallah"—God willing.

By 1 p.m. I was with a driver heading for the Lebanon border, only an hour away from Damascus but uphill all the way. The border area was having a snowstorm and we had to put chains on the van (like being back in Nebraska in the 1940s!) as we climbed higher.

It took about five hours to go through all the stops and processes of leaving Syria, entering Lebanon, then turning around (after repairing the tire chains in the ongoing snowstorm) and leaving Lebanon. All that can be done in an hour on a good day, but that day the mile or so between the borders, in both directions, was littered with abandoned cars and trucks in the snow, as well as people trying everything to get their vehicles moving again. One of the more successful ways, apparently, was to have two or three people sitting on the hood of the car to help with traction but blocking the driver's view of the road. No one seemed to have dressed for snow. From the Syrian border to the Lebanese border, and in our return, we filled the driver's van with men who were giving up on their cars and trucks.

Finally we were back at the Syrian border ready for my attempt to re-enter Syria. Inside the immigration hall, I went first to the young officer at the window for foreigners. He went through my passport several times, then called a senior officer who did the same before motioning me to follow him to the room where the officer in charge decides the hard cases.

I didn't know it at the time, but back in Damascus everyone Theresa talked to that afternoon said, "Why did Gabe leave? He'll never be back." And each had the latest stories of foreigners who weren't allowed to enter or weren't allowed to return after leaving. By then, violence had wracked the country for nearly a year.

Back at the border, the head officer told me, "No. We cannot allow you to re-enter Syria. Your visa is not valid now because you were in Syria but you never entered Syria on this visa. You must turn around and go to Beirut. You can apply for a new visa there at the Syrian embassy." The statement about obtaining a new visa in Beirut is not true for Americans (who can only obtain Syrian visas from the Syrian embassy in Washington), but the border officials don't know this. It seemed all over. I pointed out that until midnight my old residency was good and now I was entering Syria on this new visa. In a spirit of hope, I had brought nothing along but a book to read. No toothbrush, no change of clothes. I knew that not crossing immediately, before my visa expired at midnight, would mean at least a week of waiting in Beirut and probably longer. Or forever. The blizzard was continuing and I was thinking, "The driver will go back to Damascus with the stranded people we had picked up. How will I find transportation and go through this mountain storm and come to Beirut tonight? And then what?"

At that moment one new officer walked into the office and joined the discussion and apparently raised new questions. Then a phone call was made by the man in charge, who had been saying all along he could not let me enter. He had a long phone conversation with someone about this American who wants (imagine that!) to go back in. When he hung up the phone he pushed my passport toward me across his desk, saying, "Welcome to Syria."

Back to the snow! Back to Damascus! Thanks be to God!

Snowfall on the slopes of Mount Qassiun overlooking Damascus, January 2015.
Photo by Bachar Azmeh.

7
Reparations

We had come to Syria in summer 2005 thinking that we would study Arabic and find a way to start making some tiny reparations, some sensible reparations, to Iraqis.

Iraqis continued to stream into Syria, most of them settling in Damascus and the surrounding area. Iraqi children could attend Syrian schools without charge through 12th grade. The UNHCR (High Commissioner on Refugees) registered Iraqis as refugees and offered some services, including monthly food packages and legal support (including toward resettlement). Some Syrians grumbled about the newcomers driving up rents, but it seemed to us remarkable that a poor country of more than 20 million people and lots of economic problems would keep its borders open at all.

Why Are You Here?

We asked an Iraqi friend to stand on a busy corner in a neighborhood where many Iraqis were living and to ask random passersby why they had left Iraq. Most of those asked were eager to talk; not surprisingly, they all had stories of violence to share. (In January 2007, the UN reported that 34,000 Iraqis had been killed in 2006 alone. The violence was so severe that by 2007, 2.2 million Iraqis had been internally displaced, and 2.5 million were legal refugees in Jordan, Syria, and other countries in the region.) Here is a sample of the kinds of stories he was told:

- I came from Baghdad six months ago. My kids are the most important thing to me in this world. Their school was targeted by an improvised explosive device. When I heard the news, I was like crazy, running everywhere. I did not know what to do. When I saw them and they were okay, I thanked God for keeping them safe and decided that I would not wait for another IED to take them away. So I bought four bus tickets heading to Syria. We all get homesick and we wait for Iraq to become a better place. I would love to go to the United States, but I think it is too difficult for me to get a visa and live there. But I would say to Mr. George W. Bush, "You destroyed my country."

- I left Iraq eight months ago. My husband was killed and I was afraid for my three children because they are the only thing I have left in the world. Criminals killed my husband after they stole his car. I did not know what to do after he was killed but decided I could not stay in Iraq because I don't know if those people who killed him would come back and finish his family too. The thing that really made me angry was that he was killed just 200 feet away from the police checkpoint.

> ## Twas the Day After Thanksgiving...
>
> The competing television news images on the morning after Thanksgiving were of the unspeakable carnage in Sadr City—where more than 200 Iraqi civilians were killed by a series of coordinated car bombs—and the long lines of cars filled with holiday shopping zealots that jammed the highway approaches to American malls that had opened for business at midnight.
>
> A Wal-Mart in Union, N.J., was besieged by customers even before it opened its doors at 5 a.m. on Friday. "All I can tell you," said a Wal-Mart employee, "is that they were fired up and ready to spend money."
>
> There is something terribly wrong with this juxtaposition of gleeful Americans with fistfuls of dollars storming the department store barricades and the slaughter by the thousands of innocent Iraqi civilians, including old people, children and babies. The war was started by the U.S., but most Americans feel absolutely no sense of personal responsibility for it.
>
> From Bob Herbert's op-ed column, "While Iraq Burns," *New York Times*, November 27, 2006

- The war was really horrible, more than you can imagine. Baghdad started to become a dangerous place, especially the car bombs; you never know what will blow up. And the U.S. army started to arrest people for no reason and keeping them a long time in prison for nothing. My brother and my brother-in-law were kept in Camp Bucca for 16 months with no charges. Do people in the rest of the world know that Iraqis get arrested and kept for 16 months with no charges? After that time, there was a new period. This is when our identity was being killed. If you were Sunni and were captured by a Shi'a group, you would get killed. And the same if you were Shi'a and were captured by Sunni. Believe me, there was no such thing before the war. This came with the war. You can go and ask any Iraqi woman or man, Shi'a or Sunni, about this killing. They will tell you that Shi'a killing Sunni and Sunni killing Shi'a are an American creation.

- I left Iraq because I want my children to have a better life. They are too young for the suffering there. And I cannot imagine losing one of them. I want them to be happy and to be safe from everything. In Iraq, the safety of children cannot be guaranteed.

- I lost my shop and my son in a car bomb explosion. I am sad not just about *my* son. I am sad for the fathers and mothers that have lost a child. I am sure that the Iraqi government knows everything that happens and they want this condition to go on so they can make more and more money, the Iraqi government and the Americans. When will they stop sucking the Iraqi blood and killing people and making others sad for the rest of their lives for money? They have no right at all to do what they have done. I am old and I have nothing left in this life. I used to go to the mosque every day, but over the last two years the mosque has become dangerous. The Americans started doing raids and arresting everyone who is there praying. Here I can go to the mosque without fear of being arrested by the Americans. I want any one who prays to ask for mercy on my son's soul and on all the Iraqis who died in this war. And God bless everyone trying to help Iraq.

- I used to have my own house and my own car. I worked on building my house for three years, and I worked for over five years to buy my car. Now I am living in a small apartment. But I like this city and the people treat us well. But home will always be home no matter if you are rich or poor. And I miss my father and my mother and my Baghdad neighborhood street.

- Before the war, Baghdad was the most beautiful place in the world to me. But it became a ghost city, and I can't imagine how the people still there are living. Mothers and fathers and brothers and sisters and husbands and wives are crying right now for ones they loved who got killed. I left three years ago when my husband's car was smashed by a U.S. tank. We decided to leave so we wouldn't get smashed by one of those metal monsters. It's hard to leave everything behind in one night and start a new life, but after a while we got our children in school and my husband found a good job. We have a lot of Syrian friends now, but it really hurts me when I remember my friends in Baghdad and how we used to get together. I don't want to go anywhere now. I just dream of going back home.

That spring, we received a call from a university-educated Iraqi in his 30s who had been in Syria almost a year with his wife and two children, his father, his brother, and his brother's family—nine people in a small apartment. He had been working two jobs but, because he didn't have the papers to make working legal for him, he worked long hours for little pay. He told us how much quarrelling went on between the families; the father needed heart surgery, the children were bullied and teased in school, one member of the family had been jailed and required bail, the residency in Syria needed to be renewed and that was always time-consuming and costly and could even require returning to Iraq for a month. He worried constantly about relatives in Iraq. Yes, he was "safe" in Syria, but he found it very hard day by day.

A few weeks later, an Iraqi we had known well from our trips to Baghdad arrived in Damascus with his sister and one of his six children. His three-year-old son had become sick and there was no treatment at all available in Baghdad, so our friend came here to look for help. He came to our apartment for dinner one night and told us he was resolved never to leave Iraq, no matter what happened. His family has had to move from their home in Baghdad to another part of the city because of violence. He carried a great weight of sadness: trying to care for six children in such a violent place, without any regular employment, without good water or electricity, without freedom of movement. And now he was feeling the serious illness of

IN THE LATE 1980s, Iraq had a first-class range of medical facilities. Within 15 years or so, that system was effectively dismantled, thanks to two wars (the first Gulf war launched by the United States and its 2003 invasion of Iraq) and thirteen years of U.S.–imposed sanctions that deprived Iraq of basic medicines. With the deliberate destruction of Iraq's civilian infrastructure and the denial of items that would enable the country to get back on its feet, Iraq's infants began dying from preventable conditions like malnutrition and diarrhea caused by unsanitary drinking water.

By 2007, an estimated 90 percent of Iraqi hospitals lacked basic equipment and supplies, like gauze and anesthesia. Medical personnel were targeted by combatants, with the result that Iraq has experienced a brain drain of its most experienced medical professionals.

Estimates of the number of Iraqi noncombatants killed in the years following the U.S. invasion range from a low of 91,000–100,000 (Iraq Body Count) between March 2003 and April 2009 to more than 1 million for the period 2003–2008 (British polling firm). According to the UN, 28 percent of children were estimated to be malnourished by 2007; in hard-hit areas, about 30 percent of children were estimated to have posttraumatic stress disorder. More than 8 million Iraqis are classified as poor.

For a full description of the health consequences of the U.S. invasion of Iraq, see Scott Harding and Kathryn Libal, "War and the Public Health Disaster in Iraq" and Elaine A. Hills and Dahlia S. Wasfi, "The Causes and Human Costs of Targeting Iraq." Both stories are in The War Machine and Global Health *(AltaMira Press, 2010).*

this child. We were then beginning to know what is so hard to grasp without being this close. A doctor in Damascus diagnosed Burkitt's lymphoma and began treating the child with chemotherapy and other medicines. This was, for us, one of the many encounters with serious illnesses out of all proportion to what might be expected in adults and children.

More and more, the question was becoming clear: Iraqis have been deprived of a normal life. How can Americans make some restitution for what our government wreaked on them through the first Gulf War, sanctions, and then an invasion and occupation? The Iraqis we knew were not preoccupied with who did this to them or how to take revenge, though they are very aware that restitution was and still is required of Iraq for its invasion and occupation of Kuwait in 1990. As of 2013, Iraq still owed to Kuwait $11 billion of a $63 billion tab set by the UN in 1991. During the oil-for-food years of the 1990 to 2003 sanctions, the money paid for oil from Iraq was controlled by a UN committee dominated by the United States. When oil was sold from Iraq, the money came to this committee and Kuwait's reparations came off the top. See *A Different Kind of War* by Hans von Sponeck and *Invisible War* by Joy Gordon.

Who makes reparations after our government has done such damage as it did in Iraq?

Fools Rush In

Four years had passed since the occupying army of the United States stood by as Iraq's National Museum was trashed and looted and the National Library was burned. Various militias seized control of Iraq's universities, and academics had fled the country in droves, fearing assassination. The fate of Iraq's refugees was the focus of a UNHCR conference convened in Geneva in April 2007. Governments were being asked to put in place more generous policies for accepting refugees and providing aid to Syria and Jordan, which hosted two million Iraqis. This Geneva assembly became an opportunity for some of these governments to raise questions: Why is it that the United States can brutally assault other populations and then expect the UN, various NGOs, and, in this case, Syria and Jordan to do the clean up? If the United States can afford the hundreds of billions to invade and occupy Iraq, where are the mere tens of billions it would take to care for these refugees and eventually to begin to rebuild?

We received an email from Cathy Breen, a woman who had gone to Iraq with us and others as part of a Voices in the Wilderness delegation three months before the U.S. invasion in March 2003. She was among those who stayed in Baghdad throughout the U.S. invasion and later had continued to work with Iraqi refugees in Jordan. She wrote in spring 2007 of the many hardships for Iraqis in Jordan, including the closed doors of university study, and she made this challenge:

> Perhaps one way would be to find scholarships in the U.S. for Iraqi students at high school, undergraduate and master's levels. You could

help them obtain student visas and welcome them into your homes and communities. Small as such an endeavor might seem, it would be a first step we could take so that the light in these young peoples eyes is not extinguished all together. We can direct you to students, to young people we have come to know and treasure as if they were our own youngsters. The time for wishful thinking is over. We are living in times of extremity, and it is time for us to take responsibility for our actions.

We began to explore this idea by email with friends in the United States, and they were enthusiastic. Still in Damascus, we gave it a name: Iraqi Student Project (ISP). Back in the United States, we discovered that something similar had been done in the 1990s called the Bosnian Student Project, coordinated by Doug Hostetter, then the International/Interfaith Secretary of the Fellowship of Reconciliation and now director of the Mennonite Central Committee's UN office. We reached out to Doug, and he offered much valuable advice. Our goal was to send a first group of Iraqi students to U.S. colleges in fall 2008, an academic year away. We found people who could help us register the project as a New York nonprofit organization. That required a board of directors and written policies. The not-for-profit status would be necessary before applying to the IRS for 501c3 status so contributions would be tax deductible. But even without that, we needed to raise money immediately.

From the outset, we encouraged supporters in the United States to think of this project as reparations and that they not shy away from presenting the idea as such to potential allies: We will admit responsibility for the destruction of the excellent system of higher education in Iraq and try to do something about it, though admittedly only for a tiny number of Iraqi students.

We began to talk with friends involved in higher education and to think of anybody we knew, and anybody they might know, who could introduce the idea to appropriate offices at colleges.

At this point, we were thinking that the majority of our candidates would come from the Iraqi refugee population in Jordan and fewer from Damascus. However, we soon found that working from two locations, Amman and Damascus, was not practical. In some ways, Amman itself was the problem: so spread out and without affordable public transportation from the areas where Iraqis were living. Even more important, we came to realize that our commitment, to both colleges and students, was to prepare candidates for succeeding in a very different educational system than the one they had known. For this, those accepted into our program would need to commit to a full academic year of preparation. And we would need to work closely with them and with volunteers whose first language was English. By then we knew many young people who were studying Arabic in Damascus or working as English teachers in Damascus and were open to working with us.

We never pursued NGO (non-governmental organization) status for ISP in Syria; we knew it would take years, and in fact there are few NGOs in Damascus. We set two principles/practices for our work with Iraqi students in Damascus: We would never take money from or any government, and we would work openly because we had nothing to hide. We ourselves were volunteers, as were our helpers. Students and their families would have expenses for university requirements like the TOEFL (Test of English as a Foreign Language), but we never asked any fee for the year's classes with ISP.

By August 2007, we were back in Damascus, and we had a board of directors and then a mission statement, which said in part:

> The education of young Iraqis is the primary goal. Beyond this, we hope 1) to offer education to men and women who will, in Iraq or elsewhere, contribute to the future of Iraq; 2) to heal at least a few of the wounds inflicted in recent years on Iraqis; 3) to provide many Americans with the opportunity to know and interact with Iraqis. In the long term, the colleges and universities of Iraq must be restored, but the immediate need is to strengthen, even by such modest efforts as this, the present generation.

Toward that goal, we would work to obtain tuition waivers from U.S. colleges and universities for qualified Iraqi students and to assist in forming support groups in various locations that would raise the money for these students' room, board, transportation, and books, and provide emotional support. In the United States, ISP had a coordinator who was publicizing the effort, establishing contacts with colleges, raising funds, and pushing through the not-for-profit status and then the 501c3.

Inshallah

Inshallah. If it be the will of Allah. Or, if God wills. In Damascus, no Arabic expression is heard more often, uttered by people of all faiths. It is not fatalistic resignation, but rather a realistic notion of how things go.

Once we started ISP in fall 2007, still living in Yarmouk, still studying Arabic but much less often, "*inshallah*" was often all that could be said.

Word-of-mouth was our first and, over the years, best way of finding candidates for ISP. The ISP website (iraqistudentproject.org), which was up and running early in the fall, also helped steer interested parties our way. We placed

Erasing Iraq: Educide and Sociocide

War cannot be summed up in a body count and a refugee count. The present violence in Syria, wrongly called a civil war, has from the beginning been told in terms of number killed and number of refugees. Is that the sum of the harm done? Is the ceasefire the end? The U.S. war against Vietnam was an exercise in "body count" of dead Vietnamese. The counting stopped when the U.S. military fled from Saigon, though the people of Vietnam continued to die from poisons and wounds and hunger caused by the war.

In Iraq, though, the U.S. invaders/occupiers had never counted Iraqi bodies—not those buried alive in 1991 as they fled from Kuwait, not those newborns who died from depleted uranium, not even those who died in the six years of sanctions after Madeleine Albright, then secretary of state, said that the half-million children already dead as a result of sanctions were "worth it."

Lives ended or disrespected by torture and hunger cannot be reduced to the price of whatever the U.S. government said was worth it. What then are we to say of the communal lives and culture of the cities and villages of Iraq? As the U.S. occupation of Iraq began with the looting of the National Museum and the burning of the National Library, both unprotected by the occupiers, and as the universities of Iraq saw faculty killed or kidnapped or fleeing the country, the terms "cultural cleansing" and "educide" began to be used and documented. The challenge is to make these meaningful in the United States, where so little is known of the efforts of the last century by Iraqis to renew the "house of wisdom" and "cradle of civilization" in their schools and universities and museums, in their respect for the poets, the music, the architecture and the many-dimensioned population.

Iraqi academics from many fields have worked with non-Iraqis to tell the story and record the details—even while the cleansing continues. Some of this work has been published in English and is listed in the Recommended Reading (page 263). The following is from the book *Erasing Iraq*:

> Taking into account the destruction of Iraq's cultural treasures, the surge of violent fundamentalism, the decimation of its economic and social infrastructures, and the hardships experienced by women, children, and minorities, it is arguable that the U.S. aggression in Iraq has resulted in sociocide—the obliteration of an entire way of life.

For what purpose? For whose gain? The old *cui bono?* question. We heard this "why" from Iraqis during the sanctions, we heard it and still do as friends, Iraqis we knew in Damascus, write from Baghdad again. "Why did all that made this city so dear have to be destroyed?"

posters in the British Council, the American Language Center, other places where young Iraqis were studying English, and the UNHCR food distribution centers. We went to the UNHCR offices in the Kafr Suseh neighborhood and spoke to the person who was in charge of educational programs for refugees. We explained our vision for ISP and our need to find suitable candidates. She invited us to give a presentation to the Iraqi and Syrian volunteers working in the neighborhoods where many Iraqis had found rooms and apartments. We spoke to the volunteers about our plan and stressed we needed students who had completed high school, were under 25 years old, were already fluent in spoken English, had no other options for getting a university education, and had the emotional resiliency and tenacity to work with us for a whole academic year. We were clear that ISP was not an effort to resettle Iraqi students but to send them to colleges. We would teach critical reading, lecture-quality listening, and English writing skills. We required a commitment to full participation in the year's studies and activities.

When prospective candidates submitted their applications, we conducted a family visit. We wanted to know the family and to build trust, and we wanted a chance to assess economic need in an authentic way. With the applicant acting as translator, we would hear the family's story, the "before" in Iraq, then so often the incident that made them decide they could stay no longer, and the bus ride across the desert, the often long wait at the Iraq–Syria border as long lines were being processed. That could be through a hot desert day or a cold desert night.

Were these stories exaggerated to gain our sympathy? Only rarely did we suspect so, and anyway, we weren't really asking for the story but we would listen. Our focus was on trying to assess who would become a successful student. It was enough that they clearly had not wanted to leave their home, but here they were. Many had become dependent on the UNHCR for food basics and minimal medical care.

In our conversations, there was more sadness than bitterness, more determination than surrender. These parents had often come to their own adulthood during the eight-year war with Iran (with the United States then helping Iraqi president Saddam Hussein). No family was left untouched as half a million Iraqis, soldiers and civilians, died. Two years after the truce, Iraq invaded Kuwait and the United Nations imposed sanctions, which would become increasingly oppressive over 13 years. In 1991, the infrastructure of Iraq—electricity, water and sewer treatment, railroads and highways and bridges—was destroyed by U.S. bombing while Iraqi forces were driven out of Kuwait. The 2003 U.S. invasion and occupation brought much destruction, chaos, and sectarian warfare.

These well-educated but battered parents were desperate to secure a future for their children.

As for the ISP applicants, how did they manage to hold onto hope and enthusiasm for learning in the midst of the tragedy so many of them have witnessed? Most of these young men and women have very practical ambitions for their lives: to become an engineer, a doctor, a computer expert. We knew from the start that ISP would have to find young Iraqis who were resilient. It wasn't hard.

We were asking applicant and family for a commitment to full participation in the year's studies and activities. That meant almost daily travel to ISP classes in our apartment, it meant the tension of approaching TOEFL tests and the stress of trying to improve essays in college applications, it meant homework that needed concentration and for some that would become hours spent every week at the British Council or another place conducive to study on one's own. From the second year until the British Council closed in 2012, we purchased a membership for each ISP student.

> IRAQ'S FORMER PRIDE, its education system, has collapsed. The International Seminar in Ghent was a significant first step in determining whether the extrajudicial killings, abductions, forced displacement of Iraqi academics and other professionals, the destruction of the educational infrastructure, during the war and subsequent occupation, are indeed a case of pre-meditated elimination of Iraq's intellectual elite and education system, and could constitute "educide." This word has yet to enter the international dictionary of crimes; it is a composite of education and genocide to refer to genocide of the educated segments of Iraqi society. It can only be hoped that both the International Court of Justice and the International Criminal Court will pursue the question of possible educide in Iraq.
>
> — Hans Christof von Sponeck,
> *Beyond Educide*, (page 3)

In late January, a very enthusiastic young man kept calling us. His family had come from Iraq just weeks ago and had found rooms very near where we lived in Yarmouk and when we went to visit them, we were completely charmed. The youngest was six years old. She liked us right away and brought her drawings to show us. The middle child was 18 but had not finished high school because of the violence in Baghdad. Our candidate, age 21, told us he had heard about ISP through one of the UNHCR volunteers. He explained that just weeks ago their father had been shot in front of their home in Baghdad and had died as they tried to bring him to a hospital. In Damascus, the two brothers found work: 10 hours a day in a factory that made towels. They were grateful they could help support their family. The Syrian authorities seemed not to mind so much when young people took jobs. By that time, though, we realized that the ISP academic work was too far along for any new ISP candidate to catch up with those who had been at it since September. He became part of a summer study group and joined us the next academic year.

One Step at a Time

Had we thought the project through, we might have found reasons not to begin. By early September 2007, we were becoming more aware of the size of the challenge we had assumed.

We had to find a way to assess language level, and for that we turned to the American Language Center (ALC), which had a placement test that told with great accuracy a student's language ability on an eight-point scale. The staff had been using and developing this tool for years in order to place their students in appropriate levels of English language study. The ALC teachers also knew from years of experience that their test was usually accurate at predicting readiness for achieving college-required scores on the Test of English as a Foreign Language (TOEFL). A student would need to score at least six on the ALC assessment test to have hope of a TOEFL score acceptable to U.S. colleges.

If a student seemed to meet the initial requirements, we would ask whether the family had or could obtain high school transcripts that would later be part of the college application. This was so often a challenge. Some parents had nothing and felt hopeless about obtaining them from the high school in Iraq. Yet somehow they managed.

For those applicants who met the criteria for ISP, we found volunteer teachers and textbooks and began regular daily studies in September 2007. Nearly all colleges wanted complete applications by December or January and required that TOEFL scores be submitted with the application of a student whose first language was not English. TOEFL was given only three or four times a year in Damascus. We planned to prepare our students to take the test in January; their scores would arrive in late February.

In the meantime, ISP supporters in the United States, including the new board members and the director, were assembling a list of colleges that would consider four-year tuition waivers for Iraqi students if the applicant qualified by the college's standards. Most of these were small liberal arts colleges that had shown a commitment to recruiting students in the United States and beyond who were truly needy. We quickly learned that colleges interested in accepting a qualified Iraqi student and offering a tuition waiver would give us flexibility on their published deadlines.

TOEFL registration had to be made weeks before the test itself, and could only be made online and the fee ($140 that first year) could only be paid with a credit card. The system is geared to parents who could afford not just the registration fee but TOEFL preparation classes or private tutors.

We learned that an intense preparation course for the TOEFL exam is important. This course centered not on the content of the test, but on strategies for taking such a test. We found a volunteer who had had experience in teaching a preparation course. The test included an essay question and 20 minutes for writing. Theresa began working with the students on how to write a persuasive essay and other types of essays used by TOEFL.

Very early on a Saturday morning, January 12, 2008, we stood outside the ALC building near the fortress-like U.S. embassy to encourage the first group of ISP students, eight of them, as they went in to face the three-hour TOEFL. Some parents were there also. It was the first of many such TOEFL vigils.

Common Application

As the weather warmed in February and March, we were unreasonably optimistic about finding colleges for at least a dozen of our students. We studied what is known as the Common Application, a form used by many U.S. universities and colleges, and we went to work on it with the students. TOEFL scores began to arrive as the students were working on the essay portion of the Common Application. The class schedule continued. The daily classes in listening to lectures, and academic writing and reading were done by level so all would be challenged. Usually we had enough volunteer teachers to do two groups, sometimes three, for each of the disciplines. Students worked on resumés that often began as minimalist failures.

As the students began working on the essays they would submit as part of their application forms, we were getting the sense that, irrespective of the outcome, this ISP community had ended the isolation that so many Iraqi refugees felt in Damascus. Friendships formed, but the group itself had formed as well, especially in the Friday Writers' Workshop when Theresa worked with the whole group on their writing—and far, far more.

These young women and men had come from such a range of backgrounds and identities, many with violence done to their own families. They had been scattered in all corners of this sprawling city. One thing they shared: Somehow each one discovered a feel for the English language somewhere—imparted by parents, brothers and sisters, music, television, movies, books, and, of course, some very special teacher in an Iraqi school. That, of course, did set them apart from most of their peers. Those peers also needed some hope, some community, some end to refugee isolation. We had to admit to ourselves that we could render one service, somewhat small considering the need, and no more.

Waiting

Through spring 2008, we waited anxiously to learn which of the first ISP group would be accepted at colleges. We also knew that we would be moving out of a semi-demolished building in which only our apartment three flights up remained intact; in fact, we would not return to Yarmouk when we returned to Syria at the end of the summer; we would look for an apartment more convenient for our students to reach. We knew that we would miss our rooftop garden and the comradery with the neighbors on their balcony just a few meters away, who would wave and watch our morning glories inching their way over to them far above the lane. There were other reasons we knew we'd miss Yarmouk, as this excerpt from an email we sent to friends around that time expresses:

> As we write this, a wedding is taking place next door. This is the second night of dancing in the street (men only). It began with drumming and carrying the groom on their shoulders. Now synthesizers that mimic traditional Middle Eastern instruments (is this possible?) revved up with electric sounds accompany an active vocalist who seems to be dancing right now among the family and friends. All of the rest of us are watching from our balconies and rooftops, knowing the pulsing music will go on until about 11:30 p.m. The uncles are dressed in suits with ties, as is the groom, but his buddies and the rest of the crowd are in jeans and shirts. Forty white plastic chairs line the right side of the street, touching our building, and forty plastic chairs on the other side face them. Soon they will be doing the *debkeh*, the traditional dance with all the men holding hands, stamping rhythmically. A sense of joy is filling our narrow street this hot night.

During the spring, the students had several opportunities to speak English with visitors to Damascus. A group of U.S. nuns from various religious orders working on issues of social justice came for four days to Beirut and then four days to Damascus. We knew two of them and were asked to meet with the group and explain ISP. We invited the students and any parents who wished to come also. The sisters had already visited homes and agencies and NGOs in their brief stay here. The mother of one of our students told the visitors that she had spoken recently with someone who was here to do relief work with refugees. When the person heard about ISP, she asked the mother why anyone would be working on such a thing when the immediate need was for bread and heaters. This mother's response was quick: Without education, what future would her children have?

At a time when few U.S. churches were confronting the U.S. government about its Iraq policy, these religious sisters—and it wasn't a young group—were in the struggle full time. On all sides—the sisters, the students, the parents—this was a fine gathering.

Not all encounters with visitors went as smoothly. Our students met with a group of U.S. students and the teachers leading the group, two of whom expressed great pessimism about how hard (perhaps even impossible, they thought) it would be for these Iraqis to get student visas to the United States; if they did, did they realize what a hard place it would be for young Arab people? The teachers asked why they had not considered going to another country, learning some language other than English, and receiving a good education without the frustrations of U.S. visas and U.S. attitudes. This was not what we expected to hear—we were just then beginning to work on applying for student visas, and we had our own apprehensions about that—and we were shocked that these visitors, who knew the hopes of these students and the hard work they had put into this effort, would speak as if it were all a waste of time.

Success!

Later that spring we learned, one university at a time, that thirteen students had been accepted and granted scholarships or tuition waivers. We then started to work more with the ISP supporters in the United States on building support groups ready to welcome thirteen ISP students in August. Time to brainstorm: Did we know anyone in San Rafael, California, or Buffalo, New York? We already had friends in South Bend and St. Louis, so setting up support groups there was easier.

We had a few more hurdles. Our students were being accepted one by one to various institutions, and it was beginning to dawn on us that each college was going to do things a little differently, and that each support group was handling their tasks (such as securing financial help and providing support) separately. Students who had been accepted were excited but a little apprehensive about the journey ahead; those who had not yet been accepted were worried by the delay.

But the hurdle that terrified us (because we listened to people with experience) was securing the U.S. visa for students, called the F-1 visa, which requires proof from the university that this student is accepted and that the university is satisfied that the expenses of study and living can all be met. Meeting those requirements only makes one eligible for the one-on-one interviewing at the embassy. The interviewer has power to say yes or no. If yes, the students knew there would still be days or weeks or months of waiting while the State Department turns over their file to the Department of Homeland Security. For us, those last two words summarized what our country was becoming. Homeland Security would always have the final word.

For a student, this process is very complex even if coming from a "friendly" country, even if the papers required are easily obtained. Our work was trying to understand the rules, helping the students find all the documentation required, registering them online for the visa interview. We also paid the fee that, for that year, was required in *new* U.S. cash: $131 that year. For all that, the interviewers themselves were almost all kind, concerned, and welcoming.

To improve our students' chances and increase their confidence level, we did rehearsals of the interview. We asked a friend, an American citizen who himself had come to the United States as a foreign student, if he would play the role of the interviewer as each student was called to "the window." He was able to pick out the weakest link in a student's application and zero in. It might not have been the real thing, but that was quickly forgotten. The group discussed between interviews what had gone right and what wrong. Some were done twice, some more. It worked. In the following years, we always sought such help and in 60-plus visa applications, we had only one student turned down at the interview. (She applied again, wore a different outfit, asked for a different interviewer, and was approved.) But no one could predict the length of the Homeland Security step. Some were over in a few days. Some took six nervous weeks.

Most of the interviewers concluded with "Welcome to the United States!" They knew that Homeland Security could reverse their decision, and we suspected they weren't pleased with that oversight at all.

We always waited outside the U.S. consulate offices until the student emerged smiling from the interview. Often a parent or another relative would be waiting with us or another of the students. One day during such a wait for her son to emerge from the embassy, a mother said to us, "Whether my son gets to college in the United States or not, this program has changed his life." She said that now through ISP, he has developed friendships, began studying again, and has a sense of purpose. We were humbled to hear that. And we realized that even though we listened to their stories, and to many stories like theirs, we could never fully appreciate the cataclysmic effect of the war in Iraq on their lives—not only what happened in Iraq, but the shock of change in what was now "home" outside of Iraq, and the disorientation of not just a new city and neighborhood, but a new identity ("refugee"). We recalled an Iraqi mother saying to us, "In Iraq, I was an engineer. Here I am a refugee."

The Dish Party (aka Potluck Dinner)

As our time together was ending that first year, some of the ISP students wanted to have what they referred to as a "dish party" (a literal English translation from the Arabic term for what we call "potluck supper"). We invited the fifteen ISP students, four or five friends from England or the United States who had been volunteer teachers, and other friends. All found their way to our Yarmouk neighborhood carrying things they had prepared. Little group by little group, they called to say they had found the neighborhood landmark. This was the Cinema Najoum, the "Cinema of Stars," a movie theater and pool hall 50 meters from our door. Every *serveece* driver and passenger would know where and could help these first-time visitors to Yarmouk. One of us went down to lead them to the apartment on top of the otherwise-deserted building. We had candles on the stairs because the only electricity working was in our apartment.

The students each brought their family's favorite Iraqi dish: a huge pot of fragrant *biryani*, a heavy plate of *freekeh* (crushed wheat) with toasted almonds on top, a big bowl of the tomato-based *yabsa*, and the spectacular *dolma*, which would be flipped over from its cooking pot to the

Freekeh: The Spring Wheat

Freekeh is "spring wheat," kernels of wheat that are gathered as they begin to ripen. Delicious! It was a wonderful treat in Damascus. Freekeh, like rice, is brought to a boil, but then must simmer until the texture is right for eating.

> 1.5 cups freekeh
> 1 large onion, chopped
> Olive oil
> 4 cloves garlic, crushed
> 1 tablespoon butter (optional)
> 3 cups water
> 1 teaspoon salt
> 1/3 cup slivered almonds (garnish)

Measure the freekeh into a deep bowl and cover with water. With your fingers, swirl the freekeh. Unwanted material like husks and debris will float to the surface; pour the water off to remove these substances. Repeat this process a few times and then let the freekeh soak.

Sauté the onion in olive oil. When almost brown, add the garlic and butter.

Strain the freekeh to remove the water and add to the onion mixture. Stir so each grain is glazed with the oil.

Add the water and salt to the mix.

Bring to a boil and then simmer, covered, about 45 minutes.

In a skillet, brown the almonds in a little olive oil.

Fluff the freekeh with a fork and serve on a large platter. Garnish with the almonds.

platter. We made our famous garlicky hummus. The students insisted on waiting until the whole group was there before eating the Iraqi salads and main dishes. Then came an abundance of desserts, including Rana's lemon cake.

By early June 2008, thirteen students had or expected their visas. One of the ISP volunteers offered a summer-long English intensive for those who would be staying with us another year for more study before applying to colleges. Some of the students' families volunteered to store some of our things while we took time off to return to New York City. When we returned in two

Hummus

Our hummus is hearty and a bit chunky. Adjust all the quantities to your taste.

 1 can chickpeas (15 oz. or 425 grams)
 1/3 cup tahini
 1/4 cup lemon juice
 1/8 cup olive oil, plus more to pour over hummus when serving
 4–6 large cloves garlic (or a lot more)
 1/2 teaspoon salt
 Few shakes sumac

Drain and smash the chickpeas in a bowl using a potato-masher. A few chickpeas can be kept aside to use as decoration.

Add the tahini, lemon juice, and olive oil to the chickpea paste. Mix with a wooden spoon until well blended.

Crush and mince the garlic. Add to mixture with the salt. Stir to blend all flavors.

Spread the hummus in a small, shallow platter. Make ridges along the edges of the platter; add olive oil to the surface (to taste). Garnish with the whole chickpeas and sumac.

Serve with pita chips, bread, apple slices, or carrots.

months, we looked for an apartment where the next group of students could take the minibus from whatever area they lived to the center city of Damascus. We would do the work and teaching of ISP in our apartment and another nearby apartment where one of our volunteer helpers lived. So our scattered belongings and those of ISP were brought, a box at a time, by students or parents to the new apartment near Sahat Arnous in late August.

For us, the two years in Yarmouk were blessed with a wonderful friend and teacher, Mazen. And blessed too with the crazy adventures of our rented rooms. And blessed by Yarmouk's aromas: bread and nuts roasting and coffee in burlap bags outside a grocery store! Blessed by a three-story wall covered with bougainvillea, a greater blessing to our eyes than Times Square will ever be. Blessed by the appearance of just-harvested bundles of garlic taller than we are, and with all the other delights of the souq and its gracious merchants, and blessed even with "belt souq" at the east end of all the crazy clothing shops on Lubya Street. And the presence of the man, Abu Mohammed, who stood a few doors away so many days and seemed to pray the whole day. Blessed also with so many who welcomed us to their community. And we were so blessed to be living amidst the Palestinian presence in its third generation and among so many who welcomed us to their community.

8
Springtime in Syria

During our summer in the United States in 2006, we realized once again that most of the people we talked to, even those who were politically active, knew little about Syria. So many people asked us, "Are you safe there in Syria?" Were they asking because they knew that the United States imposed sanctions on Syria in 2004, claiming that the Syrian government supports "terrorists" in Iraq? Were they wondering how two U.S. citizens could feel safe in Syria when year after year, the United States put Syria on its "sponsors of terrorism" list? Whatever the reason for their concern for our safety, they always expressed an interest in learning more. And so, when we returned to Syria in the fall, we wrote what would be our final email of 2006 to our list of about 100 friends in the United States and included an invitation to them to visit us in Syria. We saw so few U.S. visitors in Syria, and we saw merit in facilitating more contact among Americans and Syrians. We hoped that some might be interested.

Our letter said in part:

> Would you be interested in coming to Damascus for a week in the spring? We have this idea of hosting half a dozen or so people here for the same week. This would be low key and low expense. Guests would stay not in hotels but in homes, the better to know Syria. We would not even try to set up meetings with officials, but would have a mix of discussions with thoughtful people: Syrians, Iraqis who have come here for safety, Palestinians who did the same two generations ago. These folks would be Muslims and Christians and none of the above. We would also spend time seeing Damascus (especially the Umayyad Mosque, the souqs, the Old City, the Museum, and the thousands of interesting everyday things to observe) and take some day trips to places of great beauty and history (Bosra, Deir Mar Musa, perhaps Palmyra or Aleppo with the wonderful ruins of San Simeon nearby).

We wanted Americans to know Syria and Syrians. Tourism in Syria was then growing, with spring and fall being the "high seasons." But the tourists seemed to come primarily from other Middle Eastern countries, with good numbers also from some Asian and a few European countries. Some came on their own, but many came in organized tours; many of these tourists were Muslim and Christian pilgrims.

We knew that Americans were afraid to come to Syria. Would anyone take this invitation seriously? One person who was interested sent us a link to the "Syria Warning" that was then running on the website of the State Department. It told anyone thinking of travel to Syria to keep a low profile and suggested such tactics as never taking the same way twice. We were amazed not by the effort to frighten but by how melodramatic it was, a work of fantasy directed by politics. Happily, many of those who received our initial note were undeterred.

Introducing Syria to Americans

We wanted visitors from the United States to see the same treasured places we went to again and again. One was Bosra, an hour south of Damascus, a town the Romans only slowly wrestled from the Nabateans, the people who had earlier carved from rock the amazing city of Petra in the south of what is now Jordan. Bosra was a Christian town by the time Mohammed, before his calling to be the Prophet, would pass through with caravans from the desert. He is said to have had long conversations with a Christian monk there in Bosra.

When going north from Damascus, many times we walked in some of the so-called Dead Cities, communities built because the soil made for flourishing olive orchards and grapevines 1,500 years ago. These "cities" were then on the trade routes linking the ships at Mediterranean ports with Persia and even China to the east. The earth here is limestone, which was quarried and cut into building blocks to make barns, homes, churches, shops. Earthquakes or exhausted soil seems to have caused inhabitants to abandon this area before the tenth century, but so many of their stone buildings in town after town are still there.

We often took visitors north from Damascus about 90 minutes where, on the last mountain plateau before the desert, we climbed many steps to another treasure: Deir Mar Musa, the monastery of Saint Moses the Ethiopian, founded probably on what had been a Roman fort.

We knew what we wanted Americans to experience in Syria, and we started to develop notes to help our visitors prepare well for their trip. Eventually these would cover such things as:

- Information on applying for a visa to Syria.
- Weather.
- Health and diet, and being ready for full days and lots of walking.
- Money and how it works.
- Staying with a Syrian family in the Old City. (This came to include such questions as "Do you smoke? Can you live with people who do?" and "Do you need a toilet close to your room?" "Would you interact with the family—share photos of your family, have tea together?")
- Dress code (e.g., for women, a scarf for visiting mosques; for men, long pants, not shorts).
- What to bring (besides a flashlight, a robe, and a notebook, the addresses for your senators and representatives so you can write to them from Syria).
- A list of books to help make the most of a visit (history and geography as well as "sights").

We prepared an itinerary and sent it to those who committed to coming on the same date. The original 2007 itinerary evolved a bit each year. We moved with the date of Easter each year so that Easter Sunday would be the second Sunday the visitors were in Damascus. In 2011, for the fifth and the largest (and sadly the last) group to visit, the plan covered a lot of ground: the Old City of Damascus, Aleppo, the Dead Cities and the ruins of the huge church of San Simeon, Bosra in the south of Syria, Deir Mar Musa, Ma'lula, and Sednaya.

"We Visited a People"

We hoped to give people a fairly inexpensive opportunity to discover Syria's culture and history, but also to know the people who live in Damascus now. Each guest lived with a family in the Old City. One of these homes had Roman cut-stone remains in its basement, another backed up against the wall of the Old City, and most of the visitors' host families lived in the traditional "Arab houses" with two stories built around a courtyard. In most cases, these homes had long been in the family but could not now be kept up.

Our days and evenings were spent seeing and learning about some of the places in or near Damascus, but also we had half a dozen times when we sat down with people to talk at length: a group of young Syrians and Palestinians, a group of Iraqis who had come to Syria for safety, independent journalists from the United States who were here doing stories on the refugees from Iraq, and then a variety of people met along the way. All the guests were amazed by the way people on the streets and in the towns we visited and in shops all said, "You are welcome! Welcome to Syria!"

This magnificent theater built by the Romans is made of dark basalt. It holds seats for 6,000, plus 2,000-3,000 standing-room places. When we brought visitors, we always invited them to sing or perform on stage. Photo by Viktor Hegyi.

We saw the Roman theater in Bosra, the sixth-century churches built over old pagan temples in Ezra'a, mosques and churches and khans and Arab-style homes in Damascus. We viewed the city from high on the mountain when we climbed to the mosque/shrine believed to be the spot where Cain killed Abel and then learned about earth burial from the birds, and was shielded by an angel from God's vengeance. We walked through the Christian villages and monasteries where Aramaic is still a spoken language. We sat with Bedouin families in tents and homes in a village east of Damascus. We visited a small but amazing photo exhibit at an art gallery deep in the Old City. We experienced the crowds of people and the processions on Holy Thursday and Good Friday nights and Easter, processions led by marching bands from the various churches of Bab Touma area. And our guests came to know their way around the souqs and the food-sellers along the streets. They discovered some of the various "tastes" of Damascus. We saw some of the fabric, jewelry, and metal work for which parts of Syria are famous in the shop of our friend Papa Joseph near the Umayyad Mosque. He ordered tea for all and proudly showed a photo taken when Jimmy Carter visited Damascus and toured the large Arab house-become-workshop where our host then worked with craftspeople of Damascus.

Our visitors were full of curiosity and so open to learning from everyone along the way. We were worn out at the end of each day but also stimulated. One of the visitors remarked the night before they left, "We didn't visit a country. We visited a people."

On Easter that first year and sometimes in the following years, Theresa took the women in our group to the hammam for several hours. They loved it! Then we all went to an Easter open house at a friend's home in the Old City, then sat and visited at a coffee house with some of the folks who had met our visitors earlier and wanted to talk more. Easter Sunday ended with a group evaluation of the week.

Subsequent Springtimes

In subsequent years, we added two-plus days in Aleppo to the itinerary of the first Springtime. The best Damascus-to-Aleppo travel was by train. It left from a train station near Midan and Yarmouk. The Aleppo–Damascus line did not stay beside the main highway, so we saw vineyards and the "beehive" houses and came right into downtown Aleppo. We tried to take rooms in an Arab-style house converted to a hotel in the Old City there, a short walk from the miles of covered souqs (covered by graceful stone arches) for which Aleppo is well-known, and near Aleppo's ancient and immense Citadel.

The last group to visit, in 2011, was also able to enter an ancient, but still in use, soap factory in the Old City of Aleppo. Here the olive oil and bay laurel soaps are made and sent all over the Middle East and beyond. And, nearby, we visited a large building with a courtyard that had been built eight centuries ago for the care of the mentally ill. We saw no confining cells but rather places where the sight and sound of water and the use of music were understood as giving the residents peace.

But the best of being there in the north of Syria was the Dead Cities, that area just west of Aleppo where there were many small towns from the centuries when Roman times drifted into the Byzantine era. We would begin at the ruins of the immense sixth-century church built on the spot where Simon the Stylite, as he was known in the West, spent 30-plus years sitting on a high pillar. This was, at the time, the world's largest church—not because of the local population but because of the thousands who came on pilgrimage there.

And from these ruins, we went to some of the dozens of towns that flourished for about 500 years. Everything was built from the limestone that the earth itself is made of there, so the quarries become cisterns for water or storage places for grain and food. People still live in some of the 2,000-year-old stone houses, but they are the "dead" cities because, for whatever reasons (drought, earthquake, changing trade routes), the population mostly left their olive orchards and grapevines by about the year 900. Wild flowers, especially deep red poppies, bloom everywhere in the spring. Some of the many olive trees may have been there when their olives were being pressed in the stone presses that also survive. And all these shells of churches and homes and public buildings—everything built of the stone we were standing on, everything suggesting what is portrayed in a book published recently in the United States, *The World Without Us.*

Each year we chose new places in this Dead Cities area to explore. Our guide was a magnificent book, *The Christian Art of Byzantine Syria,* photos of the area plus the scholarship of a Spanish Franciscan, Ignacio Peña, who lived in Syria from 1960 to 1982. The English edition of his book was published in 1996. The photos are as much of a treasure as the text.

Some years we rented one or two minibuses and invited others to come along: a day in Bosra, and another visiting the Christian villages of Sednaya and Ma'alula, and on to our favorite place of all, Deir Mar Musa, where we had several hours after we had climbed the hundreds of steps up the mountain to the monastery. The buses were often filled with singing and almost dancing! We saw Christians and Muslims praying together at Sednaya, walked the St. Tekla ravine at Ma'alula, visited with Paolo and other friends at Deir Mar Musa. The guests also went with us to visit churches in the Old City on Holy Thursday night when the streets are jammed with people doing this visitation, and then on Good Friday, we saw and heard the drums and brass of the church bands—always heard, and sometimes seen, parading on the streets and narrow lanes of the Old City from Palm Sunday through Easter Monday.

Arranging the annual Springtime in Syria tours became a focus during our years in Damascus, second only to the Iraqi Student Project. And in fact, many of our Springtime in Syria guests got deeply involved with Iraqi Student Project while they were here. Annie, Theresa's daughter, shared the teaching at Writers' Workshop. Several who came over the years joined us with home visits to students' families, meeting parents and siblings; one made it possible for one of our students to pay for her braces and another became active in engaging the university in his hometown to take an Iraqi student.

Our last tour was in spring 2011, two months after the protests began in Dara'a and spread throughout Syria. Our driver for the Saturday trip to Bosra that year took roads further east and more roundabout; we were able to see both the surveillance on the roads and how much Bosra, like Damascus, was suffering from lack of tourists. In 2012, we did not even attempt to invite visitors because so much had changed. We could not by then easily go to Aleppo or Deir Mar Musa or Bosra. Public events, including many traditional processions through the streets of the Bab Sharqi neighborhood during Holy Week, had been canceled.

Christian Art of Byzantium

Sometime soon after our first visit to the Dead Cities area, we found a treasure of a book by the Spanish Franciscan brother, Ignacio Peña. Peña lived in Syria and led the exploration of the architecture and art of the Dead Cities from 1960 to 1982. His book, *The Christian Art of Byzantine Syria*, was published in English in 1996. Peña focuses on what happened in this area between Antioch (Antakia) and Aleppo in the second to the seventh centuries and thus spans the peaceful passages of Roman rule to Byzantine rule to Islamic rule. The photos and text are organized not by site but by function: for example, chapters on baptisteries, monasteries, centers of pilgrimage (like the immense church built to honor Simon Stylites), places of pagan worship, burial monuments, Islamic adaptations beginning in the seventh century.

With few exceptions, we found in our visits to the area that very few of the villages and their buildings have any signs to indicate their age or use, so Peña's work was with us on all subsequent visits. Each time we went with our guests, we visited only a few of the long-deserted villages where all was built from the stone quarried in this limestone massif.

Peña's introduction to the book includes the following paragraphs:

Few countries of the world offer such a rich and varied range of past civilizations as does Syria, whose artistic wealth is comparable, if not superior, to that of Mesopotamia, Asia Minor, Greece, and even Egypt.... The history of Syria is conditioned by its geographical position.... Syria was at a crossroads, a meeting-point for the most renowned civilizations of the ancient world....

The Dead Cities of northern Syria—*civitates desertae*—are a collection of around 820 settlements, villages or towns from the 2nd to the 7th centuries [CE] spread over a mountainous rural landscape between Antioch and Aleppo. They were abandon around the time of the Muslim conquests in 636. Today they form a scattering of venerable ruins, signs of a brilliant and little-known civilization and "unknown ground" among historians, a civilization whose beneficent influence radiated throughout the whole of the Mediterranean basin for three centuries....

It is no exaggeration to state that a rich treasure-house of ancient religious art exists in the Dead Cities, one of the most important centres of historical, ruined monuments in the world. Nowhere else is there such well-preserved vernacular architecture. The study of these remains has allowed us to fill in the blank that existed between Roman classical art and the art of the early Middle Ages, or, to be more specific, between Roman imperial art and European pre-Romanesque.

Part 3

Sahat
Arnous
(2008–2009)

*Night creates its own impression of
Damascus. With a limited amount
of electricity, people find new ways
to illuminate their dwellings.
Photo by Bachar Azmeh.*

9
The Apartment in Center City

Our move to central Damascus in August 2008 had to do with the number of qualified young Iraqis who had applied to work with ISP that academic year. Yarmouk was a good place for us, but the Iraqis given refuge in Syria were on their own for housing and in fact were in many areas of sprawling Damascus and nearby towns. Once we decided that classes would be five or six days a week, our location had to be near the center of Damascus, where the large and small buses from all directions come.

Our apartment that year was on a very ordinary residential street on the second floor of a four-story building. The only commercial activities were a busy furniture shop just outside the entrance to the apartments and, across the street, a vegetable seller. We could watch the fresh produce being delivered each day. We visited with the merchants in the neighborhood, and Theresa came to know an elderly woman who would often sit outside on a small porch by the front door of her building. Theresa stopped by and they talked about the many plants on the front steps and on the open porch. Other flowers and vegetables were in the tiny front yard between the house and sidewalk.

We liked this apartment for the very long and wide dining and living area that could easily hold 25 students on a Writers' Workshop afternoon. We had a balcony wrapping around the west and north sides, and on it a lovely porch swing. The apartment's door opened from the stairs and landing on a space just waiting for up to 50 shoes/boots/sandals as teachers and students entered. The kitchen was large enough for a table (for a meal or for a small group studying) and we had two bedrooms, each large enough for several students to talk about a book together in Literature Circles. The classes were usually four or five students, so several were happening at the same time.

Our *sahib al-beit* (owner, landlord, but literally and, in this case, truly, "friend of the house") did not own the building, only this one apartment where his family had lived before moving further from downtown; now they used it as a rental. We came to like him very much. If anything needed fixing in the apartment, he and his father would be there together to fix it.

Our Neighborhood

As usual, we never knew our address, but we came to know the landmarks in our neighborhood. One street further west was Sahat Arnous, a much-used park whose official name is Eighth of March Square, named for the date of the coup that brought the Ba'ath Party to power in 1963 and well-known for its immense statue of Bashar al-Assad's father, Hafiz al-Assad, president of Syria from 1970 until he died in 2000. Mazen had explained to us that many streets and parks and neighborhoods had two names: The newer one often carried a political message or memory, but the older name was used in everyday speech even if it didn't appear on street signs and maps. Sahat Arnous offered good places to sit in the sun and the shade, a paved area for skateboarding, and an area in which a stage was set in the summer for nighttime theater. (The map "Central Damascus" is a way to follow this neighborhood walk; see page 34.)

Running south from the park was Salihiya Street, closed to motor vehicles and wonderful for strolling. Many people would know where we were living if we said "Near Abu Abdo's" even more than "near Sahat Arnous." Abu Abdo's was a juice bar. A famous juice bar! Damascenes would agree on this—their city was the best place on earth for pastry and juice! They love their fresh-squeezed juices and are likely to have a strong preference for which busy juice bar is the best in the city. Several of the top contenders were near Arnous. We too became partial to Abu Abdo's juice, served over a counter with the customers ordering from the sidewalk and keeping 6 to 10 young and old men busy filling orders. Who comes for juice? Everybody comes! Teenagers, grandmas and grandpas, guys in ties, guys in *dishdashas*, the religious and the not. Juice was the main thing, but fruit and even ice cream sometimes was part of the attraction.

Heading west from Arnous would take us to Zenobia Park with many shade trees and play areas and a large pond. The park was named for Zenobia, who reigned in the Roman city of Palmyra in the late third century CE and created a short-lived Palmyran empire independent of Rome; eventually she was defeated by the Roman armies and taken prisoner. The park was much used and filled with people in the evening hours of summer. Children came to play and teenagers were always passing through on their unhurried way to or from school. Working people came to take their lunch break outside. Old people enjoyed sun or shade on the many benches. But the park was Zenobia only on the maps; for reasons that remained unknown to us, everyone called it Sibkey Park. This park, like a few others, still had the above-ground entrance to

Every part of the city features its stacks of sweets, beauty in pastry!
Photo by Viktor Hegyi.

a bomb shelter built, we were told, to protect residents during the tense years of the French Mandate.

Across the street on the north was the Cervantes Center, the cultural center in Damascus not only for Spain but for all Spanish-speaking countries. It had a fine library and offered hospitality, Spanish language and other classes, films, and many other reasons to belong.

Going south from the park, one might pass a string of embassies and the British Council, whose welcoming staff made us and our students feel at home. The BC, as most called it, offered various levels of English as a second language, a library, and artistic and musical events, and it administered the IELTS (International English Language Testing System) test for English proficiency, the British equivalent of the TOEFL exam. Some British Council teachers worked as ISP volunteers and taught the classes that focused on academic listening, reading and writing. The roof had an impressive view of Mount Qassiun. Equally notable at the BC was an elderly woman, originally from Britain but a resident of Damascus for many decades, who occupied the sofa near the entrance and turned it into her salon, chatting with everyone who entered.

Books at the Border

We had done the first year without textbooks. Most of those we were familiar with were not about learning English for college study. But we talked with a friend in New York City, Emily Perry, who worked at the Oxford University Press (OUP) offices in Manhattan. We were looking in particular for books intended for students who had become proficient at spoken English but needed to work toward the listening, writing, and reading skills expected of college students at U.S. universities. Not only did Oxford have a series intended for each of those academic skills and presuming already good spoken English, but they had several levels in each of these skills. Emily asked the publisher to donate several copies of each book in the series and to ship the books at their expense. They agreed to this, but the four heavy boxes of books could go no further than Lebanon because the Hariri assassination in Lebanon more than a year before had given the United States an excuse to blame Syria and increase economic pressure. So books to help teach English were not able to cross the border into Syria, but we never quite understood who said so and why.

Bringing four heavy boxes into Syria using public transportation was complicated; three drivers would not let us board their minibus with the books for the drive to Damascus. A fourth driver took us on, but we had to promise that if we caused border delays of more than an hour because of the boxes, we would stay behind and the driver could take the rest of the passengers on to Damascus. This worry was not about breaking U.S. sanctions but about four boxes at the border and how that might slow everyone down. Our worry was having the books confiscated or having to pay large fees.

The moment of truth came when a Syrian inspector at the border took a look at the fourth box (which was bigger than the other three) and asked that it be opened. The driver struggled to cut through the packing tape with his keys and then reached in and pulled out a fat chunk of bubble wrap. Theresa took hold of it and started popping the bubbles and with each "pop" gave a whoop. Then two women who were passengers in this backseat began pulling out and popping more pieces of bubble wrap and making the shrill whooping noises as if it were New Year's Eve. In all the racket, the inspector looked more confused than upset and finally just threw up his hands, smiled, and waved the driver on. We still cannot imagine a Transportation Security Agency officer at a U.S. airport or a U.S guard at any border doing such a thing as laughing, giving up the search, and waving us through. We began to use the books immediately, with enthusiasm from the volunteer teachers and great success with the students over the next four years.

The Audacity to Express Outrage

In fall 2008, George W. Bush's term was almost over, and Syrians were far more optimistic than we were about Barack Obama's election. But the month before saw harsh verbal exchanges between the United States and Syria. It also saw massive anti–U.S. protests, some of them near where we were now living between all those downtown squares. We wrote at the time in our letter to family and friends about what had happened:

> We hear that Syria finally surfaced in the U.S. media, briefly of course. It wasn't so much the story of several U.S. helicopters crossing from Iraq into Syria, landing in a Syrian village not far from the border. The soldiers dismounted long enough to attack and kill eight people, then flew back into Iraq. None of the invaders was harmed.
>
> That itself would not have made the U.S. news. But Syria has had the audacity to express outrage toward the U.S. and Iraq. Placed alongside the nearly daily killing of civilians in Pakistan by U.S. drones or by troops crossing from Afghanistan, this little violation of Syria's borders to murder eight civilians isn't big news. These extensions of existing wars, this willingness to honor a nation's territorial sovereignty only when it suits us, is taken for granted when practiced by the United States. And even when we challenge such attacks, we seem to be accepting the U.S. aggressor's right to be in the country from which the attack was made.
>
> We may not like the idea of territorial sovereignty at all, a relic of a time when nation states seemed like a good idea. But until we agree on some better system, we have this little Syrian village whose families thought they lived in safety.
>
> Just suppose Indonesia conquered and occupied Canada and occasionally sent Indonesian troops into Minnesota where, it was rumored, anti-Indonesian rebels from Canada sometimes gathered. But the Minnesotans killed in those raids included more U.S. citizens, adults and children, than Canadian insurgents. Imagine the outrage and retaliation of the U.S. government when voters in the U.S. demanded that Indonesia be punished after watching TV news when families in Duluth buried their dead.

ISP, Year 2

We met a young man from the UK, Matthew McNaught, during the first year of ISP. He had studied Arabic with Mazen and, to support himself, was teaching English at the British Council in Damascus. He accepted our invitation to be in charge of recruiting, training, and evaluating volunteers for teaching with ISP. Matthew set about this while we focused in late summer on interviewing student applicants, testing their English skills, and doing home visits to know the family. Some applicants weren't ready, and we encouraged them to study on their own and apply again in a year. We made the contact for all students accepted to ISP to become British Council members with ISP paying their membership fee at a reduced rate. So Matthew and the BC and our move to central Damascus made this second year possible with more than 25 students, twice as many as the first year. We had classes six days a week in our apartment and in Matthew's, and made the BC a place to go between classes.

Volunteer teachers, many of them in Damascus from the UK, United States, Ireland, Australia, or Canada to study Arabic, provided a faculty of great diversity. We even had a few faculty meetings-with-breakfast at our apartment, and many, many smaller meetings. Matthew recruited and interviewed volunteers, and shared in evaluating their work as teachers. The texts from OUP were used and used again. Our apartment seemed never empty of teachers and students, always dozens of shoes around the apartment door and weighty backpacks here and there.

The weekly Writers' Workshop, followed by the ISP meeting, and the twice-weekly Literature Circles brought all the group together three times a week. For the classes focused on individual skills—reading, writing, listening, speaking—the students were in groups of three to five. All classes were two hours; most met twice a week. And there was homework.

ISP had a busy weekly schedule, with the daily classes providing stability for students and volunteer teachers alike, while the "crisis events" of TOEFL, Common Application, and visa application gave an overall structure to the year. And we had field trips both inside and outside Damascus as well as special guests who visited ISP.

One of these guests was Dr. Dina Khoury, associate professor of international affairs at George Washington University, who was in Syria to interview Iraqi refugees who had been in Iraq's armed forces during the war with Iran (1980–88). When she spoke with the Iraqi students in Damascus, she had the syllabus for a course she was teaching with her. We made copies for all of our students so that they could see the expectations set for university students: how much reading was required, participation in discussions, the assignment of short and long papers, and the use of internet communications between professors and students.

Our own notes from Dr. Khoury's conversation and her class syllabus became part of ISP in the following years. The syllabus was such a fine example of what the students were going to find at U.S. universities. It became part of our effort to make them ready for the U.S. system so they would make good use of it. We ourselves were learning how much would be different from their educational experience so far, but also how the universities they applied to now have incorporated various ways to provide for their international students. And once the ISP students in the United States started to share their experiences with us, we learned more about the use of writing centers and counseling services and the role of academic advisors.

Dr. Khoury also told the students about the research that brought her to Damascus where she could interview Iraqis about the Iran–Iraq war. These students were born after that war ended, but it had touched almost every family. Dr. Khoury's work, *Iraq in Wartime: Soldiering, Martyrdom and Remembrance*, was published by Cambridge University Press in 2013.

Each year brought the extracurricular part of being in ISP: special TOEFL preparation and the exam itself; then the college applications—navigating the Common Application and any supplements, including the short and long essays; then, when accepted at a university, studying the I-20 form. In it, the appropriate university officer affirms the student's acceptance and puts dollar amounts on the expected expenses of tuition, room and board, and various fees for the first year. The official who signs for the university is affirming that the university is convinced that this student has the ability to pay, considering fees waived, scholarships given, funds pledged, campus jobs, and such. That is a crucial piece before there can be application for an interview at the U.S. consulate to obtain an F-1 non-immigrant student visa. Besides discussing what the visa was and wasn't, each year we tried to find someone the students didn't know who would come to play the part of the visa interviewer. It helped prepare for the real thing.

All this, and somewhere along the path each student would realize that it all might happen as they wanted it to happen, but when it did, they would face a long time away from their families.

A variety of crises kept coming, some serious and some just time-consuming. Many related to the troubles of the families of the ISP students. The present troubles in Iraq had split some families—some members here as refugees, others in Iraq with the continued occupation and deterioration. There were times when suddenly an ISP student's family would be told to prepare for resettlement. Some of our own worries came from the troubles a few of the ISP students from last year were encountering at their U.S. colleges.

This was the year that the American Language Center was closed for some months by the Syrian government to protest the U.S. military actions discussed earlier. We had to find somewhere else for the TOEFL exam required by the universities for students whose first language is not English. We all went to Aleppo on the train with the students the afternoon before the test. That night we had a surprise birthday dinner for one of the students that included a birthday cake. That helped reduce the TOEFL tension. All of us stayed that night at a youth hostel so the students would have a good rest (didn't happen). The next morning, we all went to a school on the south side of Aleppo where the four-hour test was given, then back to Damascus on a bus.

This 2009 winter and spring were, briefly, a season of hope as Barack Obama became president of the United States. And there was that winter also a rare day when snow fell in Damascus.

The Iraqi Student Project was the subject of an article in an English-language monthly magazine in Damascus, clear evidence we had nothing to hide. And a good and timely event, because the next crisis came suddenly in May. The owner of the apartment we were renting, who had been so helpful all through the year, came by very upset. Someone had complained to some officials that young Iraqis had been coming in and out of our apartment and that there was sometimes singing in our apartment during the day. No one had complained to us or to the owner about this, but clearly he was frightened by a neighbor's complaint to the government. They had called him in.

We had told the owner about our work earlier but now he was the one at risk more than we were, so we said classes would end in the apartment immediately. We managed to have more classes at Matthew's apartment, and some of the teachers who lived close to the area also hosted their classes at their homes those last weeks. We found an apartment further up the slope of Mount Qassiun and were able to move our books and other possessions there before we left for the United States in the summer. We were in NYC to greet some of the students as they arrived in the United States on their way to college.

Cultural Centers

Matthew's apartment was used as an ISP classroom most days of the week. We realized that with 25 students following at least four patterns of classes, we needed some sort of place for the students to go and study between a morning class and a later afternoon class.

Enter the cultural centers mentioned earlier, especially the British Council (the BC), a five-minute walk away. We worked each year with the BC in Damascus to provide each ISP student with a membership and thus use of the internet, library, and café.

The BC was not the only cultural center we came to know that year. The Goethe Center, in addition to its many German language classes, had excellent art exhibits and cultural programs, including now and then an interesting series of films. It was this center that had a fine exhibit of the photographs of Bachar Azmeh, who graciously provided many of the photos for this book. One summer, the Goethe Center had a film series where we saw some excellent short films from Iraq. One of them led to much discussion about the Iraqi reality in these years. Like Sinan Antoon's novel *The Corpse Washer*, this film seemed to tell the Iraqi reality after sanctions, "shock and awe," and now the occupation and the sectarian violence. In one film, we are on a city bus, a small one. Passengers get on, passengers get off. Someone asks what day this is. Someone answers. Another passenger says, "No, this isn't Tuesday; it's Monday. Says right here in today's paper." Another passenger says they are both wrong and gives another day. The argument continues.

The French Cultural Center was the only one not housed in an older Damascus building. Built in the early 1980s, the center is a modern building that nestled and was somehow very much at home among its much older neighbors in the Souq Saruja neighborhood. Later we came to know the Cervantes Center, which had a fine library and, while we were there, was relocated to the downtown area, the north side of Sibkey Park and became very active with programs for the public.

Our favorite was the very large Russian Cultural Center near Yousif al-Azmeh Square. The Russian support for the government of Bashar al-Assad did not come as a surprise. Through the Cold War decades, Syria and Russia had a strong relationship. We knew many Syrians who had done graduate studies in Russia and spoke Russian. There were many Syrian/Russian couples who raised their families in Damascus. This cultural center seemed a much more lively place than any of the others, with occasional displays, book sales, art exhibits, or craft fairs in their large front lobby.

The whole inside space seemed always busy with language, music, and dance classes and recitals; it had a large theater for concerts, an internet facility, and a seemingly always-open café. In that café, we could almost believe we were in Moscow as Russian mothers had coffee and chatted while their children were at their ballet or violin classes. And when all of the above-mentioned cultural centers had closed in 2011 or early 2012, the Russians stayed open. The Syrians we knew appreciated that, and so did we.

10

Hammam

The public bath (hammam) in Damascus opened a new world to me—the world of history, the world of women, the world where I (Theresa) would hear the stories of women of Damascus and women from around the world. All of us were happy to let our guard down and be free.

When I think about the hammam, I remember dancing with women around the fountain, sharing homemade *makdous* (pickled eggplant) and bread, telling stories about our mothers-in-law, our husbands and families. The hammam became a place of sisterhood for me and the best classroom for practicing Arabic.

Daughters of Damascus

These baths, like the mosques and great houses, are architectural works of beauty and an integral part of people's lives. I had wanted to visit a public bath ever since I read the following description in Siham Tergeman's *Daughter of Damascus*:

> As was the case in the majority of the old houses, we did not have facilities for bathing in our home. For this reason during my childhood I had the pleasure of frequenting the famous public baths. The weekly visit to the bath in the suq was as enjoyable as my sisters and myself at a picnic. How we used to love to slide on our knees in the bath on tiles covered with soap and suds and endless streams of soapy water! Our innocent laughter echoed in the big chambers of the bath, rising with the steam to nestle in the ceiling like a fog and then return to us. The domes of the bath were illuminated with "the light of God" streaming through the many moons of colored glass. (page 11)

The Bakri Hammam is more than four hundred years old and still has its original stone basins and marble work. It was once one of more than twenty public baths in Damascus. Other hammams still in use date back to the 1100s. Every Sunday there became an adventure for me.

The first time I stepped into the hammam in the Old City, I pushed aside a heavy Persian carpet that was tacked up above the lintel of the doorway to provide privacy. I entered a huge, mosque-like, white-domed space with an ancient brass chandelier suspended from the center of the dome, hovering above a rose-water-scented fountain.

Three sides of the room had raised platforms with wooden sofas covered with beautiful Middle Eastern carpets, pillows, and cushions. Small, delicately carved tables, silver trays, and draped textiles made me feel as if I had entered an orientalist painting by Matisse. Three cozy areas provided places to sit, relax, read, undress or dress, and have tea after the ritual of the bath. Colored glass in the dome above muted the light that seemed to dance around the room, mixed with the voices of happy women.

Sahar, Umm Daoud, and her daughter-in-law, Najwa, ran the bath, and they mothered me through my first experience at the hammam. They provided me with what looked like half of a blue-striped cotton bedsheet to wear and use during my stay at the hammam. It would later be my mat to lie on while being scrubbed down on the floor, then it became a cover for the massage table.

I went up three marble steps to one of the carpeted platforms and put my clothes over brass hooks on a mother-of-pearl inlaid wooden frame, awestruck by the intricate details. I wrapped myself in the stripped cotton sheet and chose a pair of sandals from a low wooden rack. Upon leaving the domed room I entered a series of rooms with marble floors and either stone or marble walls with intricate geometric designs. All of the rooms had heavy marble basins of water filled from spigots in the walls. Metal pans were there for us to throw water over ourselves. Children used them to bang on the marble floors.

The largest room was warm and there were heavy stone basins on the floor around the perimeter. Women were sitting on small wooden stools rinsing off at the basins or washing their hair or bathing children. In this room, patrons would sit or lie on the marble floor and receive a vigorous scrub down with olive oil soap and jute from Sahar or Najwa. Inlaid stone graced one of the walls, reminding me of the traditional quilt pattern Ohio Star. It felt magical for all of us women to be using such a beautiful structure.

The next room was extremely hot—the steam room—and further away was a cooling-off room. The fourth room was tiny and was used for massages, one person at a time.

I asked some of the other bathers how to best use these four rooms. They suggested: first the steam room for 10 minutes, then have the vigorous scrubdown from Sahar or Najwa, rinse off at the basins, return to the smallest room for a massage, go back to the large room to wash hair, bathe more at the basin, or make use of a shower. All that and a glass of tea for only $8 including the tip.

When I finished the work of the hammam, I returned to the domed room and was greeted by Umm Daoud with two Turkish towels. I went back to the carpet-covered platform to relax and sip tea. Some women spread out picnics and made a day of it, sharing food with everyone near them. I realized the tea time was more like a hair dryer, because after slowly sipping two cups my hair was almost dry and I was ready to join the outside world of the Old City. I felt fresh, renewed, and delighted.

Hammam on Sundays

One week when I exited the inner rooms of the hammam, all clean and massaged, I wrapped a towel around myself and settled into a lovely corner in the domed room near the fountain to air dry my hair, sip tea, and read. Deep reds and blues of old worn carpets blanketed the divan and traditional music came through speakers overhead.

Suddenly another bather stepped into the room and shouted, *"Alhamdulillah!"* She was giving thanks to God for a clean body and a good bath. Umm Daoud at the desk uttered the customary blessing to one who has just taken a bath and again the bather, a Moroccan woman named Fatima, shouted words of happiness. She broke into a dance and Umm Daoud raised the volume on the radio. Fatima beckoned Umm Daoud to join her and soon the two were dancing, then ululating joyfully.

I had learned to ululate in Iraq, so I added my voice to theirs. Then Fatima laughed and said, "A foreigner? She can ululate?" and Umm Daoud confided to Fatima, "And she speaks Arabic!" Fatima beckoned me to dance with them and so I jumped down from my divan and the three of us danced around the fountain. Soon Fatima began a sort of "call and response" where she would do some dance moves and we would imitate her. As the music got faster, we each did kind of a solo with the others clapping. What a way to celebrate cleanliness!

Over the years, I met local women from ages 14 to 85, as well as many foreigners: a Japanese student in wooden clogs, a Malaysian mother and her daughter, a family from Baghdad, two Sudanese workers, and the wife of the British consul general. All of us were equal in the hammam.

One Sunday, two Damascene grandmothers came in with their grown daughters and the grandddaughters. When the granddaughters pushed their way through the heavy suspended carpet that cloaks the doorway, they gasped, delighted to see the bright dome, the fountain, the goldfish tank, lanterns, and plants. The grandmothers handed bags of food to the mothers and they spread out a pre-bath picnic. Later as they all undressed together before entering the inner rooms, I reflected on the ways that women reveal their attitudes toward their bodies here in the freedom of the hammam. What an opportunity to observe how generations relate to one another!

Once I met a lawyer from Spain who was taking her annual three-week vacation in Damascus. She arranged a home stay in Bab Touma and brought along the Lonely Planet guidebook, visiting the major sites in Damascus by herself. She reminded me of my sister Julie in her enthusiasm for the Old City and her delight in all its history. She had taken buses from Damascus to many major sites: the Roman ruins in Palmyra, the massive fortress from the Crusader era called Krak des Chevaliers, Ma'alula (a town near Damascus with the Convent of St. Tekla), Deir Mar Musa (the sixth-century Monastery of Saint Moses the Abyssinian), and other ancient monasteries. She would be off the following day to Aleppo to see the citadel as well as the Dead Cities of the Romans and the Byzantines. I shared my enthusiasm for Syria with her and tried to speak Spanish, only to find that my Arabic was interfering with my Spanish. (Perhaps language immersion in Arabic was really working!) When we parted, she gave me her contact information and offered to host me in her home if I ever went to Spain.

Once a foreign woman in the hammam asked why I was learning Arabic. She was from Australia, very active in the peace movement, and very concerned about Iraqi refugees. Since meeting her 10 years ago, we have continued to receive enthusiastic notes from her. Here is a passage from her response to our monthly letter:

> The Middle East is such a maligned part of the world and the people have suffered so much and it never seems to end! The misery is compounded as time goes on. Out here it has amazed me how many people were shocked to think that we two women had been to Jordan and Syria as though the people there are all terrorists—I explain over and over that the people are generally gentle and kind and welcoming—we had no bother at all unlike southern Europe where I was robbed twice and bailed up for money once. Anyhow congratulations on having such wonderful hearts and souls. I often think of you.
>
> —Margaret

Another special friend at Bakri Hammam was Najwa's baby. Najwa had worked throughout her pregnancy giving massages and scrubs. Soon after the birth of her son Ali, she was back at work, bringing him along with her. He became the delight of the hammam. When he was first strong enough to lift his head off the blanket on the floor under the dome of colored glass, he looked like a little turtle. Over the months, I was able to hold him and see him grow and watch him learn to crawl. He sometimes sat in a little walker and scooted his way around the fountain. When he learned to talk, his mother taught him to call me Teta (Grandma), which touched me greatly. That respect for elders in Syrian culture was a grace to me in the form of this little child.

The Bakri Closes

One spring week at the hammam, something looked different: The three women who work there were not at their usual stations. Umm Daoud and Sahar were sitting at the long table beside the fountain sorting huge bundles of fresh parsley. They carefully pinched off the ugly leaves and stroked the long stems into bright green bouquets. Najwa was checking potatoes boiling on a small one-burner apparatus on the floor while baby Ali, almost one now, practiced walking around the fountain, one hand on the cool tile. We all laughed when I asked, "Is this the hammam or your kitchen?" and they explained how during this exam time in Damascus, all of the mothers were home while their children were preparing for their exams. Classes are suspended for several weeks and the mothers break their normal schedules. I was the only customer in the entire hammam!

I asked Umm Daoud not to turn on the lights because the sunlight through the colored glass cylinders on the domed ceiling created plenty of natural, beautiful light. Amber and moss green shafts of light illuminated the stone basins. I enjoyed the 400-year-old hammam that day all alone, adjusting the steam room to my personal tastes, throwing water lavishly over my hair at the basin, singing my favorite songs. Najwa came in to do her family laundry in the old marble basins, Ali's play clothes in one and all the light colors in the other. It was easy to pick up on her sense of relaxation, getting ahead on her family chores here at work. As for me, there were no other women demanding massages and scrubs and so I had longer-than-usual sessions. A dream come true!

When I came out to the domed area, lunch was being served: boiled spring potatoes, salt, and parsley on flat bread. We munched this simple feast in between bites of green onion. Dessert was strong tea with sugar. Ali went down easily for his nap, and the women and I talked together.

After two years as a customer at the hammam, Umm Daoud invited me to her home for tea over Eid holidays after Ramadan. Although my Arabic was limited, we were able to introduce our husbands to one another, sit and chat, and laugh. She served tasty honey-soaked baklava and sesame cookies.

Sahar's husband died in 2009. She missed 40 days of work in order to fulfill the rites of a widow in mourning, and later when she returned to work, she seemed tired and fragile. Soon after, the Bakri closed for renovation and I lost touch with these three women.

For a while I resisted settling in with another hammam community. I realized that the Bakri had provided me with companionship of other women in a very intimate yet public setting. I missed the simple shared meals with Sahar, Umm Daoud, and Umm Ali. Somehow the salty boiled potatoes tasted yummier there than anywhere else, especially when eaten with homemade *makdous*. I also missed the informal Arabic language practice at the Bakri. And I no longer heard Ali's childish voice calling me Teta. The Bakri, sadly, never opened again during our years in Damascus.

Hammam Amounah

After sampling other hammams, I settled into the Hammam Amounah, one of several hammams built in the twelfth and thirteenth centuries. During this time, the population of Damascus was growing beyond the walls of the Old City. Hammam Amounah was north of the wall, near the gate to the Old City called Bab Faradis.

The walk to the hammam took me past the immense Dahdah Cemetery, said to be the place where the Roman hippodrome, site of various entertainments and sports events, had been. I entered the hammam from a narrow street where only a single car could fit. The familiar flapping cover hid a beautiful wooden door and entrance to a spectacular domed room. As is so often the case in Syria, the outside gave no clue about the inner space.

The wood of the raised platforms had been replaced and updated with drawers below for storing our clothing and possessions. But the structure of the dome, the colored glass and intricate windows above created the same lovely mood as the Bakri. The fountain was rimmed with potted plants and the sun glistened through the windows above onto the brass chandelier.

Umm Mustafa, a young woman with a hearty laugh, managed the front desk. We spoke Arabic together, but when she wanted to make sure I understood her (especially her views about the political situation), she switched to English. Lina was the matriarch of the hammam, and I mostly saw her brewing coffee, making tea, and telling stories. Two other women were responsible for giving scrubs and massages: Shakira, who committed herself to minimizing the pain I felt in my hip, and Umm Ahmed, who had a beautiful voice as she sang in the inner massage rooms of the hammam. I would miss the vigorous massage of Shakira on days she was absent, but it was worth it once in a while to experience the astounding vocal range and vibrato of Umm Ahmed, her voice amplified by the dome in the warm room.

I would try to arrive early to avoid the rush and have a quieter experience. This hammam was a popular site for engagement parties, wedding groups, families with teenage daughters, as well as old friends of Lina. When the old ladies gathered for tea, their laughter was mischievous and loud. I liked to go when it was less crowded and to lie on the stone floor during the loofah scrub watching reflections in puddles of water of the colored glass in the dome above, sudden shifts in sunlight.

Being the first arrival meant that I could join the women who worked there while they were still sipping their morning coffee over in the corner near the tiny cooking area. They smoked continuously and told hilarious stories and the news of the neighborhood, challenging each other with lighthearted remarks about who had the best information on a particular topic.

Sometimes Umm Ahmed's children would call with a question or Umm Mustafa's son would call with a request. That early time together gave me an insight into the struggles they had as working women trying to raise families, especially during the end-of-year school exams.

Umm Mustafa was excited when nonviolent demonstrations broke out in Damascus in 2011. She wanted wider job opportunities for herself and her two brothers, all college graduates. She wanted a better educational system for her son, and she wanted economic growth in Syria. But she added, "I love our president. My son would die for him!"

As the violence in Syria escalated, the early-morning chatter became more serious. In a letter that Gabe and I wrote to friends and family in July 2011, I described my impressions of that time:

> The women who work at the hamman weep for Syria, for all the dead, for the disruption of normal life. And they support the President in every way. They most clearly distrust the hand of the United States in all of this: in its call for U.S. citizens to leave Syria, in its constant use of sanctions against Syria, in the blustering of Hillary and Barack and others against Bashar, in its support of Israel and its butting into the affairs of Syria. They are well informed about the role of the United States in Iraq, Afghanistan, Pakistan, and of the U.S. role with Israel. They said, "We know that in the United States there are people who sleep under bridges and people who can't get health care." As if to say, solve the problems your people have at home—don't meddle here.

When my 60th birthday arrived, I decided to celebrate it first thing in the morning at the hammam. I brought a huge watermelon to float in the fountain where it could stay cool for later in the afternoon. I also brought fresh chocolate croissants from the nearby bakery to go with our morning coffee. Conversation turned to our ages and Hannah laughed at me, saying what a baby I was at only 60!

In late fall 2011, our own beloved Damascus began to be affected by the sounds of gunfire and explosions. Umm Mustafa was angry one morning and asked, "What makes your country think it can tell us what to do? Do they think

Hammam in Winter 2014, Damascus

It is freezing cold these days. I need to take a bath but no hot water. The house is cold too because we don't have power most of the day and night. I thought, "There must be a few public baths left in quiet areas."

There used to be over fifteen hammams in Damascus before the war began in 2011. There was one in our area I used to go almost every weekend in winter, but it's closed. The neighboring shopkeeper told me two years ago that they shut it down because they had too few customers in the first year of the war. Another problem is how much hammam would cost after this insane inflation. Well, there must be a plan.

I have been to the hamman so many times in the past, especially with my students from Europe. It was a refreshing cultural adventure. Unlike the regular tourist guide, I offered a historic introduction to the hammam starting from the ancient period to the Ayyubid period (Saladin, 12th century) and finally the Ottoman period (16th to 20th century). Then the quick death of the hammam in the 1970s and its revival in the 1980s. The funny part was when the discussion continued into the steam room where we are sweating excessively and can barely see anything.

Most hammams are concentrated in the Old City and all are very ancient buildings, so unlike their counterparts in northern Europe, our Damascus hammams are like a visit to an ancient castle.

—Hussein Maxos

we don't know and hurt for what's happening in Syria? Why can't they keep out of it and let us fix our own Syria?" Again she reiterated that they stood by their president.

Fewer and fewer foreigners came to the hammam, and sometimes Shakira or Umm Ahmed went home directly after morning coffee—for them, a day without income. Umm Mustafa worried about the loss of revenue from the dearth of tourists. One day she told me how they had heard gunshots outside in the narrow street near the cemetery. A group of non-Syrian patrons heard the shots and started to scream, then dressed and demanded their money back. Umm Mustafa reassured them that staying inside the hammam was much safer than going outside, but they left anyway.

By 2012, no music was played in the morning at the hammam and the women spoke in sad voices of the increasing violence. Instead of gossip and jokes, the conversation was more often than not about al-Midan, a neighborhood southwest of the Old City where there had been violence the previous night, or about an explosion in Qudsaya, one of the many neighborhoods that climb the mountain along the Barada. Often they discussed the many people coming into Damascus to escape the destruction of their neighborhoods of Homs or Hama.

A few weeks later, Umm Mustafa lamented, "We are just pawns in this chess game. The French, the United States, Saudi, Russia. Everybody is acting like it is their country to decide. No one cares about us."

As the academic year of Iraqi Student Project began to wind down midsummer, I told Umm Mustafa, Lina, Shakira, and Umm Ahmed that Gabe and I would be leaving at the end of July and not returning. Umm Mustafa bitterly predicted, "In some years, you will return to this hammam. None of us will be here. You will say, 'Allah yirhamhon.'" God rest their souls.

11
Deir Mar Musa

During our first year in Damascus, many Syrians, Muslims and Christians alike, asked us whether we had visited Deir Mar Musa, the Monastery of St. Moses. We decided to go and to discover what prompted such enthusiasm.

About an hour and a half north of Damascus, following the highway that eventually arrives at Aleppo, the bus stops in the town of Nebek, halfway between Damascus and Homs. The monastery is north and east of Nebek.

We first viewed the monastery from this road, recognizing that high above, some small portion of the mountain's rocky face had become architecture. The Romans might have been the first to build here, some sort of fortress for spying anyone approaching from the east, perhaps from the ancient Silk Road city of Palmyra, itself a desert oasis. Over time, the deserted fortress became a monastery founded by Musa al-Habashi, Saint Moses the Abyssinian. ("Habash" was some variation on "Abyssinia," the east African area later known as Ethiopia.)

Over centuries, the monks built a basilica-style church from the well-cut stones that had once been the Roman tower. Nearby caves suggest that monks in some centuries lived as hermits. Then as now, the community raised vegetables and gathered herbs and tended their flocks of sheep and goats. Earthquakes did their damage now and then, but a monastic community stayed in place until the early nineteenth century.

Then church and all stood empty until the 1980s, when a young Italian Jesuit, Paolo Dall'Oglio, arrived. Paolo had studied Islam and spoke Arabic and came to live there. Little by little, he began to rebuild the church. Others joined him. Over two decades, they worked together to understand, imagine, and bring monasticism back into this Syrian place. They slowly rebuilt the ancient buildings and formed a community of men and women, residents and

THE ICON AND FRESCO TRADITIONS as practiced in Syria are the subject of Erica Cruikshank Dodd's *The Frescoes of Mar Musa al-Habashi: A Study in Medieval Painting in Syria.*

Elizabeth Bolman of Temple University wrote in her review of the book:

While distinctly Syrian in character, it belongs to the shared visual culture of the Muslim-controlled territories, which included the work of both Muslim and Christian artisans. Its closest surviving relatives are Christian paintings in Lebanon and a Fatimid work. Dodd maps out the complex network of hybrid styles in the eastern Mediterranean, which has been made clearer in recent decades by the work of Weitzmann, Jaroslav Folda, Annemarie Weyl Carr, and others. She adds a new element to this scholarship by claiming a major role for Syrian paintings. She proposes that they served as mediators between the Islamic and Christian realms in both the Mediterranean region and northwestern Europe. The visual products of this contact paralleled the role of Christians in Syria vis-à-vis their Muslim rulers and the Crusaders.

visitors, Christians and Muslims, Syrians and foreigners.

On our first visit (and every visit after), we climbed the pathway up the steep eastern slope of the mountain, hundreds of steps but with such views of what's behind and what's ahead. The steps do switchbacks and so make the eastern walls of the monastery appear and disappear repeatedly as the visitors pass small herb gardens and hear roosters crowing and sometimes the monastery bell ringing. Slowly the architecture becomes more distinct until the twisting path ends just outside the door to the ancient monastic area. One must crawl or bend very low. Some would say that such doors were meant to put the one entering at a disadvantage. It does that for sure. But perhaps this crawling on our knees or bowing low for us adults always had something of a game about it, and a remembering as in the Shaker hymn: "I will bow, it is the token, I will wear the easy yoke...."

We were then in an open area with the church on our left, and the kitchen, library, and offices on our right; the courtyard stretched before us. At the far end of this courtyard were tables for guests and residents to take their meals in the desert sun, and beyond the tables, a low wall where we could look down on the zig and zag of the pathway we had just climbed.

The midday meal was always here; one of the tables would be filled with pots of hot soup or rice, a large bowl of yogurt, and an array of fresh fruits. Visitors were invited to add to the communal table any food they might have with them: nuts, olives, dried fruit, sandwiches, baklava, and other bakery treats. Like the multiplication of the loaves and fish, so it happened. Round, flat bread was stacked on each table with a bowl of monastery-made jam. We ate at low tables, sitting on small stools. Before the dishing up began, Paolo would do introductions of any group there and lead the blessing of the table and company. No matter how many people sat around the table, the food was always enough, reminding one of how loaves of bread and a few fish had fed the multitudes in another time.

Deir Mar Musa, once a Roman fort, can be seen but not easily from the east, from where the desert is becoming the wilderness and then "the sown." Even on a clear day one has to look closely to see that the stone cliff at some point has become architecture, a fort for the Romans, a monastery for 13 or so centuries, abandoned then until the 1980s.
Photo by Viktor Hegyi.

In those years of our visits, 2006 to 2011, the courtyard was alive with conversations in various languages: young people from the East or the West trekking through Syria, and people like us accompanied by guests. Some guests would come for some specific purpose, like the time 30 Syrian beekeepers held a work conference there, climbing those 350 steps for a few days of sweet discussions.

And always there was hospitality from Paolo, the community, and those temporary residents who found reason to stay weeks or months or sometimes years. If we had just entered or if he had just come from the library or his office, this tall and so absolutely visible man might notice us and shout out, "Tereza! Gabbey!" ("Gabbey" being how "Gabe" sounds when every letter counts.) Paolo became a good friend to us in those years. We would usually arrive bringing the Springtime in Syria visitors or the Iraqi students we were working with at that time.

Hundreds of stairs climb and twist up from the road until they reach Deir Mar Musa.
Photo by Ryan Rodrick Beiler.

A Room for All

Near the dinner bell on the outside wall of the kitchen was the entrance to the church. Outside the entrance, all removed shoes and left them there as one would on entering a mosque or on entering homes in much of the world. Then, at the doorway, we moved a canvas drape aside to enter a much cooler space sometimes lighted only with beeswax candles.

Our feet, shoes left behind, felt the softness of an array of well-worn carpets, some pomegranate and dark blue wool, others forest green with maroon and mulberry yarn, one fuzzy brown with brick-red fringe. The room had no pews, no sense whatsoever that this was a place to be an audience. Instead, just cushions and pillows and those carpets and a few benches against the wall. The room created a great sense of calm.

After taking a few moments to adjust to the dim light, we slowly became aware of the frescoes that covered walls, columns, arches and alcoves, an experience we had every time we entered that space. Life-size images of women, saints from scripture and the early centuries of Christianity, gazed down at

162

Father Paolo in His Own Words

I traveled twice in the Middle East and Palestine before joining the Society of Jesus in 1975. During the month of spiritual exercises, I received a spiritual call to offer myself in the mission of the Catholic Church in the Islamic world, in its specificity as Islamic. From that time, Charles de Foucauld was already important for me, in order to think about the manner of a Catholic mission in the Islamic world. I started to think how to transform the presence of the Church *in* the Islamic world into a Church *for* the Islamic world. From 1977 onward, I was sent to Lebanon to study Arabic and I went with a strong desire to inculturate Christian faith in an Islamic cultural, religious, and spiritual background. This was immediately conjugated with inculturation in the Oriental Church. I always said at that time (and still do) that the Universal Church will not be able to meet Islam by jumping over the Oriental Churches and Christians, but through them....

—From a presentation Father Paolo gave in 2010 to a conference held at Heythrop College, University of London.

We think that the monastery has rediscovered and redeveloped the role of the oriental monastery, especially the role of the desert monastery, in a social, symbolic, and spiritual context for both Muslims and Christians. On the Christian level, many people from all over Syria and other countries come from *all* churches. It is also evident that local Muslims are interested on a level that goes deeper than mere cultural curiosity as they come in their thousands, especially in the spring. On another level other people, tourists or foreigners working in Syria, coming from a variety of religions and cultural backgrounds, see the monastery as a symbolic spiritual place relevant for them....

We live our vocation building on this extremely rich experience of Christian witness accumulated by the Oriental Churches in common life with Muslims for fourteen centuries, and deeply harmonized with them through the Arabic language. And we walk on the path of Saint Francis of Assisi, Ignatius of Loyola, Charles de Foucauld, Louis Massignon, and Mary Kahil, feeling the love of Jesus to each Muslim man and woman. We now consider Islam as being the human group to which we belong and in which we are happy to live, thankful that we have been chosen by God to participate in the life of the *ummah* [the Muslim people].... We understand the monastery as the spiritual home of those Christians, disciples of Christ, who feel a vocation of deep and humble love for Muslims and for Islam, as much as a spiritual port for Muslims feeling a vocation for deep friendship with Christians. For both, it is a place of harmony and a prophecy for peace in our region and further than that.

—From Father Paolo's writings

us from every archway. Texts in various alphabets—Greek, Arabic, Syriac, Roman—were scattered here and there quoting scripture and identifying the scene or the persons. One "cycle" of frescoes was painted over a cycle created centuries earlier. At Mar Musa, the most recent cycle was probably done in the fourteenth century. It covered the previous cycle of saints and stories as that cycle had covered the one before. Today much of that fourteenth century fresco work is what is seen, but in many places its images have fallen, perhaps from those years when no one lived here and the roof itself fell, leaving the walls and arches open to the rain and sun.[1]

Paolo in NYC

When we visited the monastery in spring 2007, Paolo told us he would be going to Fordham University that summer to attend a gathering of those Jesuits working in predominately Muslim countries. We planned to be in the United States during part of the summer, in New York City, so we asked him if we could arrange an evening where he could speak to some New Yorkers about the monastery and its mission. He agreed and our friends at St. Peter's Lutheran Church in Midtown Manhattan helped to put together a sponsoring committee of Christians, Jews, and Muslims.

On Paolo's first day ever in the United States, we met him at Fordham's campus near Lincoln Center in Manhattan, and he rode the crosstown bus to St. Peter's with us. Sixty people attended to hear Paolo speak of Syria and its continuing willingness to accept refugees (from Palestine, from Lebanon, from Iraq) and about the Middle East's long history of different faiths living mostly in peace. He said, "Syria is a hope, not a problem." He asked why the West cannot understand "security" as a necessity but not a solution. In response to a question, Paolo argued that none of us can separate our religious traditions from the violence that believers have committed, "All must bear the sin of our common violence." Looking at this interfaith assembly, he said, "Syria does not know this face of the West."

We went back to the monastery one weekend in November and stayed overnight, taking with us a couple who were visiting from Philadelphia. We all joined the evening prayer in the church, and Theresa sang and played guitar at one point in the prayer.

---

1. For images of the monastery, including the frescoes on the arches, pillars, and walls of the church, see a brief 2006 documentary by Yasmin Fedda, *Milking the Desert* (http://bit.ly/1nL4HxR). For a later, longer film, see *A Tale of Two Syrias* by the same filmmaker (http://bit.ly/1Un0VFn).

It was so cold at night! The men's dorms were full so Bill and Gabe slept in the chapel (watched over by all the saints in the frescoes). Theresa and Betty climbed another 150 steps in the dark, going further up the mountain to the women's building. Then Theresa, who usually loves a warm bed, loved the stars more, and decided to sleep on the balcony, covered with heavy blankets and staring straight up into a star-filled sky.

The next morning we were there for the Sunday liturgy. Father Paolo presided in four or five languages for the various visitors, always careful to include the children present. Afterward, we spent time in the monastery's growing library.

Voice for Dialogue and Spiritual Jihad

The nonviolent protests began in the south of Syria in March 2011 and almost at once met a violent response from the regime. The following excerpt is from a letter that Paolo sent that Easter to friends of the monastery:

> Syria is wedged between Lebanon, characterized by confessional divisions, Iraq, characterized by general insecurity and sectarian divisions, and Israel always perceived as the enemy. Because of the forces and interests involved in the conflict [in Syria], it is our national unity that is threatened. The loss of it could provoke a long and bloody civil war. We are convinced that a large majority of Syrians recognize themselves as a united community existing in a shared civilization. We still hope that true freedom of expression will exist to allow opinions of many people to be heard. Only this will make change possible without bloodshed....

Later in 2011, as the violence in Syria steadily worsened, Mar Musa was always in our thoughts. In this bit of the world, the "people of the book," lived peacefully for the most part and most especially in those centuries when together Muslims, Jews, and Christians constructed that "House of Wisdom" that was also house of poetry, medicine, science, translation, architecture, mathematics, and more. So in these hard months, working with what would be our last group of Iraqi students, we tried to listen to the voice of that monastic community, whose space had become a place of hospitality for all.

In early September, the community invited its friends in Syria to join them in "spiritual jihad, through fasting, prayer, and *sakina* (God-inspired peace of the soul) for reconciliation between the children of Mother Syria."

The invitation said in part:

The Community of Deir Mar Musa al-Habashi in the mountain of Nebek wishes to dedicate eight days to fasting, prayer, and *sakina* for imploring of God Almighty, Father of All Mercy, for reconciliation between citizens on the basis of a common option for non-violence as the only method able to ensure sustainable reform and to avoid the slide into civil war and the vicious circle of revenge.

We hope that our brothers and friends, and all citizens of Syria of whatever orientation, will support this our pious deed: We are family! We weep for all the martyrs, because they are our children.... If only we could reach the heart of all those who have slipped into the use of violence, be it justified by fear, interest, duty, religion or ideology. We ask for the miracle of reconciliation in Syria, amen—a miracle that we will receive from God if we keep our hearts turned towards one another, daughters and sons of this homeland. Our country is wounded, souls are full of resentment and fear of the other....

There is a great disparity in the way we assess events. Extremism carries us away, annulling the space for a possible national agreement in the sphere of common social life, driving people to division within the same house, the same monastery. In the end, it leads us to somehow justify the violence of the party to which we believe we belong.

How do we free ourselves of this deadly maelstrom that disfigures our humanity? How can we, on the one hand, achieve for the benefit of all the reforms that some desire, while keeping on the other hand the good things of the past, dear to others? How can dialogue occur between two sides that consider one another as liars, as enemies of the country and of humanity?

And now we wish to entrust ourselves in the hands of God, the Friend of humankind, through supplication, *dhikr* (recalling the name of God) and spiritual discernment. May God have mercy on us, grant us light, show us the way to reconciliation and open to us the doors to forgiveness.

The document then specified two such doors to reconciliation. The first opens to freedom of expression and plural sources of news coverage while recognizing how imperfect the international media is. And the second door opens to conflict resolution without violence from internal or foreign sources. The community notes that all foreign military intervention is to be rejected, but not help from "movements for peace on the part of friendly countries, to help the people of Syria achieve reconciliation and reform and avoid the vicious circle of civil war and revenge."

The letter concludes:

We invite you to those days of fasting, prayer, and *sakina*, because such a stand cannot be taken without asceticism and detachment from any personal interest not in accord with the common good. These are days of encounter and exchange of views in peace and quiet and respect for the dignity of every individual and every person's opinions.

In their letter at Easter 2012, the monastic community of Deir Mar Musa wrote:

The spring has returned, and the Merciful gives us the grace to remain witnesses to the vocation of the Syrians, their divine destiny to live as good neighbors in spiritual harmony, mutual religious esteem, participation in the same civilization, social solidarity and unity in the good and bad days.

"Loving Islam, Believing in Jesus"

On one of our last visits to Deir Mar Musa, Paolo gave us a copy of the just-published book he had written in cooperation with Églantine Gabaix-Hialé: *Amoureux de l'islam, croyant en Jésus (Loving Islam, Believing in Jesus)*. It is not an autobiography, but in fact no better title could be found for Paolo's life story. Loving Islam and believing in Jesus have been both Paolo's scholarly study and his life's daily labor and daily joy.

A few months before we left Syria in July 2012, Paolo's residency permission was withdrawn by the Syrian government and he was forced to leave Syria. The community continued. Several times unknown persons with unknown backing came to the monastery. More than once computers and phones were smashed, and once sheep were taken and their shepherds kidnapped, but all were later returned. The community continues, but the flow of visitors had nearly stopped by then.

In summer 2013, Paolo entered northern Syria from Turkey. This was the time when the Syrian opposition to the regime was itself becoming more widely divided. The group then called Islamic State in Iraq and Syria (ISIS) was in control of more and more territory in northern and eastern Syria. Paolo's intention seems to have been to meet with ISIS leaders in al-Raqqa, perhaps to speak with them about the prisoners they were holding. Paolo was taken prisoner at that time. Later there were reports of negotiations for his ransom and release, as well of reports of his death. Many who knew Paolo believe he is still alive. The community he helped to create at Deir Mar Musa continues.

Women saints are on both sides of all the arches, as seen here. Through the arch, we see the west wall of the chapel. Photo by Gabe Huck.

12

Portraits

The people we knew in Syria made that good place our home. These pages, portraits of some special women, tell about a few of them.

Noor

"I'm leaving Syria and before I go, I want to leave you with something—a new friend." With that, fellow Arabic language student Richard Cozzens explained that his Syrian friend Noor would be a wonderful companion for us. Noor was fluent in English and she was enthusiastic and outgoing. He thought she would be able to help us by becoming our Arabic conversation partner. The moment we met Noor, we were so at ease and we agreed to meet every Thursday. Noor offered to teach us how to cook one of the most difficult Syrian dishes, *yalangy*. That first Thursday, she burst into our tiny kitchen on the roof in Bab Touma with a stack of grape leaves, lemons, rice, and all the spices she would need.

Noor quickly began giving us directions: I (Theresa) plunged the grape leaves into boiling water, retrieved them, trimmed the stems, and cut a small "v" where the stem had been; Gabe peeled and diced onions, then juiced the lemons. Meanwhile Noor chattered on, describing her work at the University, her sisters and their disagreements as well as her parents' expectations for her to marry. She was mixing the rice with lemon juice in a glass bowl and simultaneously, it seemed, chopping parsley and tomatoes. How many hands did she have? Soon we were learning how to roll the rice mixture into the leaves forming a finger-like shape. Noor laughed at some of our overly chubby *yalangy*. "You remind me of the ones I made when I was a little girl!"

After scores of rolled up grape leaves were placed in a huge soup pot, she added some tomato juice and stewed tomatoes. She weighted the stuffed grape leaves down with a dinner plate and covered the pot. Now it was time to wait.

Feeling like a child, I whined, "You mean we have to wait over an hour to eat?" but Noor said not to worry—she had brought along a board game.

This ancient game was embroidered on black velvet and it resembled the Parcheesi board of our childhoods. We shook shells instead of dice as we moved around the board toward "home." Noor loved teaching us this traditional game and we passed the time playing and chatting as the scent of the stuffed grape leaves wafted through the roof garden.

A graduate of Damascus University in biology, Noor was working in an office at a local university, but her real love was her intense involvement with the Red Crescent. In summer 2006, she did that almost around-the-clock as the young volunteers helped to provide housing and food and health care for the tens of thousands of Lebanese refugees who fled to Damascus as Israeli planes attacked their homes. Noor told us some of her experiences: the birth of a baby to a young mother accompanied by two other children while her husband had stayed home, the tragic meeting at the Lebanese border with a large family that had to flee without one of their children, learning later that he had been killed.

We had the opportunity to see some photos of the work these young people had done for the refugees when Noor invited us to participate in an upcoming blood drive. Large photos were displayed in a Red Crescent tent where we went to donate blood. With people fasting during the month of Ramadan, the blood supply drops and we were happy to become part of the effort to restore the blood bank. We were impressed by the commitment of the young people who volunteered for the Red Crescent. Their incredible energy and enthusiasm were apparent as we learned more about their projects with refugees, children, the blind, the elderly, and those most vulnerable.

In general, giving blood was somewhat simpler than in New York, far fewer questions to answer. But one question eliminated Gabe entirely—his age! At 65, he was considered too old to donate blood. After I gave blood, I received a little basket of local chocolates with a red ribbon tied onto a handwritten note that said, "Thanks for donating your blood."

One night during the holy month of Ramadan, Noor came for *iftar*. She kept the fast of no liquids, no food, dawn to sundown, all the 29 days of Ramadan. The *iftar* meal begins with a special prayer, which Noor recited, followed by dates and lots of water. Noor could not ever just be a guest with us without bringing half the food herself. We especially enjoyed the pastries she had purchased in al-Midan, a neighborhood famous for its sweets. After we ate, Theresa played her guitar and we sang together. Noor wanted to sing an Eric Bogle song she had learned from a CD we had lent her, "No Man's Land (Ballad of Willie McBride)," a powerful antiwar song.

In 2006, Noor was selected to participate in an environmental project collaborating with science students from the Japanese International Cooperation Agency (JICA) who were researching water quality in Utaya, a village about 40 kilometers southeast of Damascus. Some of the villagers are Bedouin who follow their flocks in spring and summer, and others are farmers who stay on their land year round. The Syrian and Japanese students came to Utaya in response to problems the villagers were having with water shortage, poor water quality, and problems with the sewage system. Doctors from the village provided data on water-related illnesses. The students all stayed in the village with families, witnessing their poverty. The work of the JICA team showed that the water, which came from the city system in Damascus, was toxic. The treatment plant had never been fully completed to do the work it was intended to do.

Noor was excited to be part of this joint project with JICA and to write recommendations. At the end, they gathered all the villagers together at the municipality to share the findings with the community (everybody came, even the children). The students prepared and served a Japanese meal to everyone at the meeting. The Syrian half of the team presented their findings to their government in hopes that the problem would be addressed.

Later that spring, Noor brought us to Utaya and we were invited to come inside a Bedouin tent to meet a large family. This was the first time for us to be inside one of the long, rectangular tents we had often seen from a bus or train while traveling in Syria and Jordan. Inside the tent were a dozen or more family members seated on cushions or on beautiful overlapping carpets. We felt honored to drink tea with them, exchanging greetings and trying out our basic Arabic.

After the visit, Noor took us to the home of the family she had stayed with while on the JICA project and we shared a lovely meal with them. They had prepared lamb, herbed rice with toasted almonds, and fresh yogurt. After dessert and hot tea we went for a walk to see their vegetable garden and fruit trees. Noor expressed her pride in one of the daughters, who was now the first young woman of the village to make it to college. Since Utaya had no high school, she had taken it upon herself to travel by bus to another town to attend high school.

Sibkey Park and many parks in Damascus became the setting for some of Noor's Red Crescent projects. She taught local children lessons on ecology, led them in cleanup efforts, and taught art lessons using trash they had collected. Every Mother's Day, they planted flowers in the park. Each child who participated was given one potted plant to bring home to their mother. How touching it was, six years later, when Noor met a teenager who told her that she had planted the potted flowers every year and it was because of Noor that her family now had a garden. Women like Noor are the hope of Syria.

Long before the troubles in Syria escalated into violence, Noor left her family and moved to Spain to complete graduate work in international relations. While working on her PhD, she became a researcher for UNESCO (United Nations Educational, Scientific and Cultural Organization) and Chair for Intercultural Dialogue in the Mediterranean.

Noor Today

We asked Noor to write about her life since leaving Damascus:

I work now for the European Institute of the Mediterranean in Barcelona in the Euromediterranean Women´s Foundation within their online platform for gender equality and women's rights. I am still volunteering with the Spanish Red Cross, and in the Center of Cooperation for the Mediterranean. We organize workshops and youth camps for young volunteers from all over the Mediterranean. Always we are working with the youth for the culture of peace and nonviolence.

In Barcelona and Tarragona, I have another project called "Cena Siria." I organize Syrian dinners! People can come with their friends or just come and meet new people. The idea is to prepare Syrian foods and talk about Syria, talk about politics, do poetry readings, make music. People from different nationalities come to these dinners. Also I am in a dance group in Tarragona and we organize social dances to support different causes.

Sometimes I travel in the Catalonia region and give talks about Syrian refugees and the situation inside Syria.

Finally I am translating a book of poems written by my little sister Salam, who is still in Damascus. She is 14 now and she writes beautifully! She is amazing, my little poet! One day she will have a Nobel prize for literature!

Three Poems by Salam, a Teenager in Damascus

1.

We felt so much and finally our emotion has spilled out,
spilled and flowed away to a hidden place.
Only the good-hearted know where it is.
We want bread, not blood.
We want justice, not commands.
We want peace, not truce.

2.

On one morning, just smile, sister!
Let the roses crown your innocent heart,
let that shadow of your dream
hold the reckless imagination from the seas of your world,
let hope sleep with the melodies of the heart.
Maybe love will shine, rose-colored with the shine of your eyes.
Or a goodness will accompany you, to live that day with you.

> 3.
> Friend, rise now and try,
> try to live the moment, enjoy this thing called life.
> Know the happiness that lies in details, in simple things.
> Listen to the spontaneous laughter inside you.
> Try to see that shine in your eyes!
> Burn, just for once, the castles of your luxury,
> your strict laws, your worn out pretensions.
> Try just this once to live
> inside your wooden hut
> and your imprisoned soul would be free.

Umm Rita

"Mumkin ukhti...yani...aindy ukhti...mumkin...?" I struggled with my first-year Arabic to ask a neighbor if she had a room for my sister Julie who was coming to visit us that week. Our landlady was uncooperative and said my sister could not stay with us in our room on the roof, so I was searching the narrow streets of the Old City looking for a family that would rent a room for a week. After four unsuccessful attempts at four different dwellings, I knocked pathetically on the door of a two-story home. A small woman answered the door and smiled cheerfully, inviting me in. Her name was Umm Rita. For the next hour and a half, we spoke in Arabic and a bit of French. She must have thought I spoke French like the many Europeans who come to Damascus to study Arabic and live in the Old City. It didn't matter; somehow we communicated as we drank tea and laughed over our attempts to share news of our families and situations. I had no idea then how close we would become during the next seven years and how our families would intertwine.

We sat in the courtyard of her old-style Damascus home, but the open courtyard had years ago been covered with an opaque roofing material. Various rooms spoked off the courtyard, including a tiny kitchen, bathroom, and two bedrooms. In better economic times, the fountain in the center must have functioned, but now it was empty and there were signs of deterioration in the adobe-like walls surrounding us. We were encircled by an array of holy pictures tacked up here and there of Mary, Jesus, and various haloed saints. A nearby glass cabinet held special teapots, a silver sugar bowl, and small cups for Turkish coffee.

Umm Rita told me about her daughter Rita, who worked in a nearby doctor's office as a receptionist. Rita should be married by this age, according to her mother, and actually had been engaged once to a doctor. That seemed promising but later did not work out. Umm Rita wanted Rita to become engaged soon since she wasn't "getting any younger," although from Rita's photo she looked to be in her young 20s. I brought out pictures of our own grown children. That made Umm Rita call upstairs, and after a bit, her son George came ambling down to say hello. He seemed to be jobless, like many of the young men in Syria. His father worked in the family business making wooden mosaic boxes and inlaid trays, intricate backgammon sets, and mosaic tables. Umm Rita whispered to me that George wasn't interested in working with his father and two uncles in the generations-old workshop.

A perky, long-haired, high school student descended the cement staircase smiling like a model. This younger sister, Mariam, was delighted to practice her English with me. She learned to speak English in two ways: in school like most Syrian children and at home with foreigners. Umm Rita rented out rooms downstairs to make expenses meet, since the economy was increasingly feeble. I learned that the family had all moved upstairs to free up the entire downstairs for boarders.

My sister Julie did move in with Umm Rita and her husband, Jabreel, for her week in Damascus. We arrived at their front door after midnight that first night, rapping quietly, keeping our voices low. Suddenly the upstairs window burst open and the family leaned out and waved, shouting happily in welcome, pulling a rope from upstairs that released the front door. When Umm Rita saw us, she cried out excitedly, held my sister's hand, bowed, kissed her shoulder, and welcomed her as if she was a movie star. Repeated kisses, another embrace and Umm Rita exclaimed, "You didn't tell me your sister was a nun!" I hadn't mentioned that Julie is a Daughter of Charity, the same order of sisters who run the hospital right outside the walls of the Old City. Julie was wearing the same navy blue habit and veil of the sisters who live in Bab Touma.

One late evening while Julie was staying at Umm Rita's, a couple came over with their son, about 10 years older than Rita. The room felt full of tension as a well-coifed Rita and her parents visited with the dressed up young man and his parents. Coffee was offered, but at the end of the evening it had not been touched. When Julie met us for breakfast in our upstairs kitchen she asked, "I don't get it. Why didn't they drink the coffee?" It was then that I recalled what our Arabic teacher had told us: Drinking the coffee would have meant a sealed commitment, an acceptance for an arranged marriage.

Whenever we had visitors to Damascus, we always had one or more stay with Umm Rita: an Iraqi Student Project candidate and her mother from Baghdad, the vice principal from the New York City public school where I had taught, Springtime in Syria guests. Umm Rita always made them feel a part of her family.

We often stopped by to visit Umm Rita and, besides the hammam, this was an excellent place for me to practice speaking Arabic. As years passed, we finally attended a wedding for Rita and, in time, the celebration for the birth of her son Butros. Like many grandmothers everywhere, Umm Rita took care of Butros when Rita went back to work.

In 2011, as fewer and fewer tourists ventured into Syria, the work at Abu Rita's woodshop slowed down. We were mindful to bring our guests to the workshop, where Jabreel demonstrated the techniques for creating the mosaic boxes for which Damascus is famous. That year, one of Jabreel's brothers died of a heart attack, and the sorrow was deepened because none of their sons wanted to keep the family business going.

Dr. Reema

Discovering the need to see a doctor while living in a foreign country could become a cause for anxiety, but a friend gave me the name of Dr. Reema and assured me I could communicate my medical needs in English. When I reached the doctor's receptionist on the phone, I was proud to be able to speak enough Arabic to set up an appointment.

Dr. Reema, a graduate of medical school in Syria, completed her specialty studies in London. There she met her husband, also Syrian, working on his specialty in surgery. He had lived in Oklahoma as a youngster while his father was working on a PhD. Their two sons were born in the UK, but later the family returned to their home country so the children would grow up in their own language and culture. Both doctors spoke proudly of what it meant for them to return home.

Dr. Reema's personal office was filled with open shelves displaying geological treasures, small ceramic figures of children, and remembrances from families whose babies she had delivered. Her voice was soft and musical and her eyes twinkled joyfully when she spoke about her practice. I explained what had brought me to Damascus, and Dr. Reema listened and asked questions and offered to help in any way she could. Only then did she turn the conversation back to my health.

In Damascus, they worked together to design an environment for their offices that is mindful of the people with whom they work. Dr. Reema's husband told us, "We do not think of the people who come to us as patients or clients. We think of them as people who are mostly healthy, coming to us with their concerns." This was obvious in the great dignity with which I was treated. Dr. Reema took my health history herself in her office, a living-room-like space, large and welcoming. She went with me to the exam room, never leaving my side after that. From simple things, like subdued lighting and lovely colors on the walls, to complex top-of-the-line equipment and computerized images, everything I experienced was positive and comfortable. She made me feel like I was her only patient.

After my physical exam, she sent me to a lab a few blocks away, "Don't worry. The pathologist there speaks English. He studied at Harvard." I remember thinking as I walked to the lab, "If this is cancer, I'm just going to stay in Syria and have Dr. Reema take care of me." I didn't have health insurance in my home country anyway, and from this short time together with Dr. Reema, I had complete trust in her.

When I returned from the lab, Dr. Reema suggested I have a bone density test when I returned to New York City, but I said that without insurance, it would cost hundreds of dollars. "Nonsense. You can get it down the street for twenty dollars. I'll write the prescription. You can walk there from here."

Between 11:00 a.m. and 3 p.m., I met with Dr. Reema, walked to the pathologist where I delivered my lab work, later a walk to a nearby clinic for a mammogram and the bone density tests, then a return visit to the lab for additional blood work. I was impressed by the speed, the lack of red tape, and the dignity with which I was treated at these three places. The best part is that they all believe the patient should hold onto her own records and medical files. How reassuring to have these records and results in my own hand! The cost for the entire day of exams and tests was less than $80. The next day Dr. Reema and her husband met with us to discuss my health.

As time went on with Iraqi Student Project, we were able to refer students to Dr. Reema. The students were always treated with respect and dignity, and in most cases they were treated free of charge. We were grateful for the way she and her husband met with parents of students to explain medical concerns.

Dr. Reema and her family later moved to an area outside of Damascus. When violence came to this area, the family decided to relocate outside of the country until peace returns.

Huda

Up in a small, smoky internet café in Muhajireen sat a mother with a college-age student. As all mothers of intelligent offspring, she was wondering how they could ever manage to pay for college, especially since they were Iraqi refugees in Damascus. Syrians who did well in high school were entitled to free college education. Non-Syrian young people had free access to elementary and secondary education, but not university.

Internet cafés then were small and tightly packed, so a young American overheard these two speaking fluent English. He leaned over to say, "If you want to go to college for free, look at the website of Iraqi Student Project."

That was the beginning of our friendship with Huda and Muhanned, an Iraqi couple our ages. A year later, in the first group of ISP students, their child left for studies at a college in the United States, but we adults stayed friends until all of us left Syria years later. At the beginning we had tea at each other's apartments, Muhanned always stepping briefly out to the balcony with his pipe. And we began having meals together, Huda's wonderfully rich chocolate cake often served for dessert. We took walks together to Abu Abdo's juice bar. Huda and I would walk arm in arm window-shopping, laughing all the way down Afeef Street toward the park at Sahat Arnous. Gabe and Muhanned strolled ahead.

Over time we heard stories of how Huda was educated by the Sisters of the Sacred Heart in China when her father was in the diplomatic service for Iraq. She told of the strong education she received from the nuns and how her family respected them. As everyone who attended Catholic school, she had many tales of special sisters she loved. She told us about childhood capers with her brother in Russia during their time living in Moscow, when their father was assigned to the Iraqi embassy. During those years, she traveled throughout Europe and became fluent in several languages. She talked about the wonderful library her father had in their home in Baghdad. And now she was a refugee.

Her husband, Muhanned, was a medical doctor who had established his own clinic back in Baghdad but as a refugee was unable to open up a practice in Syria. Eventually he found work at an oil camp in a remote area of Syria, administering medicines and first aid for the workers. The schedule was unpredictable and it required him to live for weeks at a time in a trailer at a work site out in the Syrian desert. But he valued any opportunity to use his skills.

Frequently Huda would stop by our apartment and drop off fresh *samoon*, an Iraqi bread, wide in the middle and tapered at either end. Often the bread was still warm from the baker. Our students loved these visits and this "bread from home." They split the *samoon* open and covered it with spicy Anbar sauce and hard-boiled eggs and potatoes, or filled it with falafel, or just ate it plain. If a student's mother or father wanted to talk with us about a specific problem, we often asked Huda to come over and meet them. She had a graciousness about her and was able to calm any fears of ISP parents. She was very comfortable coming over to our apartment when classes were going on, and over time, she came to know most of our students.

When I asked how to make *biryani*, a favorite traditional Iraqi dish, Huda came over to our apartment to teach me. As she completed each step, I wrote the directions she gave me with a blue dry-erase marker on the white tile walls of our kitchen: Dice the potatoes into small squares, fry the potatoes separately, use freshly shelled peas, have the special spices ready. That recipe ran from the floor to the ceiling and it stayed up until the day we left our apartment in 2012. When we finally served the biryani that afternoon, the students were thrilled. For some students, especially those whose parents returned to Baghdad for work, Huda became an honorary auntie. She had a special place in her heart for our last group of students.

When Huda's brother came to visit from Portugal, she invited us over and prepared Chinese food. Since she and her brother had lived in China decades before, these were authentic dishes Huda learned to make. She found all the special ingredients she needed in the spice souqs of Damascus. The dinner conversation flowed between reminiscences of their old days together and the current woes in Iraq.

Despite the ongoing violence in Iraq, Huda exhibited hopefulness, her faith a source of strength. Beneath her optimism were the realities brought on by the sanctions and invasion of Iraq and the subsequent violence that had caused her and Muhanned to come to Syria. Normal family tensions—and "family" always means more than mom and dad and the kids in this society—were magnified by three decades of war, brutal economic sanctions, the way mutual respect between Iraqis was collapsing. Families were separated by the need for safety, some living as refugees in one country, some resettled in another. We saw this over and over. New sorrows sometimes seemed to arrive by phone or email with regularity. In all this, the four of us came to know each other well.

Huda took advantage of the many classes offered by UNHCR (UN High Commissioner on Refugees). Posters, especially near the places where refugees went to pick up their monthly food packages, announced classes in English, jewelry-making, and glass-painting. Huda soon joined other refugee artists who exhibited at a church hall located just outside the Old City. Iraqi women from all religious backgrounds proudly displayed their best crafts. Huda sold some pieces in each show and soon began to specialize in jewelry making. The bead stores in Souq al-Hamidiyya offered a wide range of glass, clay, enamel, and wooden beads, and she loved creating different designs, often reflecting her impression of ancient treasures of Ur or ancient necklaces in the National Museum in Damascus.

But artistic expression was not enough for Huda. She began volunteering in Jaramana, a neighborhood off the Airport Road south of the Old City. Jaramana was, some said, the Little Baghdad of Damascus with its thousands of Iraqi refugee families. She visited people who were alone, especially the elderly. She arranged for clothing or food to be delivered to those most needy. She helped find and deliver a sofa and table to a shut-in who had no family. She found funding and once a month arranged for a local café to serve breakfast to a whole group of older people who then stayed for a few hours singing Iraqi songs together and listening to music from home. Huda found joy in bringing beauty and happiness to others.

As the troubles in Syria escalated, Huda and Muhanned returned to the chaos and violence of Baghdad. Ironically, after more than five years of living as refugees in Damascus, they were then contacted by the UNHCR and told that their request to resettle in the United States was being terminated because they had returned to Iraq.

We stay in touch.

Hadya

The sufferings of sanctions, invasion, and occupation are, in their duration and breadth, more terrible and destructive than we had imagined. We turn the page and move on at such a distance, responsible but never lingering to observe, let along grieve.

In fall 2007, just as the first ISP students were being interviewed and classes were beginning, a friend from Chicago contacted us. He was asking us if we could locate two persons who had just fled Iraq and come to Damascus. Our friend had received a call from a relative of theirs who had long lived in the United States. Their first names were Hadya and Salem. Could we try to locate them and make sure they were safe?

We will tell Hadya's story the way we experienced and wrote about it in letters from Damascus beginning in late 2007.

October 2007

Later today we are going looking for a brother and a sister from Iraq. She is 71; he is 59 and has, we're told, something like Down syndrome. They arrived here in Damascus recently after being threatened in Baghdad. A neighbor gave them money to take the bus to Syria, but now the money is running out. They need help getting to the UNHCR offices to sign up for refugee status so they will be eligible for food packages and medical care. We know that those who line up now at the UNHCR are given appointments five to six months away for their interviews that determine whether they are given the refugee status. Because of their age, perhaps these two will not have to wait that long.

We don't know exactly what they need. Even finding them could be diffi-cult, as there really aren't street addresses in most areas of Damascus and they have no telephone. But we have some general notion of the neighborhood and the name of an electronics store that they live near.

Later. We found the neighborhood, we found the electronics store. With the help of an Iraqi friend, we talked to many people, but no one knew of this couple. So we are trying to see if the person who wrote us about them from the United States can get more information. This is a neighborhood we had never been in before and isn't one where many Iraqis are finding apartments.

Later in October 2007

Our friend in Chicago sent a phone number for an Iraqi family who offered to share their home with Hayda and her brother Salem. We have visited them! They are living about 50 meters from where we stood last week without a clue of which door to knock on.

Hadya has many health problems, including diabetes and degenerative bone diseases. She had braces on both knees and her right arm has been in a sling for decades. For these and other long-term problems, she carried from Baghdad a large file of medical records and doctors' reports.

Her brother Salem has some neurological condition. He seems such a gentle person, but he cannot care for himself and didn't speak. Hadya has taken care of her younger brother for a long time.

A month ago, someone came to their door in Baghdad and told them to leave their home or else they would be killed. A neighbor gave them money for the bus to Damascus. They had no certain destination, but they left the bus with other passengers. An Iraqi man who had just recently come himself from Baghdad saw them walking along the highway and asked if they needed help. He ended up giving them a ride to his home and offering to share his lodging with them. So they are now living with this man and his two children: Yassin attends the local high school, and Karima was in college in Iraq but isn't sure what she can do here.

We have been trying to find how and if UNHCR can help them. They already tried to go to the UNHCR office but, because of their condition and the huge crowds, never even reached the door. But we now know that the UNHCR people are trying to accommodate special needs like this and soon Hadya and Salem will be able to register at home. When they have refugee status, they can receive some food, blankets, and health assistance through the UN programs here.

Their hope is to be resettled in the United States where a sister of theirs has lived for decades. But how can this happen? A friend in the United States who is an immigration lawyer says a family reunifying visa could take 10 years to obtain.

But when we hear their story—even the little we know—we see something amazing, how people who are all in such hard situations still help each other:

the neighbor who gave them bus money to leave Iraq after their lives were threatened, the man who found them here on the street and invited them to move into his own rooms and stay there with him and his children. His wife is still in Baghdad because her father is ill. These three have kept Hadya and Salem safe and sheltered, now so far away from their home and city.

December 2008

In the year since we met them, Hadya and Salem have made progress toward resettlement with their sister in the United States. We visited with Hadya and with the two young people who live in the house, Karima and Yassin. The father of these two has gone back to Iraq as he ran out of money—so common. Karima and Yassin prepared tea and bread with hummus for all of us. They seem very accepting of the responsibility they have now. That visit was pretty much our Christmas Day and it was good.

Early January 2009

Salem is still not speaking while we're there. Somehow the Iraqi refugee who offered them shelter and later returned to Iraq has now made it to a European country. So the household has become these two Iraqi brother–sister sets: Hadya and Salem, Karima and Yassin. They all receive some help with food from UNHCR. Last summer we met Hadya and Salem's sister in upstate New York. Their sister told us she has been so long speaking only English that she thinks her Arabic has almost gone. She asked if her sister in Damascus now could speak English. We said no, Hadya speaks Arabic.

Over the year of waiting for resettlement, Hadya's health has deteriorated and she's been hospitalized twice, once for surgery. Now apparently someone at Homeland Security finally figured out that the two of them pose no security risk to the United States and they have been approved to resettle with their sister in the United States.

A few days ago, we went with her to the IOM (International Organization for Migration), the organization paid by the United States to prepare those accepted by Homeland Security for resettlement. Apparently one of the tasks IOM is paid to do by the destination country is to check the health of those being resettled. A wonderful Syrian doctor there is doing everything he can to facilitate the travel of Hadya and Salem to the United States while Hadya is still able to travel—and to arrange for a doctor who will travel with them. Salem is in good health, but if Hadya cannot care for him, what's to be done?

Mid-January 2009

All the necessary doctors have agreed that Hadya is able to travel, and IOM has booked seats for her and Salem and an accompanying Syrian doctor to fly to New York City next week. It will be a very different life for them and for their U.S. relatives. And it will be a very different life here for Karima and Yassin. The latter hopes to graduate from high school this year, but college here is not free for non-Syrians. This week we learned that for $5,000 Karima could complete her final year of college in a private university in Damascus and become an agricultural engineer and perhaps be eligible for a job.

So in one way this story has no big fireworks. It is just how the lives of two sister–brother sets were disrupted by the violence of the invasion/occupation. All are alive, but all removed from their home place, all forced to accept charity. The older ones will finish their lives without neighbors who speak their language or familiar places to visit, trying to stay healthy in a health care system that isn't likely to make a big place for them. The younger brother and sister are full of life and energy, but their physical safety in Syria doesn't bring them opportunities to get on with what young adults need to be doing. When we Americans see what we judge as an opportunity to remake the world to our liking, do we ever consult folks like these four?

February 2009

When we wrote a month ago, Hadya and Salem were about to travel to the United States to live with their sister and brother-in-law. A week passed, and very early on a cold Thursday morning, we went to the home where they have been living with another brother and sister, young adults, also Iraqi refugees. The six of us and two cousins of Karima and Yassin came along as we took two taxis to the Damascus airport. There our group met two Syrian doctors who work for the IOM. And we met another Iraqi family being resettled in the United States. The father in this second family has a brain tumor, and there are five children 12 years old and under. The doctor who had helped Hadya at the IOM offices would fly with Hadya and Salem until they reunited with their sister. The other IOM doctor would fly with the family of seven to Salt Lake City. Why are they being resettled in Utah? Family there? No. Another reason? Not that anyone knew.

So the two doctors, the family of seven, and Hadya and Salem went through security, Hadya in a wheel chair. Many tears.

Their flight took them first to London to change planes, then to JFK airport in New York City. They would have four or five hours to rest at a hotel before going to their Albany flight from LaGuardia airport across Brooklyn and Queens. Then they would have an hour's flight to Albany, where their sister would be waiting for them. The IOM (not the doctor with them) demanded all of this, even though their sister lives closer to JFK airport than to Albany and wanted to meet them at JFK.

On landing in Albany, Hadya was taken immediately to a hospital in Albany. For the next few days, Hadya's sister was able to visit with her in the hospital. Hadya died there on that fourth day. We think she was holding on until her brother Salem had someone to care for him as she had for half a century. A strong and intelligent woman, over 70 years old, an Iraqi, a Muslim, a Baghdadi, a refugee at the end, Hadya seemed to us never accepting what nations and gangs had done to her and to Salem, yet never preoccupied with this injustice. For us, Hadya is one of scores of Iraqi women we know whose strength in bad times brings shame upon our country.

One cannot possibly unravel all the wrongs done to Hadya and Salem by sanctions and war and occupation and the unleashing of violence in Iraq. Nor will it ever be counted, told, or tolled. Apology? Repentance? Reparations? Restitution? A firm resolution of amendment?

13
Writers' Workshop

Walk down Straight Street away from Bab Sharqi, turn right at the site of the new mosque under construction across from the nut shop, continue until the lane narrows at the door with the stained glass, go right and then right again, labyrinthing deeper and deeper into the Old City, and when there's nowhere else to go, there is a building, probably hundreds of years old. Knock on the nondescript door and enter a tiny courtyard.

Those were the directions we followed to find the apartment in the Old City offered by a British journalist as the site for our first Friday afternoon Writers' Workshop. We passed these directions on to each of the Iraqi students like clues on a treasure map. Beyond the wooden door and inside the courtyard was a most beautiful small home, the setting for our first Writers' Workshop. We still have the key to the door hanging on a hook in our bedroom in New York City, a memento of the initial place we met for Writers' Workshop. As years passed, we went on to gather in an art gallery and later in our apartment when we moved to a more central location.

"Love thyself most and best, love thyself day and night, let no bad dreams make thee doubt thyself...." Woody Guthrie lyrics from a Joel Raphael CD beckoned us to settle in, trust our best selves, and prepare to write. Students gathered around a large coffee table: some sitting on the floor, some perched on soft chairs or cushions. The lyrics were posted on a large chart and everyone sang along. This opening was a time of relaxing, smiling, singing, a type of sacred moment where we all knew we were about to embark on some sort of journey together. From that day on, "Love Thyself" became our Writers' Workshop theme song no matter where we gathered.

Even now, we use the same song with Syrian refugees in Istanbul who participate in Writers' Workshop via Skype. They meet in a room at a refugee center in Turkey and much like our Iraqi students, they settle in comfortably when they hear the voice of Joel Raphael.

Writers' Workshop was not a class but a gathering where students could free themselves up to write in a trusting environment, to share their writings with others in a nonjudgmental response group, to develop their identity as writers, to build a sense of community with other students. This weekly event was filled with music, sharing, challenge, and fun. Writers' Workshop was held over a period of five years and much good came from it.

Quick! Write!

After the opening song, we went into a quick-write using an instrumental written by Kate Wolf, performed by Nina Gerber. The first three weeks we played this four-minute song through once while the students wrote whatever was on their minds. Then they shared with a partner. The fourth week we played the song twice, creating eight minutes of time to write, eventually working up to 16 minutes of quick-write, then sharing. We never "corrected" or edited these. After the pair-share, we asked for volunteers to read their text aloud. Sometimes students would encourage their partner to read their work to the whole group. Toward the end of the academic year, the entire group chose to share with everyone. Through nonjudgmental sharing we built trust, strengthened a sense of community, and became better writers.

As one student described:

In Writers' Workshop, we write from our hearts and we put all of our feelings into what we write. Listening to each other's writings, opinions, and thoughts makes us know one another better. I like sharing my thoughts with many of my ISP friends because they show a lot of support and empathy and it strengthens our friendship. I like listening to what they write to find out what's on their minds. They always seem to have interesting ideas that I can learn from. For example, one time when I was listening to Z's writing, I thought it was so beautiful that I quoted a part of it and put it in my notebook: "Being alive is not being awake, but aware...maybe not aware of others, but aware of myself."

> ### "Love Thyself!"
>
> It has been a tradition in all five years of Iraqi Student Project to sing a special song written by Woody Guthrie before we begin Writers' Workshop every week. "Love Thyself" is the joy we experience every Saturday at Beit ISP. This song was quite ordinary to me the first couple times I sang it. Now "Love Thyself" is very special to me and I love it more each time I sing it. It makes me feel joyful, refreshed, and full of love for myself and others. A few days ago, I noticed that Theresa's voice was not the most distinct voice among us as it used to be when we were too shy or too careless to sing out loudly. In fact, I could not hear one person's voice. We were all singing a glorious chant together as one. We love ourselves "loud and long."
>
> —Taleen

FRIDAY IS ONE OF THE MOST EXCITING DAYS of the week for me because after we listen to the ISP song "Love Thyself," we start the "quick-write." In quick-write, the students write whatever comes in to their minds. After that, we start to read to each other, one to one. Almost all the students write what they were thinking about at that moment so their writing is as pure as spring water. When I listen to them I understand directly what the student is facing in life, what their concerns are. I feel closer each time I share my writing with other students. Last week I was M's partner. Although what he wrote was a little ambiguous, I felt his problems and understood what he meant. He was worried about losing control of his life because he talked about time and how we shouldn't waste any moment in our life without using it. I think listening carefully to others will make our relationships deeper and stronger.

—*Mimoon*

I used to think that I'm not a good writer so I didn't have the courage to express my thoughts and feelings through writing. After I started writing every week, I realized that I have many thoughts and ideas that were locked in my head and were never shared, not even with myself.

My writing has improved. I found out that the more I write, the better writer I become. When I first joined ISP, I remember how I was able to write only three lines in Writers' Workshop. It wasn't that I had nothing in mind, but I didn't feel confident enough to write what I was thinking about. Now I feel more comfortable when I write and share my thoughts with my friends and it helps me feel good about myself as a person and as a writer.

We used the National Writing Project as the model for Writers' Workshop, utilizing prewriting as one of the most important parts of the lesson. A song, a poem, a newspaper article, a photo, a startling quote, a prompt of some sort: This leads to brainstorming of ideas, words, and phrases. Learning how to mind-map and use graphic organizers and word webs was a vital part of each lesson. Prewriting strategies helped the students not be afraid to write because we already had generated possibilities and that blank piece of paper was not scary. For example, one successful lesson was based on a song telling the true story of the Sierra Blanca massacre (*Woodeye*, by Joel Raphael). The subject matter was so evocative that the students could not help but write well. Phrases from the lyrics (e.g., "Didn't even say goodbye to my friends, not to my grandparents") resonated with some of their own experiences while leaving Iraq.

Both Author and Questioner

After the quick-write, the first lesson in 2007 featured the theme of identity (based on a lesson designed by Cece Skala, director of the Central Coast Writing Project, California). We heard a few examples of poems using a simple formula beginning and ending "I Am." The students were then invited to write their own identity poem using the pattern: eight lines, each line with its task. As they wrote, we listened to classical cello music performed by YoYo Ma. After that, students broke into response groups of three and shared their writing with one another.

We emphasized that while listening to one another, students would face each other, make eye contact, and in responding not criticize but either ask a question or offer praise. Finally we came together as a group for whole-group sharing. They sat in a circle, their faces intense and involved, a rare Damascus rain pounding outside and a golden glow from the lamps around the perimeter of the room. Students read their poems aloud, many reflecting on their love for Iraq and the friends and family they left behind. This prompted more discussion, especially how much they wanted to hold on to their identities as Iraqis. Here are two of their poems:

> In Iraq, the cradle of civilizations,
> In Baghdad, where I left my beautiful
>   memories,
> In Baghdad, where the mosque and
>   church are side by side,
> In Baghdad, the people of the
>   neighborhood are your family
> even if they don't know you,
> In Baghdad, where Tigris and Euphrates
> move along together as friends,
> In Karbala, where my dad's grave
> is calling me to bring a bunch of flowers,
> In Basra, where the Tigris and Euphrates
> meet together as lovers.
>
> —Mustafa Jaafar

I am Sarah.
I am the deep blue color of the sea under clear skies.
I am like a tigress that is ever ready for challenge.
I feel human when I cry.
I love myself when I accomplish things I didn't think I could.
But I hate it when someone says I'm too young.
The sound of Yanni's music calls me.
I am Sarah.

I am Ali.
I am dark blue the color of deep oceans.
I am like an ant that does its job everyday without getting bored.
I feel happy when I see a hope in the horizon.
I love to have something to do that moves me a step forward.
But I hate to waste my time on un-useful things.
The sound of duty towards myself and my family calls me.
I am Ali.

As the two hours drew to a close, we played the opening song again with a hopeful promise to gather again next week. As we were leaving for the day, a student whispered, "I never knew I could write a poem!"

Iraq, when I say your name
I remember my Mom!
You gave me your love,
you gave me your arm.
When I look back, I see something,
I see something different from my Mom.
My Mom breastfed me for a while,
but Tigris and Euphrates never stop.
I'm your spoiled child!
Your hands held me for so long
and still want to hold,
but I left!
When I think of what was going on,
I realize that you are in the labor!

Yeah, Iraq is in labor,
Iraq is having a new baby, a new generation.
I'm sorry Iraq because I had to leave,
but I promise I will get back and help you
to take care of that new spoiled baby.

—Fatima

Students came to love this learning about writing to different forms and sharing their writing with each other. Most of them would come every day if we had time and place to hold sessions. At the second session, we worked with a wonderful poem by the Palestinian poet Mahmoud Darwish. A long poem of 22 short stanzas, each began with the same short line: "In Damascus...." Farah and Ali alternated reading verses in Arabic, then Theresa read it in English. The students listened and discussed Darwish's poem, later examining the structure. They used this as a model for their own poems about Iraq. Subsequent Writers' Workshops featured odes by Pablo Neruda, Shakespearean sonnets, Matsuo Basho's haikus, modern free verse, always followed by the student's own poetry writing.

Learning from Snow

One day in February, snow fell right on Damascus, globs of snowflakes stuck together and falling straight down because of their weight. And melting. But it kept on, the snowflakes were smaller, the ground became colder, and soon we had an inch or so of snow on the streets, on the roof by our door, on the clothes we had hung out to dry on our clothesline the day before. Snow fell until evening, a challenge to drivers, a delight for children, and a conversation for all. When it first began that morning, the two young women who work in the building a few yards from our roof were standing out on their balcony in the snow, laughing with us and shouting, *"Mashallah! Mashallah!"* Praise God!

People told us the last time it snowed was fifteen years ago. Because none of our students had ever seen snow falling, this became our theme for Writers' Workshop. First, the students excitedly shared their impressions of snow and we created a quick web of vocabulary, phrases, and ideas. Then we listened to an instrumental, "Snowblind" by Walt Michaels from his album *Stepstone*. The sound of the hammered dulcimer reminded them of the *qanun* from Iraq. We all set to work quickly writing poems about the snow. In addition to surprise, awe, and joy, many of the students expressed wonder at how the whole society stopped working and began playing: throwing snowballs, playing in the snow, rolling or falling in it to create shapes, forming snow creatures. Others wrote about the total letting go of bad memories, responsibilities, worries, and fears as an aura of happiness filled their neighborhoods.

I (Theresa) demonstrated how to cut a piece of paper to make a snowflake. Snow was just not part of their experience in Baghdad! I told them that I had grown up in southern California and that I was 24 years old when I saw snow falling for the first time. I was then living in Brighton, Colorado, and kept looking up waiting for giant paper-snowflake-sized snowflakes, like the ones we made in grade school. I told the students how stunned I was when a classmate told me that these small bits of white *were* snowflakes!

I told the story of Snowflake Bentley, a rural Vermonter who devoted his entire life to studying snowflakes (which he regarded as the most beautiful form of water). His love of study brought him to develop techniques of micro-photography so he could preserve images of snowflakes captured on black velvet during storms. But most important for our students was Bentley's tenacity. He stayed focused and never gave up even in dire circumstances. As the students settled into the second assignment, writing a prose piece about the day they first saw snow, we realized that many of them would have many years of snow ahead of them at U.S. colleges in the Midwest.

January Snow in the Fourth Year of Syria's Violence

It is snowing now. We heard in the news that a storm is coming. People here have very little to do regarding the preparation for the storm. With no or very little fuel, power, gas, or wood for heating, almost nothing can be done to protect oneself from the cold except wearing more clothes and staying at home.

Still, when snow comes, it turns to a big festival. The rich of Damascus drive to the nearby mountains in Zabadani and Bloudan where snow is thicker so they can throw snowballs at each other playfully. They build snowmen and take photos. On the way back, they stop for tea or coffee in some warm café and show off their little adventure to friends with photos.

The poor usually go up to the roof where a thin layer of snow is piled. They also make snowballs and throw them at each other. Some people grab a bowl, fill it with a clean snow, then add sugar or syrup, and eat it like ice cream. If the snow on the roof is thick enough, they may make a snowman. For the boys, snowballs also are a way to flirt with neighhorhood girls who are allowed to go to the roof in this freezing weather or even to play on the street. Snow here makes for a more tolerant parental attitude.

Teenagers who don't have a big roof go to the street and play with the snow. Boys gather in small groups and throw snowballs at other groups. Bad guys wouldn't spare any pedestrian, including me! But nearly everyone wants to be out there for the rare snow of Damascus.

—Hussein Maxos, January 2015

PEOPLE DON'T KNOW HOW TO CELEBRATE THE SNOW in this time of war. Snow, usually full of joy and memories, is bringing some other feelings. I challenged this confusion and went out to walk in the snow. I needed exercise and fresh air. I wore my thickest and heaviest clothes, even more than usual as the news tells us that some people have frozen to death in Damascus, Aleppo, and in the refugees camps.

Outside, the snow was changing the look of our city and the city is suspiciously quiet. I met a few neighbors from whom I expected a lot of complaints, but all said the same thing: "The snow is a blessing from God." I wanted to reply, "Come on! We are freezing. We have no power or gas for heating or cooking!" I didn't. They all knew that. With friends and relatives, we complain all the time. Perhaps we help each other during the war more than in normal time because we need each other more.

I walked down the hill on Afeef toward the city center, passed the deserted French embassy, saw children playing with the snow happily. One child was holding a snowball in his hand. I looked at him just as he was about to hit me with the snowball, then stopped and turned around to make it less embarrassing. "Hit me! It's ok!" First, he was scared, then he smiled, let the snowball drop from his cold hand, and ran into a small alley before I could say anything or take a photo.

At Jiser Abyad ("abyad" is "white" in Arabic and appropriate today) four teenagers were standing at one corner behind a car. I thought they must be the bad guys who throw snowballs. Immediately a big snow ball passed near my head. I stopped and looked angrily at them. They rose from behind the car, gave a sign of apology, and pointed to a girl walking near me. I kept my angry look and defiant body language after such a bad excuse and I walked on. Maybe in my very thick clothes I look bigger than I am.

When I reached Sahat Arnous, I was looking for a warm place, realizing, "I don't feel my toes anymore! I know a café with free internet here." The absence of noisy bombing and shelling today makes us wonder: They didn't stop to be kind so maybe even the military wasn't prepared. Or did they take the day off because they thought nature was making us suffer. I made a little poem:

The sneaky snow has come.
Does it know it's not welcome?
Will just add to our fear and agony?
Bombs stopped...an absurd harmony:
Frost or bullet, death is a destiny
And it continues, the surreal symphony.

—Hussein Maxos, January 2015

Odes and Haiku and Songs

Loving the writing of Pablo Neruda made it easy to teach odes in an intriguing, enthusiastic, passionate way. I (Theresa) set up three specimens from nature on a small table: a red tomato, a fresh lemon, and a papery-skinned old onion. When I read a particular Neruda ode aloud, I picked up the vegetable or fruit that was the "star" of that ode and read directly *to* it. The students loved how funny, profound, ironic, and clever Neruda's odes were. Then I passed out copies of two additional Neruda odes and put the students in groups to read them out loud and enjoy the sound of the poet's language. We had a pink wooden lizard carved in Oaxaca perched on our lamp, so Neruda's "Ode to a Lizard" was a natural choice. The other was Neruda's "Ode to Bicycles." Then we analyzed: What are the characteristics of odes? What is intrinsically "ode-ish"? We recorded our responses on a giant chart. We looked at how odes appear on the page and we talked about the shape of Chile, Neruda's home country.

> ### Ode to My Pens
>
> My pens,
> You welcome my embrace every day.
> Gilded with ivory print,
> Golden is the halo that surrounds your tip,
> And pure white is your aura.
> You march upon paper,
> Adorned and undeterred.
> Many a test with you I passed,
> Never for my gratitude you asked.
> From dusk till dawn,
> You dance in your inky gown.
> Eternalizing feelings,
> Remembering people,
> And faithfully keeping secrets.
> To you my pen,
> Who started from stone,
> And to plastic have grown.
> To you I pledge friendship.
> To you I write an ode,
> Greedy for your kinship.
>
> —Zaid Ahmed

From there the students wrote their own odes in class, then we broke up into groups and read them to each other. They were so pleased! Once comfortable with the concept, they were able to create more complex odes. Some of these odes by ISP students over the five years were included in *The River, The Roof, The Palm Tree*, a book of student writings we published in Damascus each year at the end of the Iraqi Student Project academic year.

In that workshop, we only provided two kinds of feedback: praise and questions. Praise: "The words you chose to describe the pillow were so metaphorical and funny at the same time." Question: "Do you think you need to tell what *biryani* means in English?" Each group nominated who should read their ode to the entire group. The students actually cheered and clapped for one another. From there the homework was to type it and email it in, making any changes or edits they wanted to. We printed out copies of their odes.

The next class, when I returned their odes, I did a mini-session with each student: Did you understand why you need a verb here? What word could you

Leaving What We Love

When I left Baghdad, I took one last look at everything around me and took a mental photograph that I can still remember because at that moment, I remembered everything I went through to reach this point. I remembered when I had to run out of school and call someone to pick me up because a bomb had exploded nearby, and the time I had to call my mother and tell her to come home and see what these strange armed men knocking on our door wanted. There is no doubt that because of those circumstances, I am a stronger person today. And yet somehow, I find that leaving everything behind is a great sacrifice.

That sacrifice is worth taking in order to have the chance to do something that can affect my community, to be part of the change process. Even though I miss my simple life and my mother's cooking and my friends, it's very hard to remain uninvolved, to look the other way.

We all had to struggle to get to where we are, and that has become the thing that identifies us as Iraqis. And it is what makes us believe that if we work hard, we can overcome adversity and actually make a difference. Our pain is our strength.

—Samah

use instead of "big"? Yellow as a what? How can you shorten the last verse? Have you considered using words for gems as Neruda often does ("the sapphire sea")?

Odes were fun because they didn't have to rhyme, the exaggerated praise was humorous, and students with limited vocabulary were able to create a fascinating ode.

In Writers' Workshop, we tried to master the following types of writing: biography, autobiography, short answer essay, book review, personal essay, persuasive essay, reflective essay, critical analysis of literature, poetry. We designed many different types of graphic organizers to help the students with prewriting organization of thoughts. These included Mr. Fish, a long horizontal line with a fish head on one end, lines to indicate a tail on the other, and many lines on either side of the "spine" where students could add words or concepts or steps needed to reach a goal. Mr. Face was a line drawing of a face used to record parts of an essay. Grandma's Fan was based on the quilt block of the same name.

In spring 2010, my daughter Annie came to visit. She is a high school English teacher, and we two teachers co-led a Writers' Workshop. Annie created a lesson based on the Socratic method, encouraging divergent thinking, teaching students to think critically by asking them to design open-ended questions, moving them into literary analysis. During part of the lesson, we used large color photos showing natural and human-made delights all over our planet. I challenged our students to recognize and write "level three" questions probing deeply into the subject, "Why don't the local people have enough clean water to drink while this resort has three swimming pools?" The students broke into small groups and, through asking questions like these, wrote creative narratives based on the photos. Annie was struck by the enthusiasm and eagerness of the students, and she is still in touch with many of them today.

Singing together was always part of Writers' Workshop, and Woody Guthrie songs were a favorite. During one workshop, students collaborated in rewriting "This Land Is Your Land" from an Iraqi viewpoint. After all, Woody wrote it in reaction to Irving Berlin's presumptuous "God Bless America."

We were thrilled the next year when Taif, by then a first-year college student in upstate New York, was invited to attend a birthday party for Pete Seeger. He showed the ISP version of Woody's song to Pete, and the two of them led everyone in singing our version of the song!

Chorus:
This land is your land, this land is my land
From old Ramadi on to Baquba,
From the Zakho Mountains to the Basra waters.
This land was made for you and me.

One of the verses:
As I was walking in a lovely garden,
I saw above me the flocks of gray doves.
I saw below me the shadow of the palm trees.
This land was made for you and me!

Halfway through the academic year, and again at the end, we tried some reflective writing: How are you changing as a writer? How is it for you to share your writing out loud with another person? How has listening to others' writing changed you? What do you need to work on? What goals do you have for this month? Here was one self-evaluation, written by Sarab in 2011:

When I would sit down to write an essay, I had the same three scary words blocking my thoughts: "Words can't describe." It was as if I reached a level of emotional clutter where I didn't even know how I felt. Now, writing one paper after another and editing them, I discover that words, in fact, *can* describe. I used to think of words as enemies, never expressing my exact thoughts. But now they are my companions. They're in my music library, my books, and my mind. Words no longer scare me.

Ode to Tigris

You gently halve gorgeous
Baghdad,
O powerful,
compassionate Tigris!
On your enthralling green banks,
you cradled ancient civilizations,
nurtured the first human laws,
erected cities,
embraced diversity,
protected harmony.

You handed fish
to the poor with one hand,
and with the other
provided water for the thirsty.
You never neglected
the yearning palm trees.
On your chest,
love thrived,
the depressed found consolation,
One Thousand and One Nights drew breath.
You memorized the books
of demolished libraries,
and mourned
over slaughtered bodies.

How wise you are, how peaceful!
You healed the wounded,
defended your homeland
with no spear, sword or gun,
but with a mesmerizing smile,
an exhilarating wave.

O mighty Tigris,
how painful it is to see you
miserable,
frail,
decrepit,
helpless.

To see the smirks of your enemies,
slashing your body with concrete dams,
filling you with toxicants.

I know you will rise again,
head held high,
proud yet humble,
strong and considerate.

You will thrive
and you will tell your glory
to forthcoming generations.

—Hasan Ali

Ode to Baghdad

Oh, Baghdad,
you are the capital
of the Abbasids
and my pride.
Away from you,
I am misplaced,
lost on the earth.
Your rooted history
is as old as time,
telling stories
of the Arabian Nights.
With your pure lungs
I breathe the fragrance
of saffron and cardamom.

I call upon Tigris,
the vessel of my life,
to forgive me.
You shed tears
and mourn sadly
like Jacob,
as if I were Joseph,
your absent son.

I am Sinbad,
the exile,
looking eagerly for a ship
to take me back
to Baghdad.
Across a long distance,
reminiscences take me
back to you,
to the statue
of Kahramana
in Karrada,
to Abu Nawas Street.

One frond of a palm tree
removes life's impossibilities.

One day, someday,
in the spicy taste
of your summer,
a miraculous
date fruit will ripen
to restore wellbeing,
to create sheer bliss.

Baghdad,
you are a word
not matched by any.
Always return
to glory.
No one has been able to defeat you:
neither Hulagu,
nor the recent
murderer Bush,
the uncivilized.

—Mustafa Hmood

Ode to My Old Neighborhood

Bright mornings,
colorful twilight
and pure moonlight,
shared sadness
and joy with you.
In my childhood,
I watched you blossom
and your delicious fruit,
dates ripening
one day after another.
You were rising
with a white dress,
and an embroidered veil:
simplicity, beauty.
With you, my happiest days.
You were my smile.
Oh, what misery
when you fell like a pale leaf
in bitter autumn.
You taught me melancholy,
isolation.

Your beauty is still alive
in my wounded memory.
With a broken heart,

I had to leave you.
Will you forgive me?
Your children did not love you
as much as I do.
Your eyes, filled with tears.
Your hair,
gray as an October sky.
Your skin, cold.

I heard of your lost beauty,
glass shattered on your surface,
red tears on your emerald skin.

My kindergarten,
my elementary school,
my favorite bakery,
my favorite shop,
you are not
alone.
I am forever
your child.
In my eyes you are Mother Earth.

—Rand Zalzala

Part 4

Jiser Abyad (2009–2012)

Ahmed, Awss, Riyam and Mustafa discuss with Theresa a novel they are reading in Literature Circles. Photo by Holly Snyder Thompson.

14

Between Two Minarets

From summer 2009 until we left Syria on July 31, 2012, our apartment was just a stone's throw from the French Embassy. No doubt more than a few stones proved this between 1920 and 1945, the quarter-century of French occupation, which historians see as little more than a colonial venture disguised as a mandate from the newly established League of Nations.

More stones flew in summer 2011 when this fortress-like embassy and the U.S. embassy, a 10-minute walk further west, were attacked by Syrian protesters loyal to Bashar al-Assad. The ambassadors of France and the United States had visited the city of Hama to support those who were rallying against Assad. The Syrian government was outraged and its supporters expressed this to the embassies. This was barely four months into the struggle that had begun when peaceful protests brought a violent government response. By March 2012, both embassies would close. (It may help throughout this chapter to follow the map of Central Damascus on page 34. You will find the Jiser Abyad area, our apartment 2009–12, the French Embassy, Madrasa al-Maridaniya, and much else that will be discussed in this chapter.)

This neighborhood would be our home for our last three years in Damascus. We now lived on the lowest slope of Mount Qassiun, where a community had settled a thousand years ago on land that had been part of the fertile Ghouta.

Our neighborhood is sometimes called Jiser Abyad, the "white bridge." Did such a bridge once cross the Tora Canal, the oldest (at about 3,000 years old) of the canals that spread the spring melt from the mountains? The Tora Canal still flows west to northeast through this part of Damascus, sometimes above ground but much of it now under the streets.

"Afeef" is another common name for this neighborhood where Afeef Street climbs the lower slope of Mount Qassiun from the Square now called Sahat

Jiser Abyad, passes to the east of the French Embassy, and continues uphill toward Souq al-Jouma'a. Not far from our home was a thirteenth-century mosque sometimes called Madrasa al-Maridaniya and sometimes called the Jiser Abyad Mosque (see the furthest of the two square minarets in the Lortet image on page 19). The construction of the mosque was the project of Akhshu Khatun, a princess who envisioned the mosque as a place of quiet piety. And indeed, the mosque's simple structure creates that space inside and out. The princess was evidently a pious woman herself; she made her way to Mecca to perform the hajj and lived the rest of her days there, supporting herself with money she earned as a water carrier.

This mosque seemed never unattended. Even in unpleasant weather, it was common to see people sitting near the *sabeel* (small fountain with drinking water) or around the corner on the wide sidewalk between the mosque and busy Afeef Street.

A five-minute uphill walk on Afeef Street took us to the souq in Salihiya (see the Souq al-Jouma'a map on page 35). We loved this souq not only for its carrots and beets and garlic and the huge leaves of *silliq* (perhaps some relation to collard greens on one side and Swiss chard on the other), but for its many tombs, madrasas, and mosques. These seem "hidden in plain sight" because the visitor is likely caught up in looking at stalls and shops, at purchases being weighed and paid for, and sometimes in making way for funeral processions bringing the body of someone just-now deceased through the souq and then further up the mountainside to a cemetery. One could do worse than this mix of those selling and buying tonight's supper, the smells of nuts being roasted and garlic being peeled, the colors of grapes or tomatoes or eggplants harvested the previous day in the Ghouta and brought to market this morning, the sound of the call to prayer coming from competing voices, and the music of Damascene Arabic everywhere.

Always when visitors came from the United States and we took them here, we had to tell them now and then to lift their gaze above the olives and oranges and great bundles of garlic because they might miss the stones engraved with Arabic calligraphy, the arched entry to a mosque, the minarets, even the place of Ibn al-Arabi's tomb, where pilgrims still come to honor this teacher who loved this area when the walls of the Old City of Damascus were a forest away. Ibn al-Arabi was a 13th-century mystic and philosopher who was born in Andalusia and died in Damascus in 1240. Three centuries later, the Ottoman sultan would endow the construction of a *tekkiye*, a Sufi monastery *cum* bakery just north of al-Arabi's tomb, so that bread could be given to the pilgrims coming to pray there. They still come to honor al-Arabi and the bakery is still making bread.

Sometimes we would return to our apartment laden with vegetables, cheese, fruit—and realize we also forgot to look up and see why all of this was here on the Friday Souq.

The souq more or less follows the path of the Yazid Canal, the last (680 CE) of the seven canals dug to spread each spring's mountain snow melt from the Barada River over the area known as the Ghouta to the east and southeast of Damascus. The Yazid Canal is roughly parallel to the much longer, much older Tora Canal dug at least 15 centuries earlier by the Arameans. Roman centuries between saw the digging of four other canals. All of these made Damascus a broader, richer summer garden, a sort of paradise like the one the artists imagined in their glass mosaic on the courtyard walls of the Great Mosque.

The Old City was already ancient when this lower slope of the mountain began to be settled. This is where those fleeing from the European crusaders took refuge and where the Sufi community established itself at the time of Nur al-Din and with that ruler's blessing. Nur al-Din (who died in Damascus in 1174 CE) and later Salih al-Din (Saladin) united the Arabs to retake, over the next decades what the crusading Europeans had conquered along the Mediterranean coast. Both of these leaders are revered for their military skills but far more for their sense of justice and of service to their community.

Our Off-Afeef Street Apartment

We lived just off Afeef Street, a major shopping district of central Damascus, and the main approach to the always-busy Muhajireen neighborhood. Traffic—large school buses, small trucks carrying produce, taxis, horse- or donkey-pulled carts, bicycles, motorbikes, cycles (sometimes outfitted for a whole family)—coming down from Muhajireen met traffic coming up from downtown and they often became tangled along the mostly two-lane street.

Considering the range of vehicles and the narrowness of the streets, accidents were unavoidable, but they were handled civilly. More than once we were nearby when one vehicle bumped another. Almost always both drivers stopped where they were (and this only happened with male drivers) and came out of their vehicles. After a quick glance at what damage had or had not been done, they faced each other; it might end in a moment or turn into shouting. But within moments, the two drivers would be surrounded by other men coming off the sidewalks, out of other vehicles or even from their businesses along the street. And always this intervention calmed the situation and soon traffic was moving again. It would be like this even if one or more police officers were watching. No one invited them over and they seldom came on their own. Even when an accident resulted in injury, within minutes the injured were placed in

Construction workers in Damascus. Photo by Bachar Azmeh.

a car and heading for a hospital; no one waited for an ambulance or had insurance considerations in mind.

Our apartment was ISP's home, perfect for the eight to thirteen ISP students we had during each of those three years. Our living room held all the students for Writers' Workshop, but if they were in two or even three small groups, we had a smaller room with a table and a balcony, and the bedroom made a third space to be used for literature circle discussions in small groups. The door from the hall opened to our much-needed "shoe room": As in most homes, shoes were for the streets only. We tried to keep many pairs of slippers or thick stockings for any who wished to wear them. The shoe room was also the coat-piling place for the colder days. Those colder days were the only weakness of this apartment. It had no windows toward the south, and that could make December to February cold and dreary inside.

Still, this was a good place on a good street. Our building had only two apartments on each floor. The apartment below us was rented by a young man who moved back to his native Egypt in late 2011; the owners rented it to a family from Homs whose home, by then, had been destroyed with so many others

The Tikritiye Mosque

Often when we approached the Tikritiye Mosque on our way through the Souq al-Jouma'a, we would hear hammering, scraping, and tapping sounds coming out of the small, dual-domed structure. Peering into the windows didn't help because heavy plastic was covering every window from the inside. After two years of wondering what was happening, we saw the door was open to the domed room on the right. When we asked the workers if we could come inside, they beckoned us and proudly showed us their craft.

The flooring around the tomb had been completely restored with most of the original stones. The adobelike walls were fresh and calligraphy on one side was deeply cut and easy for us to read. But they told us the real treasure was inside the second dome. The workers were all smiling as they led us to a beautiful wooden door. When we stepped in, we stood silent, astonished. The room was completely white and every bit of every wall covered with intricately carved geometric designs, floral patterns, and calligraphy. Below the window was a stand for the Qur'an and the book was open. We all basked in the glory of this centuries-old space.

in that city. The first floor was a men's clothing store opening to the street. This store and most of the others on this little commercial area just off Afeef Street were pure Damascus: one man, owner and operator, faithfully open at least 10 hours a day (10 a.m. to 8 p.m. would be typical). Other commercial renters nearby included a barber, a man who sold flooring, and an electrician. All eventually asked, "What are you doing here and who are these Iraqis that come every day?" These merchants would visit with each other on the street, two or three together, sometimes joined by the tailor across the street.

Walking Every Direction: East and South

Damascus continued to charm and delight, even after we had lived there for many years. We loved to take walks in all directions. Often we'd go down some path that would bring us from the slope to the walk along the Tora Canal, then south on Shahbander Street with a possible stop at a tiny bakery where they made the best date cookies in Damascus. Then we continued south to where the government's central bank rather grimly faces Sahat al-Saba'a Baharat (Square of the Seven Seas), where six busy streets met at a huge circle that was always colorful with changing plantings of flowers to surround its fountains. If we veered to the left, Baghdad Street would take us east toward the Old City, and on the way see some of the second-hand furniture stores.

Many of the pro-regime demonstrations in 2011 and early 2012 were held at the Square of the Seven Seas. Often high school students from a large school nearby would march down our street, chanting slogans as they headed toward the square for a compulsory rally.

In those months, we came to know two men who worked in a small store on the circle and had no choice but to listen to the rallies. As small business owners waited for customers, they typically visited with their neighbor store-owners, drinking tea or coffee and talking. Over time, they voiced their support for change and revulsion against state violence (and noisy pro-regime rallies). This did not mean support for U.S. intervention (after all, Iraq was next door as a grim reminder of the aftermath of U.S. intervention). Their position had as much to do with the growing erosion of socialist ideals in the Ba'ath party's half-century control as it did with understanding what was happening in Dara'a or any feelings against Alawite Syrians.

Walking south on 29th of May Street, we might stop at the Russian Cultural Center for tea in their café or to see the small art exhibits that were sometimes on display. Always we would see Russian and Russian-Syrian families there for a child's music or ballet lesson, for language classes, for a recital or a film in the auditorium. Walking back toward Afeef Street, we could easily pass our favorite juice bar, waiting in line on the sidewalk to order strawberry or mint flavor. The former was simply some large number of strawberries, nothing added, turned into thick juice before your eyes in their powerful blenders. The latter was some combination of mint with lemon juice making a beautiful and delicious green drink. Many of the customers came not only for the juice drinks but for the fruit with cream.

Walking Every Direction: West and South

Our walks often took us past the Opera House (Dar al-Opera) on Sahat Umawyeen, the traffic circle that sends vehicles from central Damascus on their way to all points west and the only traffic circle where drivers seem not to care about pedestrians. The Opera House opened its doors in 2004 to performers from the Arab world and beyond. It is where we heard the masterful performance of our friend, the young Syrian clarinetist and composer Kinan Azmeh. When performing, he showed not only mastery of his instrument but also his respect for music itself and for his listeners. More than once he stood, clarinet in his hands, and did not lift the clarinet to play until there was complete silence in the house. Kinan made us all practice what another Arab musician, Edward Said, once expressed in a conversation with conductor and pianist Daniel Barenboim: "I think there's a difference between just enjoying music, which for most people really means keeping it in the background, and then the opposite, which is to foreground it and make it a central concern by knowledge and passion and commitment to it, which is not only something a performer does but also, I believe, a listener."

The Opera House welcomed in 2010 the Beijing Opera presentation of *Turandot*. The entire set came with the orchestra and singers from China. Their fine performance, in the Italian original, filled the Damascus opera house every night. But probably the performance we most enjoyed was the standing-room-only concert on World Refugee Day in 2010, where we saw and heard the Iraqi guitarist Ilham Al Madfai, a person loved by every Iraqi we knew. And most of them had stories of meeting him. We were there in that full house with the

ISP students and their families: listening, cheering, standing, and dancing as Madfai played. He brought with him a glimpse of an Iraq that was never known to Iraq's occupiers.

East from the Opera House

From Opera House to the old campus of the University of Damascus was about a 20-minute walk. Between us and the campus, in the last year we were there, we watched a huge circular construction project beginning. A billboard showed what this was to be: a hotel in the shape of an immense Damask Rose. But by 2012, everyone wondered if those huge petals would ever hold guests.

Rising above the traffic was Jiser al-Rayyis, Bridge of the President. Traffic on this bridge moved north and south, the latter soon to pass the downtown campus of the University of Damascus. Northbound traffic on the bridge was headed toward the neighborhoods of embassies and more expensive stores. The bridge provided broad walkways for pedestrians also and usually a chance to purchase pastries or flowers from street sellers. Walkways on the bridge were connected to walkways on either side of the highway below by spiraling stairs. Many stalls for sellers of books, of posters, of CDs could be found at the foot of the stairs closest to the university campus.

From early morning until late night, the area below the bridge was an arrival/departure point for dozens of *serveece* (eight to a dozen passengers) routes with passengers waiting to board or transfer or heading to classes or work.

Most of the routes south went to al-Midan or Darayya or Qadam and beyond to towns along the highway south to Jordan; or they headed west to Mezze with its new campus of the university and beyond to towns between Damascus and the Golan Heights or towns near the highway to Beirut; or they went northwest to a dozen towns that climb Mount Qassiun, as the streets follow the Barada River and, in places, the old railroad tracks still used a few times a week. In almost all of these areas, judging by the construction we would see, the populations were growing.

The National Museum Outside and Inside

East of that bridge above us, we were soon in front of the National Museum, a work-in-progress surrounded by a sculpture garden that seemed far larger than the museum itself. This lovely and entirely welcoming area, barely mentioned in the various guide books and open to all without an admission charge, was where we came not to learn about art or history, but to sit or walk among these huge trees, most of them eucalyptus, and the hundreds of stones carved into

Ancient couple in the sculpture garden at the National Museum silently speak of earlier civilizations. Photo by Bachar Azmeh.

lions or birds or markers that speak in a variety of alphabets and languages. "This is a museum," we thought the first time, "so where do we find out where this couple carved in stone lived and when? And what kind of stone is this and how did the work function?" Soon we admitted that often we spend too much time reading the signage in museums and here we just loved looking at the work of human hands and the beauty and variety of stone.

Museum Resources

By 2011, we were told, much of the museum's treasure had been taken to unknown places. Photos from the museum's collection can be found at gettyimages.com, virtualtourist. com, and many other websites. The photos include the wondrous (because it is so random and so shaded by eucalyptus trees towering above) sculpture outside the museum. Online resources can show:

- Khans (like the one on the cover of this book) in the Old City as well as the Old City's souqs and gates; Ummayad Mosque and oher mosques of the Old City; some of the finest examples of the *"beit 'Arabee"* with the courtyard and *liwan*, fountains, and family rooms on two or more levels.
- The Tekkiye area discussed in the following pages of this chapter.
- The twelfth-century mosques, madrasas, and tombs along the Souq al-Jouma'a discussed earlier in this chapter.

The shop just inside the gates had books about the museum contents and maps for tourists in several languages as well as some scholarly studies of the history and archeology and anthropology of this part of the Fertile Crescent. They also carried fiction and poetry by Syrian authors, autobiography (we found *Daughter of Damascus* here), and for a while the usual picture postcards included the unusual images from the frescoes of Deir Mar Musa and the synagogue of Dura Europos.

Inside and outside the L-shaped museum were many treasures. When we first visited the National Museum in 2006, some of the signs identifying objects inside the museum were in French only, others were in Arabic and French—and this was 60 years after the withdrawal of the French. The rooms of Arabic calligraphy—used to write not only Arabic but Farsi and Urdu and Turkish (until the 1920s)—might outshine the collections of Western museums. By late 2011, we were hearing that the Syrian government was moving many of the museum's objects to undisclosed places.

This Crescent was fertile in many ways. Iraqis and Syrians were well aware that if they wished to see some of the most amazing and beautiful objects created in these lands, they would have to visit museums of Germany, Britain, and the United States. In 2014, we visited the Metropolitan Museum's Islamic and Assyrian galleries with an Iraqi student who had finished undergraduate studies in the United States. When Alaa saw the massive relief sculptures made by the Assyrians and associated with Mosul/Nineveh in northwestern Iraq, she immediately said, "These are mine!" and placed both hands on one of them.

How many people coming from these lands must feel as this young woman did! And how few of the Western visitors ever relate the genius and artistry here to the people who live now in Iraq and Syria? We have seen at the Smithsonian's Asia museum in Washington a large map, intended to introduce visitors to the treasures of Ur, which failed to indicate in any way that Ur is in present-day Iraq. What keeps us from honoring the Middle East?

Perhaps the most visited display of the National Museum was the Dura Europos synagogue. Dura Europos was a city in the Syrian desert, very near where the Euphrates River flows from Syria into Iraq. It was settled about 300

BCE as a military outpost but became a city shared by various cultures and religions over five centuries. When the Persians conquered and emptied the city in 257 CE, Dura Europos was left deserted and eventually disappeared into the sands for more than 1,600 years.

When the sand-preserved city was discovered a century ago, no one expected to find what Dura Europos held: a third-century CE place of gathering and prayer for a Jewish community and the earliest known example of the "house church" of a Christian community. Each was a revelation. The house church revealed much about the Christian community that gathered there in a large room that was part of a home. Some of this house church is now at the museum of Yale University.

The synagogue, dismantled and in part rebuilt within the National Museum, revealed walls and ceiling covered in frescoes of biblical figures and stories. Like the frescoes at Deir Mar Musa and the mosaics of the Umayyad Mosque's courtyard, these frescoes of the Dura Europos synagogue are evidence that believers had faith that beauty could surround the community and perhaps survive to bless even us in these hard times.

Tekkiye

In the outdoor park of the National Museum with its stone-become-sculpture and stone-become-memory/memorial, hundreds of individual pieces in no particular order of century or place, we didn't look up so often on our first visits, didn't notice those high eucalyptus trees that rise so far above the stones. But once we did, we realized that we were seeing something unexpected: two minarets unlike any others we had seen in Damascus. It was the Tekkiye.

And it was right there! (See page 209.) When we left the grounds of the National Museum, crossed one quiet street, and found a gate in the west wall, we were where those minarets had been for four centuries before the National Museum was built nearby.

Just 50 years after the Ottomans of Istanbul had added the Arabic-speaking lands south of Turkey to their empire, they commissioned Mimar Sinan, already known as a great architect, to design a mosque in Damascus. Sinan brought to Damascus these slender minarets, unlike any others in a thousand years of Islam in the city. But Sinan also incorporated many of the distinctive marks of Syria's mosques, most wonderfully the alternating of dark basalt and white limestone seen in the arches of the porch.

Tekkiye and its courtyard were one, in the way the cathedrals and plazas are in Latin America. The front of the mosque was wonderful with its arched porch and the two minarets, round and thin, rising high above the dome of the mosque. The courtyard centered on a large reflecting pool and distinctive fountain. The peacefulness here in the still water and the beauty of the stone always invited us to linger.

The grounds of the Tekkiye were a place for pilgrims to stay when passing through Damascus. Like tiny row houses built of stone, the pilgrim dwellings stretch along the walls that enclose the grounds of the mosque and its fountain and walkways. Each cell or room has its own low door, its dome, and chimney. Here the Sufi monastery offered its hospitality to pilgrims. The Middle East had not only the Silk Road of commerce from China to the Mediterranean, but the hajj caravans moving to Mecca and back to their homes. Syria knew not only invaders from all sides, but pilgrims from all sides coming and going back.

Behind us, if we faced the mosque, larger rooms had served once as the kitchens and dining halls for the community and the pilgrims. Now, by 2010, these large rooms hosted occasional exhibits.

Further along, the stone walkway led to a smaller courtyard, this one in front of what had been the madrasa or school, now serving as a mosque while the larger mosque was repaired. The courtyard fountain was usually dry but it hosted doves and cats who never bothered each other. The cells of this smaller courtyard were the workshops and tiny stores of what had become the Handicraft Souq. Visitors to this souq could often take as much time as they wanted to visit with the craftspeople and view the work: weaving, silks, gold and silver jewelry, carpets, leather work, glass blowing, painted glass, embroidered clothing, tiles, brass work, pottery. Work was displayed in the walkways and from the pillars of the courtyard. It was festive, even when quiet. Nowhere else did we ever notice that such a large number of merchants and craftspeople were women.

We loved this courtyard simply for the way no stone tile was quite on the same plane as the ones next to it. Children loved these stone-tile hills and valleys. The call to prayer always brought a steady procession through this courtyard. Many who worked there would leave their shops unattended to enter the mosque for these times of prayer. Shoppers, merchants, and passersby from the neighborhood came too, women and men and children sometimes making the courtyard area even more wonderful as they went around the dry fountain to ascend the stairs to the porch, removed their shoes, took water for their ablutions, and entered the prayer room.

Over the years, we did come to know an artist who had a tiny shop—barely room for two visitors at a time—whose calligraphy was done in silver pendants that were worn as a necklace. "I'll make the silver into any word you want, a silver pendant in Arabic calligraphy," he told us. We purchased three, two for gifts and one for Theresa. Hers was "Iqra'"—Read! Another was Arabic for "Write" and another the Arabic for "Heal."

In the foreground are ancient inscriptions in the sculpture garden of the National Museum. In the far background, the minarets of the Tekkiye Mosque designed by the greatest of the Ottoman architects, Mimar Sinan, in the mid-1500s. The slender, round minarets rise far above the dome of the mosque. In the middle ground we see the smaller domes and chimneys of the cells for pilgrims that surround the courtyard of the mosque.
Photo by Viktor Hegyi.

The Cave of Cain and Abel

Our friend Mustafa, who had become a licensed guide, took us on our first visit to the place we had seen so often from below: a tiny speck on the otherwise unbuilt slope of Mount Qassiun above Damascus. Mustafa led us and his four daughters and his niece to Jabal al-Arba'een. These four daughters, ages 3 to 13 then, had been so delighted to be with Theresa at their home earlier. Now one of them had embroidered a little velvet banner: "I love Theresa" in English and then "Theresa" also in Arabic.

We came by *serveece* from downtown, then by taxi up and up until a spot where drivers and their small pick-up trucks wait for passengers for the next part of the ascent. Passengers rode in the open area behind the driver, sitting on the floor and hanging on until the streets climb no further. Mustafa and his daughters then led the way on a path to the Arba'een (the forty). But being so far above Damascus on a bright morning, we paused often to turn and look and to point and call out what streets and buildings we began to recognize far below.

The trail goes nowhere beyond the monastery, which seemed part-built and part-cave and full of legend. Ancient tales say that the origin of the word "Damascus" is in words for "blood" (an almost voweless *dmm* in Arabic) and some word for "brother," and this spot on the mountain explains that—for here Cain killed Abel. In the Qur'an, their names are Qabil and Habil.

We sat in the room whose floor was covered by many woven rugs, overlapping each other in no particular order. There, an old man told about the 40 holy monks who once lived here. In a time of famine they had only one plate of food (or one jug of water in another version). Who would eat or drink and be the only survivor? One by one, each of them refused, and all died. But why were there monks living there in the first place? A guide/storyteller led us to the cave where Cain killed his brother and told us that this made the mountain itself so angry it quaked and would have killed those first few humans, ending human life before more harm was done. But the angel Gabriel (important in the Qur'an as in the Christian New Testament) held up the roof of the cave. Here our storyteller showed us the handprint in the stone just above. So humanity was saved.

15
Literature Circles

Every Iraqi knows the aphorism: "Books are written in Egypt, printed in Lebanon, read in Iraq." And each year we had a student or two with such enthusiastic memories of a grandparent's library, books floor to ceiling, and loving memories of the grandparent who treasured that library. But such libraries and such a habit of reading seem more a fond memory than a possibility for them—until students form Literature Circles and a universe opens to them.

Students who participated in our program in Damascus focused on academic preparation for success in college, so we needed more than the excellent language textbooks we had, courtesy of Oxford University Press. From the very beginning, we incorporated Literature Circles into our curriculum. We secured several copies of each book on the syllabus, and three or four students read the same book at the same time and met twice a week to discuss the 30–40 pages they had just read. Students served as discussion directors for the groups, keeping everyone on track, encouraging quiet peers to speak out, and inviting more dominating speakers to hold back. Students decided how many pages they would read until their next meeting and held each other accountable. And students also self-selected which of the three books offered that month they wished to read.

They used Post-it notes to mark passages with striking language or phrases that held a special connection for them, or words worth sharing. Together they probed the themes that were raised, the characters and their motivations, the plot, and the possible relation of the narrative to their own lives. These books opened up discussions and differences on essential topics: war, racism, power, ecology, sexuality, faith.

Each month we had three Literature Circles meeting simultaneously, each group reading a different book. One group might read *Flowers for Algernon* by

---

Ten Rules

In a short essay about how he had changed as a writer during the year of study with ISP, a student wrote:

When I first entered ISP House, I was surprised by a little chart that indicated 10 lines of advice to become a better reader. The 10 were:

Read

Read

Read

Read

Read

Read

Read

Read

Read

Read

Daniel Keyes, another might be reading *Lord of the Flies* by William Golding, and a third might be engrossed in *Martian Chronicles* by Ray Bradbury. Each year, the students perfected the methods for student-led Literature Circles and took over every room in our apartment to meet and passionately discuss their books.

"Hold onto that thought. Does anyone else have an idea about why the parents in *An Island Like You* wanted to boycott Rick's memorial service? Was it because he was gay?" Alaa was questioning her peers in her role as discussion director.

Fatima led her group for *Esperanza Rising*: "How did you react to the scene where Esperanza and her mother are being interrogated by that guard at the border?"

Ihab was already making connections when he asked his group, "That neighborhood in Newark in *We Beat the Streets* sounds a lot like Baghdad: violence, poverty, uncertainty. If those guys can make it to Seton Hall we can make it to college too! Is there a character that you really relate to?"

In the spring we would have a week-long interim, a breather to read easy books with complex themes. *The Acorn People* by Ron Jones explored deepening relationships of special needs children at summer camp and how the teenagers who came to camp to be their counselors were changed. This book inspired one of our students to study special education when she went to college. *Sadako and the Thousand Paper Cranes* horrified our students and generated a discussion about the United States dropping the atomic bomb on Hiroshima. They talked together about people in Iraq who were exposed to depleted uranium and had become sick. *Heartbeat*, written as a poem by Sharon Creech, explored the expected birth of a new sibling balanced with the impending death of the grandfather, giving many students the opportunity to talk about losses in their own lives. *House on Mango Street* was a Latina teenager's view of her own community in Chicago. The first time we offered this book as a choice, it was selected only by our female students. The second time around, three young men chose this book and were exposed to a feminist view of life.

In late 2011, two students interested in chemistry and physics asked if we could set up a few Literature Circle books with a more scientific focus. We had discovered *The Disappearing Spoon* over the summer in the book reviews of the *New York Times* and purchased several copies to bring back to Damascus. Author Sam Kean created a clever portrait of the periodic table of elements through "true tales of madness, love, and the history of the world." The most challenging nonfiction was Stephen Hawking's *A Brief History of Time*.

Over time, the Post-its students used to mark favorite passages became treasures and we created the Post-its Hall of Fame, a poster of all kinds of quotes, some memorable, some shocking, some inspirational, some lovely examples of writing. Perhaps the most meaningful passage selected by a student was from *Farewell to Manzanar* by Jeanne Wakatsuki Houston and James D. Houston: "When your mother and your father are having a fight, do you want them to kill each other? Or do you just want them to stop fighting?" The students discussed how this quotation had so many implications about Iraq.

We advised students to always keep a book in their backpacks and to read while they were waiting for an appointment at the UNHCR monthly food distribution center, at the dentist, at the bus stop. One of the best "waiting" stories occurred toward the end of the academic year when Ali was reading at the U.S. embassy as he waited for his visa interview appointment for travel to the United States. He took his book with him to the window when his name was called.

Interviewing officer: Good morning.

Ali: Good morning!

Officer: Do you want to be interviewed in English?

Ali: Of course.

Ode to Books

When I carry you in my hand,
I am carrying a key.
Not a key for a door,
a key for the whole world.
Not a key to enter my home,
a key to enter the world.
A light not just in the night,
a light of the morning.
Water in the desert.
Warmth in the winter.

—Anas

Ode to the Dictionary

Always kept in my backpack,
Wherever I go,
during the hot summer or snow.
It's you, Dictionary!
When I feel lost and a stranger,
You get me back out of danger.
When I go to a new city
with no friends yet,
You always have me as a friend.
In the thirst, water.
In the darkness, light.
For the lost, a map.
For the blind, sight.
When all the world fails me,
You never let me down.

—Awab

Odes to Books

As I read you, I feel happy.
I lose my sense of time.
I find my friends.
Between your pages, I see my future,
I see my history.
I can touch your fascination.
I can tell you my secrets.
I can know your information.

You make me smell the flowers of spring.
You make me feel the heat of summer.
I see the world from the east to the west
between your pages.

—Raed

Books, dear books,
you are my friend,
my teacher, my light,
my way to knowledge.
I wish you the best.
You are my leader
and I will raise the flag
of your child, knowledge,
who conquers the world
with an army of peace,
your words.

—Ahmed

Officer: What's that book you were reading?

Ali: It's *Farewell to Manzanar.*

Officer: I don't think I know that book. What's it about?

Ali: It's about how your country put its Japanese citizens in prison camps during the war with Japan.

Officer: Really?

And then the interview began, with questions about what Ali would be studying and how he would pay for tuition. A minute later he was told, "Ali, welcome to the United States."

Farewell to Manzanar inspired Ziad to create a presentation for his group featuring speeches by survivors of the camp who have created a memorial on the site in Manzanar, California. The students were dismayed to learn that the U.S. government had erased most signs of the camp's existence and they discussed the idea of "erasure of memory" and why the author's spouse had urged her to write this book. One student asked, "This could never happen again, could it?" Residents of Yarmouk who hailed from the ethnically cleansed village of Lubya could assure her that it has in fact happened again.

Another book that particularly affected readers was Jerry Spinelli's *Maniac Magee.* In this young adult classic, there was a street in the middle of the town that divided whites and blacks. The theme of who is the "other" struck them, and students began discussing sectarianism in Baghdad since the U.S. invasion, based on newly created boundaries. They marked passages to share and read them out loud focusing on the ignorance of one group's racist perceptions of the other, including a question posed by a character: "Do they use toothbrushes?"

Literature Circles gave students an opportunity to discuss sensitive issues and draw parallels. When they read Columbia University professor James Shapiro's *1599: A Year in the Life of Shakespeare,* some students remarked how the treatment of Ireland by England in 1599 is similar to Palestine's treatment by Israel today, especially land confiscation. *Lord of the Flies* brought discussion on the disregard for law and the breakdown of society following the U.S. invasion of Iraq.

During Fatima's first semester in college, she sent us an email saying the syllabus for her Gender Issues class included *House on Mango Street*. She told us how her professor was surprised that an Iraqi refugee had read Sandra Cisneros's book. Fatima beamed, "We read it for Lit Circles in Damascus!"

Over time, we had developed a library of close to 900 books. Each year after our summer trip back to the United States, we lugged some books over to Syria, but hardly enough to make this library. What made the library grow? English-readers leaving Damascus (especially our volunteer teachers) often left books with us. Fulbright students who came to study Arabic in Damascus heard about ISP and would stop by with a stack of books. Family members who traveled to visit us carried along books for us. And sometimes when visitors were coming they'd ask if they could bring anything for us. We might respond with something like, "Yes! Five copies of *Martian Chronicles!*"

In addition, there was a neighborhood bookstore within walking distance with an excellent collection of books in English. We could order books there or pick up multiple copies for Literature Circles. Once we took a field trip there and the owner talked to the students about how she selected books and the joy of becoming a lifelong reader. Each student was invited to select a personal favorite to take home.

Halfway through our years in Damascus, we found we had overflowed the roughly 32 to 35 feet of bookcase shelves that a neighborhood carpenter had built for us. So he quickly built us another 18 feet of shelf space. We kept the Literature Circle books out of sight until they were needed. They were behind the front row of books on these deep shelves. We had three to five copies each of more than 20 different titles for our Literature Circles. Except for the Literature Circle books, our teachers and friends and students could take any book home after checking it out in our purple ISP sign-out book. At any given time, perhaps 20 books were out.

As summer 2012 unfolded, we knew the conditions in Syria would prevent us from taking on another new group of ISP students. We asked ourselves, "What should we do with our books?" We decided to share them with Syrian students. There was a new institute called the Advanced Learning and Training Center (ALTC). This institute was created when the U.S. government closed their American Language Center (ALC) early in 2012. Syrian women and former employees and teachers at ALC formed this new teaching center and found Syrian funders. They then rented the same space the ALC had occupied and hired staff and teachers. They registered the ALTC with the Syrian Ministry of Education.

One hot day in July 2012, we hailed a truck heading down our street and asked the driver if he would take us over to the ALTC. Our students loaded the truck with the wooden bookshelves made by our neighborhood carpenter. They packed in boxes containing over 600 books suited to students studying English. Off we went! The poignancy of knowing we would soon be leaving Syria was offset by the joy of creating a library. The experience also provided a sense of closure for our Iraqi students who would soon be off to their colleges in the United States. As of this writing, it is possible to look at the website of the ALTC in Damascus and see what a vibrant language center it has become! And those Literature Circle books are still circling.

16
Holy Ones

No matter where we lived, we were always accompanied by the call to prayer, the powerful chant beckoning Muslims to pray. Often a muezzin would have a particularly beautiful voice and the sound brought us into mindfulness of the Creator. For us as for many local people, the call to prayer simply became part of the rhythm of our day, the fabric of life. A stirring call to prayer was sung from inside the Umayyad Mosque in the Old City.

One night toward the end of Ramadan, we were seated at our kitchen table studying when we heard an almost mystical chanting. We looked up at each other and were struck silent, astounded by the sound. We knew it was not the call to prayer, but we had no idea what we were listening to, only that it was beautiful and ethereal. We later found out from our friend Noor that it had been *laylat al-qadr,* the "Night of Power" when the entire Qur'an is chanted. Muslims believe that on this night, which commemorates the revelation of the Qur'an to the Prophet, sins are forgiven and prayers are granted. For us it was a moving experience simply to listen, but Noor described what a blessing it had been for her to pray at a mosque in Yarmouk camp on that holy night.

Perhaps that call to prayer heard five times a day, like similar public sounds (church bells, for example) in other places and times, is a sort of blessing on all who hear. It led us to think about something we did not hear so much as witness. Some religious traditions around the world have a belief that the world will survive whatever evil we do to each other, as long as some small number of the just, maybe 36, maybe less, remain faithful in their prayer.

The Faithful Few

In Damascus, we observed some of these faithful ones. When we lived in the Jiser Abyad/Salihiya neighborhood, we would often pass an old man who sat on a box and prayed outside the Madrasa al-Maridaniya mosque many hours of the day and almost always during the evenings. Even on the coldest nights of winter, we would be on our way home hurrying up the hill and there he would be wearing a black wool cloak, sitting on a box under a palm tree near the bus stop. His white mustache and white hair shone on full-moon nights, but on darker evenings he seemed to blend into the neighborhood unnoticed. Even in the midst of the time of troubles, he would be on his box near the mosque, a constant, reassuring presence.

Walking home on a quiet street called Ibn al-Moqaddam, we would soon pass a smaller mosque named Dlamiye. The Friday call to prayer at noon often brought more people than the mosque could hold. We would see the faithful on the sidewalk and into the street, mostly men and many fathers with their sons. They were listening to the Friday sermon as well as joining the prayer: standing and bowing and kneeling in the rhythm of that prayer's verses and its silences. But if we were walking home in the evenings, we would see an old woman who sat and prayed outside the mosque's door. She had a simple scarf tied over her hair and usually wore a long cotton coat. She would sometimes stand near the doorway in the light or she would sit on a box with her back against a wall that had intricately carved medallions right above her. It was comforting to see her on our way home, her presence exuding a calmness and sense of peace as we headed up the hill.

The first time we were at Deir Mar Musa (see Chapter 11) and we gathered in the church for night prayer, it was not Father Paolo who presided but a Syrian woman, Sister Huda. When she read the scriptures, her voice echoed in the candlelit chapel beneath arches covered with frescoes of ancient female saints. The chanting of prayers flowed back and forth between Sister Huda and all present. We had known the monastic community was famous for interfaith dialogue but we had no idea it was also a model for shared inclusive leadership. From a letter addressed to friends of Deir Mar Musa in 2014, a year after Father Paolo was kidnapped in northern Syria, we learned that Sister Huda had become superior of the community. Her faithfulness, scholarly work, and courage surely bring the strength and peace needed in such hard times.

Up in the street leading directly into the Souq al-Jouma'a, we always saw a small, elderly blind man sitting in a plastic chair, a string of prayer beads in his hand. The setting was almost ludicrous: cigarette sellers on his left, mounds of watermelons behind him, vegetable booths with bright red radishes, a nearby sidewalk stacked with boxes of corn flakes. The scent of warm peanuts filled the air, the sound of the spinning roaster making a strange music. Children ran by, playing or approaching the peddler with his candy cart of colorful sugared shapes. Yet here was this silent man creating a sacred space, perhaps one of the two or 12 or 36 good persons who keep the world alive.

During the two years we lived in Yarmouk camp, one of our simple, good experiences was seeing Abu Mohammed nearly every day. He was in his 60s or 70s, tall and thin in mended dress-pants and a wool vest, usually wearing his white skullcap. He had a store about as big as a large closet, perhaps 15 meters from the door to our rented rooms with Umm Ali's family. Abu Mohammed sold some milk and eggs, but mostly he sold candy and the ever-popular tiny packages of chips that children always seemed to be eating. He would arrive about 7 a.m., sweep the narrow street, and bring out the candy, the rack of chips, and his chair. While it was still quiet, he also brought out a

> ## Simon Stylites
>
> In 2006, our first visit to the church built for the pilgrims coming from all directions to honor Simon Stylites, we talked with Syrian school children, Muslim and Christian, who were there on class outings to explore the hilltop church and the famous pillar. A hundred yards south was the baptistry building.
>
> In the Aleppo area 1,500 years ago, a few Christians sought their sanctity and caught the eye of the world because they lived day and night on top of pillars. Simeon (or Simon), whose pillar was west of Aleppo, was and is the best known. He stayed 37 years atop a pillar, about half his long life. And still the pilgrims came after Simon died. And continued to come when church authorities in Antioch took Simon's body. The pillar stayed. Finally, we came too and saw the ruins of what had been the largest church built to that time. The icon of the old man, in which Simon and his pillar seem one creature, is familiar in Moscow and Alexandria, Istanbul and Athens, and far beyond. Who really is the center and who is the eccentric? And why?

little table and on it something to support a large Qur'an. When we would take our morning walk we would see him sitting and reading, entirely absorbed in prayer, and so turning this fairly ugly little lane into something with beauty. Also beautiful was his manner with very young children. He was the funny grandfather you love to visit whether you are with your parents or out by yourself. And he was always happy and kind with us.

One day in October during our second year in Yarmouk, we noticed from a distance that something was out of joint. Abu Mohammad seemed a little more bent than usual and when we were closer we could see his face was sad and suddenly older. He told us he had been knocked down by a bicycle. He had gashes on his face below his left eye. His left hand had been cut and his leg bruised. A doctor at the hospital had put in stitches. Worse, some of his teeth had been broken and his bent glasses needed repair. We brought him some ointment for his hand and leg to prevent infection. This man who always cheered others was grieving not for his wounds but for the way it had happened: Kids on bikes, rushing down this lane, had knocked him down and gone right on without stopping. Abu Mohammed's good spirits returned, but only gradually over the next two weeks. We saw him then joking with children as before, praying in the morning in his chair. He was another of those people that seemed to witness for us how the very existence of the earth and of ourselves depends, moment by moment, on some small number of the just.

A Mandean Ordination

The Mandaean people lived for more than two millennia in the area that is now part of southern Iraq. They had contact over centuries with Jews, and then with Christians, and then with Muslims, but they remained faithful to their own traditions. The rites of their religion centered on water. Even under Saddam Hussein, they continued to maintain their traditions and to pursue the trade for which they are well-known: goldsmiths and metalsmiths. The U.S. invasion/occupation ended that. Nearly all of the estimated 35,000 Mandaeans fled from Iraq. About 10,000 of them sought refuge in Damascus.

Our friend Rana, who was our housemate for over a year, knew some of the community. They invited her to what might be called an ordination rite, the transition ritual for someone who has prepared to join the ranks of the leaders and holy men (called "the believers"), and they agreed that we could accompany her. About a hundred people gathered in the morning in a rural area near the road running southeast from Damascus toward the airport. There we stood under fruit trees among fields of green onions, fluffy parsley, and huge cabbages, as the community began a ritual that would last seven days.

Members of the Mandaean community had created a small river of sorts in the irrigated field. Water flowed over clay steps leading down into a pit where two or three adults could stand waist deep in the water. The leaders wore loose, thin white robes made of cotton and strips of white cloth wrapped around their heads. Over and over again, the seven bearded leaders and the new candidate went into the water to wash themselves or pour water over one another, at times even drinking the water. Sometimes in their wet robes and long white beards and twinkling eyes they seemed like every caricature of that holy man on the mountain who is supposed to know the meaning of life. Other times they just seemed like the vested clerics of any religion performing the rituals they had received with more or less insight.

These religious leaders came for this rite from various places where Mandaeans are now living, including the United States. Outside the water, they would chant at the same time from various places in their holy books, books written by their prophets beginning with Adam. The books were written by hand, not printed. The written alphabet and the spoken/chanted language were some variation of what Chaldean Christians and some other Christians here use in their rites: Aramaic. Like Arabic and Hebrew, it is part of the Semitic language family.

They had built a fire of wood and palm fronds, and they sometimes used this fire to dry off after immersion in the tiny river. Near the book table there was a clay vessel for incense that burned throughout the ritual.

Through all of this, the non-leaders in the assembly paid varying degrees of attention. They wore street dress as we did and felt free to visit or wander off for a while. Informal moments alternated with more formal moments. Three grandmothers sitting on chairs seemed to be the matriarchs. The mother of the man being initiated kept close by, periodically adding incense to the clay vessel. One of the most delightful aspects of the day was the way all the women would ululate to show their joy on hearing their scriptures read. We tried but failed to imagine Americans cheering when our holy books are read.

After four or so hours, the leaders moved to a small, open space set up (also outside; nothing happened in any enclosed space) by tying a few pieces of bamboo to define the walls. They sat crowded on the ground inside the structure as the one being ordained read through the scriptures with the old leaders correcting him at times. In all, they stayed outside in that open "room" for eight days. The real ordeal of this ritual for those being ordained is not being allowed to sleep during that time.

We were only a half hour or so from home but it felt like we were in another world. We were amazed to be so welcomed by the group as they celebrated this event. We had the opportunity to use our Arabic and that really surprised people. One man adopted us after the first hour and tried to explain to us some of the Mandeans' beliefs. When it was time for us to leave in the early afternoon, the presence of water, clay, fire, and the incensed air stayed with us.

17

Learning to Be a Refugee (Again)

In January 2015, as we were writing this account, I (Theresa) went to visit friends in Istanbul. We had spent a month in Turkey when we left Syria in summer 2012. At that time, Turkey had already become greatly involved in the Syrian struggle. In the early months of violent clashes in spring and summer 2011, the Turkish government sought to build on what had been increasingly friendly relations with the Assad government. Turkey's offers to broker negotiations between the Syrian government and various opposition groups were rebuffed by Syria. After that, the Turkish government moved quickly in support of the Syrian opposition by allowing arms and opposition fighters to cross Turkey's 500-mile border with Syria; it also allowed Syrians fleeing their homes to enter Turkey as refugees.

Syria's total population in 2010 was estimated at something under 22 million. By winter 2015, half this population had left their homes, often because the home was destroyed or in an area in which it was too dangerous to remain. More than four million Syrians were estimated by the UN High Commissioner on Refugees to be outside Syria, the vast majority of them as registered or unregistered refugees in Lebanon, Jordan, or Turkey, with smaller numbers in Iraq and Egypt, and increasing numbers of asylum seekers in European countries. Another six million were internally displaced. Syria had until recently been home to over a million Iraqi refugees, and now half of its population were refugees themselves. Whether still in Syria, or in Turkey, Lebanon, Jordan, Egypt, or Iraq, half of these Syrian refugees were under age 18.

When we left Damascus in summer 2012, the number of Syrian refugees in Turkey was estimated at 40,000. Turkey has now become a temporary home to about two million Syrians, some of whom will move toward central European countries. Most of the Syrian refugees in Turkey stay near the border with

Syria, especially in the city of Gaziantep; Istanbul, 500 miles to the northwest, is home to a much smaller but growing population of refugees.

Mazen, our teacher in Damascus, is now 53 and has been in Istanbul for several years. He is teaching Arabic at a major university. I visited Istanbul for two weeks in January 2015. I was helping at a project Mazen started there called Ad Dar (home), a space where young Syrians, often there without family, can meet, study, talk, and discover how years of education lost could be begun again. Mazen is a "not by bread alone are we to live" person, but he can also create wonderful food from the humblest ingredients, and he loves to feed guests at his apartment or at Ad Dar.

Mazen and his eight siblings are the children of Palestinian parents who were children themselves when their families fled the Palestinian town of Safad near the border with Lebanon to the north and Syria to the east. Safad was home to 9,500 Palestinians and 2,500 Jews. In late May 1948, Zionist militias drove out all but 100 of the Palestinians. Most became refugees in Lebanon.

The refugees from Safad were among the 700,000 Palestinians who fled their homes in 1948. This was the Nakba, the Catastrophe. Mazen's parents came to Syria by way of Lebanon. Mazen had played a huge role in our lives in Damascus, not only as teacher of Arabic, but as friend and helper in understanding what and how everything from Ramadan playgrounds to Syria's politics worked. I asked if I could interview him and perhaps publish the text. He agreed to this.

Theresa: When Gabe and I sat each day with you for almost two years studying Arabic, you were living on the ground floor of a corner apartment in Yarmouk. Very often, especially if we were sitting in the garden space outside your kitchen and library, you would have visitors, and no one came more often than your father. Tell us about him.

Mazen: My father was born in 1933 or 1934 in Palestine. His family lived in Safad in the north. As a teenager he heard of massacres by the Haganah and about resistance, but the Palestinians had no weapons. When the Palestinians fled from Safad, they planned to go back. On the way out, many were attacked and killed. My aunt told me about this.

In 1948 the family went to Lebanon, to Tripoli in the north, near Nahr al-Bared camp. Family members ended up in many different camps. My father eventually found work as a mechanic in Syria. He slept in mosques and schools. In 1953, Palestinians started to live in Yarmouk Camp south of Damascus. It was like a farm then. In 1957, some of our family moved there. My father's sister and her husband had also lived in mosques or schools before they came to Yarmouk. The UN was involved in buying/renting and distributing land to families. My parents had a plot of land close to Damascus. In 1953 or 1954, UNRWA [UN Relief and Works Agency] was forced to provide services.

In 1953, we didn't try to build walls; it was more like tents, twenty people in one place. The first houses were very simple with corrugated roofs. Until the end of the 1960s, the buildings were one story. People named streets for villages and towns in Palestine and often people from that place went to that street or area in Yarmouk to live. The people who came from Lubya named their street Lubya Street. Many of the names were for towns that entirely disappeared. My parents lived near Safad Street. In 1975, they built the family's present house, where I was living and teaching Arabic when we first met in 2006. People built schools and clinics. There was more economic growth and Yarmouk became like a city.

Theresa: Do you want to add anything about your father?

Mazen: I love him.

Theresa: We never met your mother because she had died before we came to Syria. But you would often talk about your mother and how she had earned the respect of the entire Palestinian community in Yarmouk. Did Umm Mazen know your father already in Palestine?

Mazen: She was born in Safad in 1935. Her family had come from Haifa. Her father was a butcher and traveled around to sell meat. In 1948, she was 13. The family went first to Lebanon, then she came alone to Damascus in 1948. She found a friend of her father and that family raised her. They taught her to be a tailor and she used that family's ID card to go to work in an army clothing factory as a tailor with a fake name that she kept the rest of her life. This new name wasn't Arabic: Houjah. Later, when I came to Turkey and was teaching Arabic, the Turkish students called me *houjah*. The first time that happened, I looked up surprised. They were calling me by my mother's name! In Turkish, her name means "teacher."

My mother is like a character in a book. My father wasn't home a lot because he worked in Kuwait and sent money to us. She was strong and she forced us to study. She worked hard as a tailor and raised nine children by herself. She was a very social woman, a woman everyone trusted. People came to her with questions. She invited my friends to come and play music. She had a very good memory and looked after details. She knew what was going on with all nine of her children. She made sure they had hand-me-downs. Her own family came later and she helped them.

She had cancer and knew it. My mother sent me to a woman to say, "My mother wants to see you before she dies." She planned which women would wash her body when she died and who would buy the shroud. So many people came when she died, even from Lebanon and Jordan. Such a number of people walking behind the body!

She influenced her neighborhood. She would tell children, "This is not your country. If you don't educate yourself, you will not survive. What protects you is your degree, your education. They can take away your house, but not your education." All of my brothers and sisters were educated; we had no choice.

I was studying to be a mechanical engineer. But I missed my fifth year of college because I was in jail. My mother left me money to finish college, and after jail I went to theater school.

Theresa: How did your parents relate to being part of a Palestinian community in exile? Did they eventually feel at home in Syria?

Mazen: They never felt at home. My mother tried hard to make my father buy a house and land, but always he said, "No, we're going back." And he kept a bag with his Palestinian stuff packed in it. When we were young we asked him, "Why do you have this bag?" "Because—one day—we'll go back to Safad."

Theresa: What are the names of your brothers and sisters?

Mazen: Shehinaz is oldest and has three children. Her name is Persian. She lived in Yarmouk but now is living up the mountain in Qudsayah. Mohammed is next, then Jamal; he lives near Damascus with his wife's family. The fourth is Haseebee, who no longer lives in Damascus. I'm the middle child of the nine. No one noticed me. People listened to Mohammed or Jamal, but not me. That's why I'm special.

Then the twins, Safa' and Sana'. Safa' is married to a nurse; he was working at Damascus hospital, and one day he took care of an injured person who was a fighter. Soldiers came and demanded records, accused him of hiding papers; he was arrested, tortured, humiliated. He and Safa' and their children are now in Toronto.

Sana' is in Zahara, and our sister Wafa' lives with her. The youngest, Muwaffaq, lives in New Zealand; he named a son after me. Muwaffaq was a senior in high school when I was in prison and he didn't do well, so he was restricted in what he could study in college. My mother would tease me, "If it wasn't for you, your brother would be a doctor now!"

When the troubles began, Muwaffaq told my father, "You should come to New Zealand and live with us." But my father said, "This is my home. I will not leave it as I did in Palestine." When the bombing started in Yarmouk camp, my oldest brother, Mohammed, said he would stay with my father, but all of us told my father he had to leave Yarmouk. Now Muwaffaq has the papers for my father and he will come to take my father to New Zealand soon. Everyone has a story.

On the day the bombing of Yarmouk began, Safa' was at home with the twins (they were three years old). She called the others who were still in Yarmouk to say that there was shooting and bombing, "Come get us!"

Now most of the camp has been bombed and destroyed. My entire family went to a "safe" area and lived together for two or three months. But a massacre occurred in that area. People had no water, no food. They were under siege.

Theresa: When we were still in Damascus, we visited you after the fighting had begun in 2011. We had heard that some Palestinians in Yarmouk had been killed on Nakba Day when the tradition had been for many Palestinians in Syria to go to the area Israel had taken from Syria in 1967, the Jaulan (Golan Heights). People would go as far as the strip controlled by the UN peacekeepers and protest from the Syrian side.

Mazen: That year the Assad regime tried to show the world that it had been protecting Israel for years because in previous years it had not allowed people go to Jaulan without permission from the Syrian government. When the revolution started, the regime wanted to show international society that Israel would be in trouble if the regime fell. If opposition groups took over Syria, Israel would not be safe. So pro-regime Palestinian militias encouraged people to go to the Jaulan that year on Nakba day, and people went. Israel didn't expect that anyone would have the courage to cross the border. But people did. And there were no land mines, so they just walked right in. They were in Palestine!

But then some were shot. Some were arrested. They dreamed their whole life to go back there. A few days after the funeral and burial in Yarmouk, people asked about going again and some went. The Israelis were waiting. When people returned to Yarmouk this time, they were angry with the pro-Assad Palestinian militia. They felt used. After the funeral and speeches, the people went on to demonstrate at Yarmouk headquarters of the pro-regime Palestinian group. Fifteen demonstrators were killed. People said: Yesterday, Israelis shot at us. Today, Palestinians and the Syrian regime shoot at us.

Palestinians don't want to be involved with the Syrian regime because it tried to use us. Maybe 10,000 are in Yarmouk now. Yarmouk is destroyed. What the regime did was a service to Israel, to destroy the largest concentration of Palestinians. Seventy percent of the Palestinians in Syria have left for Indonesia, Libya, Lebanon, Iraq, Turkey, Algeria. Some headed for Europe in death ships. Yarmouk is still under siege. The regime doesn't want people to come back. Some died; others left.

Theresa: How was Yarmouk regarded by Damascenes through the decades?

Mazen: In general, they didn't like Yarmouk. We were the immigrants, the poor, the needy. Only those in business and in direct contact with Palestinians liked us. When I was a kid, I was sick and thin, so my mom put me in a government school, not a UNRWA school for Palestinian children. Then my school moved out of Yarmouk. That made me feel different because I was going to a school far away that had only four students from Yarmouk (out of a total student body of 1,000 students). So I was lucky and I was different because generally Yarmouk kids never left the camp. Always there were some Syrians who sympathized with us but on the whole, it felt like they were doing it because they were religious and felt they should. Many people, even much later, would act like, "Oh no, don't go to Yarmouk!" Since the beginning of the troubles, the regime encouraged that attitude: Don't go to Yarmouk.

Theresa: Were Palestinians ever required to serve in the Syrian military?

Mazen: Yes, if they were born in Syria or were registered in Syria. My father's family was registered in Lebanon, but he registered in Syria. All people registered must serve two and half years at first, later changed to two years. I didn't do it because I was in prison. We were told "political prisoners don't have the honor to serve"—or obtain passports or civil rights.

Theresa: Can we talk about your time in prison and your reading there?

Mazen: I was arrested in 1985. Then my brother Jamal was arrested. Then Safa'. They shot Jamal, then interrogated him, then took him to the hospital. My mother was amazing. She tried to find us and defend us. She was able to figure out where we were, and she dressed as a cleaning woman, got into the hospital, and went in to visit Jamal. She spoke with him. It seems Jamal had figured out a way to let her know where he was—and she came.

My mother was very attached to her children. If one of us was late, she'd go and wait for the bus to come. Jamal was an activist. She worried about him and thought he'd be in trouble with the police. But she never expected Safa' and I would get into trouble. She didn't know where they had taken us so she visited the *mukhabarat*, the secret police, and sometimes stood for twelve hours at a time to find out where we were. They accused us of being in an opposition party.

When I was in prison, I jumped from the window and broke my back and was taken to the hospital. Then they put me back in jail but with a group of Syrian prisoners. We learned through oral stories. One person would read a story to the others. One helped us memorize poetry. We shared the literature we read and taught each other. I met all types of people—fundamentalists, rapists, robbers, Jehovah Witnesses who taught us about Christianity and the Bible, Muslim guys who taught us the Qur'an. All of the guys were educated. Some had PhD degrees and had studied in Germany. Some had been ambassadors!

Finally we went to our comrades who had a library. They were a leftist group, treated better than we were, and they had books. Some of the books were smuggled in; some we paid the guards to bring. We learned so much. I stayed with them for one year. Later they moved us to Sednaya with prisoners brought from Tadmur. So we made reading groups. We took turns. We would each read five pages and then pass books on. But evenings we each had our own book. It was a great system. I learned good Arabic there. I learned my English. Very concentrated knowledge. It was a good opportunity for me.

Theresa: Did you ever think of leaving Syria for good after that?

Mazen: Leave Syria? I didn't think about it. I did apply for a Fulbright to study and to do research. We were thinking it, but not one comrade left Syria. Jamal went to France for a bit but he married a Syrian. We didn't even have ID cards or passports.

Theresa: When Gabe and I lived in Yarmouk, many could afford to live in central Damascus or Mezze. Why do they stay in Yarmouk?

Mazen: Yarmouk is full of life. The people live in small apartments so the streets mean a lot to them. If it's hot, they can go out and sit in the streets, meet their friends. They know each other and they talk. Outsiders started to come in, businesses started to grow. Outsiders (Syrians) came because it was cheap and it was safe. I loved the feeling of Yarmouk. It felt like a safe place. You know the people, you have a good relationship with them despite all the problems. I always had a lot of students in Yarmouk. I had my own place to use in my way. Some foreigners came to live in Yarmouk because I was their teacher.

Theresa: What's the story of that little park that was just outside your door?

Mazen: In the camp there is no park. There were a few big "forbidden to go in" areas just outside Yarmouk. So people started to think about making parks. They made a few like the one near the family's house. Once it became public, the government controlled it. Then there was street planning and city planning and the people had no control over it. The municipality (Ba'ath Party) had control. So we had a big campaign and wrote petitions. Years later, religious people wanted to build a mosque on that space. Others said no, we have enough mosques. So there was tension, but then nothing happened; the municipality did nothing. So our neighbor, Abu Ramzi, planted and cared for the little park until he died. Then I started to look after it. When I was in jail, my family brought me flowers from the park. Often the guards took them, destroyed them. When I was released, we dug a well. We wanted to keep the municipality from giving it away by having things there. I added three ping-pong tables for kids. I kept the keys for the park. One day the police were playing ping-pong for half an hour. Then they started to steal the tables. I went to the municipality. We had to pay 3,000 lira for each table to get it back. We only got two of them back; the officer took the third one home for his kids.

Theresa: When we lived in Yarmouk, we loved the streets because of the surprises we found there—a funeral or a "hajj house" or an engagement celebration.

Mazen: In the streets, it's a big market, a big theater. You can find a family saying, "Our son did well in baccalaureate." They go in the street and dance the *debkeh* to celebrate it; you can't do that in a small apartment. If there's a circumcision, there's a party in the street. There were small shops, the goods always out on the street: candy, ice cream, sweets, pickles, fruits, nuts. They took up part of the road and sometimes made it hard to walk. It was a kind of "occupation" of the streets by the people. Girls and boys went to the streets to meet each other. Bad things happened in the streets, too.

Theresa: Mazen, what are your thoughts about Gabe and myself as your students in 2006 and 2007?

Mazen: One day this woman came to my house and asked me all these weird questions in front of all my friends! At that time, I was trying to find my own meaning. Most of my students are there six months or less. I lived my life with no stability. You gave my life meaning. We would eat together. It was your way that you deal with the people. Your relationship with the plants in my house. Your stories about your life. And Gabriel, his stories about history and the Unites States. I was teaching you Arabic, but you were teaching me. Gabriel taught me. You were very regular. I watched you develop your student project in my house. Sometimes I was anxious and eager to see you. I looked forward to your coming. You brought me pistachios and pine nuts, the best gift, better than meat. And after your project started, I always continued to have visits with you. The way you walked the streets, you and Gabriel. Everyone knew you, knew you were coming to my place. You asked me to talk with the family that owned the house where you rented your apartment, or with the *mazote* guy.... That time Gabriel was sick, I walked in the room and I had an image of Trotsky laying there sick, wearing his glasses.

Theresa: What did you tell us once about the sound of Arabic in Damascus?

Mazen: It's Sham! It's an easy accent. It's like music. It's different. You hear it on the TV shows and in the music here. Linguistically, Damascus is the richest region—Aleppo, too. Lots of big families, they improve the sound.

Theresa: You had us read some of the stanzas of the poem "The Damascene Collar of the Dove" by the Palestinian poet Mahmoud Darwish. We came to love the poem and its sound in Arabic and the way every one of the 22 stanzas begins "*Fi Dimashq.*" Do you have a favorite stanza of that poem?

Mazen: I like all of it. It is a treasure. You love that city more and more. You love it, but now you can't talk about it. I remember how I played a recording of Darwish reading his poem on my laptop with pictures of the city.

Theresa: Later, when we took some students to an exhibit of Arabic calligraphy at an embassy, we found another fine poem about Damascus by Nizar Qabbani.[1] At the next gathering of the students, we had the six lines in Arabic and we learned about translation and how hard it can be. This was an amazing lesson in language and poetry for all of us. We keep the best translation, coming from the work of the whole class, on our wall now in New York:

> Never can I write of Damascus
> without my fingers becoming
> a trellis for her jasmine.
> Nor can my mouth speak that name
> without savoring the juices of her apricot,
> pomegranate, mulberry and quince.

Mazen: Damascus isn't simply the city here, it is the Ghouta, the rich farm land that is east and south of Damascus, watered by the Barada and its canals. From it comes the juice, the apricot; every house had these trees in their courtyard.

Theresa: What would you tell us about the Syrian scholar Sadik al-'Azm?

Mazen: He was my teacher! In the drama school at the university, they chose him to teach us Western philosophy and the history of thought. I love his character. He was an old man at that time. I hope I grow up to be like him. I liked how he dressed. He wasn't directly involved in politics, yet he studied to understand religion and how it works in society, our relationship with religion and how it affects our political point of view: the Arab mentality, the patriarchal system related to Islam, how we make our authorities like God. So the president? You can't talk about him.

If I wasn't old, I would go to the field, to Syria, all that's going on, to see their dreams, to achieve something with them. We need different tools. We can fight with education. If I was there, I want to have a conversation over a bowl, a dish of *mujaddara*. I don't want to talk to NGOs. Bring us back to the table. We used to eat together. This is why we love Mahmoud Darwish. You hear it as a poem and we see it as our reality right now.

---

1. Samples of Qabbani's handwritten poetry, including the one below from which the title of this book is taken, are available at http://nizarq.com/ar/hand_writen.html.

Theresa: Mazen, can we use your name when we write about you and share this conversation?

Mazen: Yes. I do not think I will have a chance to go back to that part of the world.

Theresa: Here in Istanbul you began Ad Dar, "Home." Why?

Mazen: You have met Hattem, the theater teacher at Ad Dar. He is from Deir al-Zohr. His family's home was bombed and his brother was killed. He was injured and still has shrapnel in his neck. We want to protect these young Syrians by education. It would be too easy for them to become angry and pick up a weapon. Better to give education—thus Ad Dar.

I started Ad Dar to help students. It's for young people who lost years without school. We put on plays. I learned a lot from how you worked with Iraqi refugees. But I never learned how to be organized. We take Syrians and Palestinians who were refugees in Syria. We protect ourselves as a small group—young people so vulnerable, most of them have never lived away from their family before now. Now they have come alone here to be safe in Turkey, but they are on their own and face all the dangers like drugs and alcohol. It is so important to give them a sense of home and a safe place.

When Palestinians came to Syria in 1948 and after, Syrians welcomed them. Suddenly Syrians are refugees too. We are living in a circle, still in conflict. I stopped being sure about anything. I moved from Syria to Lebanon but I was not comfortable there. I moved to France and received asylum, but I felt too far away. I came then to Turkey. Friends here, former students of mine in Damascus, knew of jobs I could apply for in teaching and translating, and they helped me obtain a work permit. So many refugees here, Syrians and Iraqis and many others in Turkey.

I've been a refugee all my life. But watching these young people now, I still need to learn how to be a refugee.

18
And Ask a Blessing on the Town

When 2011 began, nonviolent protests in Tunisia were spreading across North Africa. Young people began the occupation of Cairo's Tahrir Square, and weeks later President Husni Mubarak resigned. The momentum had already spread to other Arab nations. In Syria, the reforms expected when Bashar al-Assad replaced his father 11 years earlier had offered Syrians more access to the internet while further enriching those close to power. Promises of ending a "state of emergency" police state remained just that—promises—but broader access to communication meant Syrians knew what was happening in Tunis and Cairo. The "force more powerful" of nonviolence seemed now in the hands of savvy young people in countries where half the population was under 21.

The Square

A young Egyptian who had been a volunteer teacher and conversation partner with ISP in Damascus went home to Cairo to be part of that day-and-night presence in Tahrir Square. In Damascus, the mother of an ISP student saw him interviewed on the television news: "I just saw your conversation partner demonstrating in the Square!" Iraqis in Damascus were hearing that, with the United States due to end its occupation of Iraq the next December, protesters in Baghdad were openly denouncing the corruption of the U.S.-sponsored Iraqi government. Our teacher who had gone to Cairo returned to Damascus in February and came to Writers' Workshop to tell of his experiences in Cairo. He had seen "power to the people" and was very enthused.

Soon after that, in March 2011 in Dara'a, which we knew only as the first Syrian town after the bus from Amman crossed into Syria, "Arab Spring" came to Syria. It began with the abuse of police power against middle school boys.

In Cairo, the Egyptian-American filmmaker Jehane Noujaim, who had come to Writers' Workshop in 2010, was in Cairo at this time beginning what would become *The Square*, a documentary nominated for an Oscar in 2013. Soon after this Arab Spring began, Jehane was doing interviews with several young participants from very different backgrounds. She stayed with the same individuals through Mubarak's departure, during the months of the military government before a constitution and election of Morsi, and she was still doing these interviews until the summer of 2013. Her conversations with these same young people were continuing until the military under General Sisi imprisoned Morsi and brought new violence against those who opposed the return of military rule. It must have been hard to take the film that far and even harder to leave it there.

This brought Syrians to the streets. Everyone knew at that point that massive nonviolent protest had brought down decades-long dictatorships in Tunisia and in Egypt.

In an April 2011 letter, we wrote of what seemed our reasonable fears:

> We know the dead are mourned widely here in Syria even by those whose only wish is a return to the secure feelings of a few months ago. We do know that U.S. threats of sanctions against Syria—and some sanctions already exist—are resented by nearly everyone here. At the end of the liturgy on Holy Saturday evening, the Patriarch, Gregory III, was giving Easter bread to people one by one. We and some of our Springtime in Syria guests from the U.S. were the last in line. He asked where we came from and with great kindness and sternness urged us to tell President Obama to stay out of Syrian matters.

We were then only a few weeks into the nonviolent protests and the violence of the Syrian regime's response. The Patriarch recognized how little people in the United States knew about the Eastern churches. He feared, as would later happen, that some in the United States would urge U.S. intervention to protect Christians. He and other bishops in Iraq and Syria, throughout their struggles, stressed that these churches have lived in peace with Muslims and Jews through the centuries. And he had seen what the U.S. interventions in Iraq since 1990 had done.

Those guests who were with us at the Easter Vigil were eight in number, the sixth and final Springtime in Syria visitors from the United States (see Chapter 8). They came for the days before and after Easter in late April 2011. Roads were being closed, outdoor activities banned except for pro-regime demonstrations, and the warnings about traveling to Syria on the State Department website, always grave, had a hysterical edge. But there we all were and, if nothing else, that was taken by most Syrians the visitors met as an act of solidarity with them.

From Patriarch Gregory's Easter Letter, 2011.

We should like the League of Arab States and the Organization of the Islamic Conference to be able really to deal with this state of revolution in the Arab world by developing together a new program for a new Arab Middle East: a really new program, that we, not others, will set out, containing the conditions for a worthy life for all Arab citizens, Christian and Muslim, in this Middle East, cradle of religions, cultures, and civilizations.

The unity of the Arab world is an important condition for coping with the serious development of these popular revolutions, or intifada.

If Arab countries do not manage to resolve together, univocally, these tragic, bloody developments, with wisdom, prudence, sense of responsibility, openness, and a really clear plan that is transparent and sincere, the future of the Arab world looks very dark for all of us. No Arab country can be outside the evolution of this revolution.

Today more than ever, and not tomorrow, we need a sense of awakening, counsel, and a joint Arab social plan. Today, more than ever, we need a vision of an Arab Muslim-Christian future with immense horizons. Otherwise, our Arab world, with its various denominations of Muslim and Christian citizens, is liable to dislocation and division. This Arab world will crumble into isolated confessional statelets, fighting and hating one another....

We shall pray in our churches, monasteries, parishes, homes and in the intimacy of our families for our dear, suffering Arab world and for the whole world, for more fellowship, love, and unity. We shall pray for the army, the security services, and the police that God may give them wisdom, prudence and sagacity to take suitable steps in these tragic situations.

We shall pray especially for our governments, kings, presidents, and all those who bear responsibility in our countries. We shall also pray that they respond to the demands, requests, hopes, sufferings, longings and needs of all their citizens; that they endeavor to establish a social and political program, and so contribute to ensuring a worthy life for all citizens of their countries.

Nonviolent protest in solidarity with the people of Dara'a came to Damascus, especially after prayers on Friday afternoon. Government violence, so immediate and deadly when the nonviolent protests began in Dara'a, spread to other towns in Syria. This use of deadly force against unarmed protestors seemed unreal and counterproductive even to Syrians long opposed to the regime. Many who had been content to accept Syria's modest progress now seemed to be telling even visitors like ourselves that it was time for the Ba'ath party and the Assads and their circle to move out. But few wanted outsiders to come and move them out. Syrians would do it.

Many had hope that spring when President al-Assad announced that he would address the Syrian parliament. There were press reports that some in the government were predicting that the president was planning to offer important concessions. Would he apologize and resign or at least show sorrow for the actions of the Syrian police and military? Would he abolish the emergency law that for nearly five decades had made the rule of law impossible? Would he order an immediate end to government violence against and imprisonment of nonviolent protestors? Would he release political prisoners and show some indication that he and those close to him understood what grievances had led Syrians to such deep opposition?

We felt ourselves and in others not only disappointment but shock that al-Assad said no such things. People said he seemed to enjoy his appeal to patriotism and to damning those ever-useful agitators from outside. This day seemed to us an end to any hope for real change in response to the continuing nonviolent protests. The disappointment was immense. Syrians had been patient over the years. The protests begun in March were not violent and the government surely knew many wanted to see that nonviolence bring a nonviolent response. But both the words and manner of the president left no room for hope. He betrayed their long patience.

As the violence moved toward major cities like Homs and Hama that summer, a few Syrian friends continued to tell us it would all be over before this or that holiday, and in 2012 the tourists would return, but the images of whole blocks of apartment buildings in cities to the north—so similar to images of south Lebanon after Israel's bombardment of that territory in 2006—followed by the arrival in Damascus of refugees not from Iraq or Beirut or Palestine, but from Syria itself this time, was heart-wrenching to watch.

Brutal violence against nonviolent demonstrators and against people leaving the mosques after Friday prayer in some areas continued. By early summer 2011 an armed resistance was beginning, coming primarily from those in the Syrian armed forces who deserted after the early government violence. Some would soon form the Free Syrian Army (FSA) and find in Turkey, near the long border with Syria, safety and more.

Nonviolent protests, coordinated by the Leadership Coordinating Committee, continued even as the Free Syrian Army was beginning a violent opposition to defeat the regime. The regime offered some steps to make allies: Some Kurds, who had not been allowed citizenship in Syria, now were offered citizenship. Some government officials, who were known to use their positions for profit and were widely hated for this, were dismissed. That spring, the hated 1962 emergency law, a suspension of citizens' rights to due process, was abolished. This had been a demand of the Syrian opposition for decades, but now it made little difference to the conduct of the regime.

When the schools were in session that spring, on into June, one or two mornings each week, students released from nearby middle and high schools came streaming down the street below our apartment, then turned toward Jiser Abyad and so joined thousands of others in yet another pro-government demonstration, usually at the square in front of the Central Bank. From the street below our windows, it sounded not so organized, more like teens on their way to a pep rally.

That August 2011, the fourth group of ISP students were off to study at U.S. universities. In the months before, many of our volunteer teachers received calls from Mom and Dad in the United States or UK or elsewhere: Come home now! But the spring events of TOEFL scores, ups and downs from colleges considering admission and tuition waivers, visa applications and travel arrangements were fairly normal. The Damascus airport was still open for the international flights.

We took our usual summer journey to New York City, returning after eight weeks to begin another year with Iraqi students. While we were in the United States, some who were helping ISP by serving on its board opposed our returning to Damascus to do yet another year. What carried the day was the advice by a board member who, as a conscientious objector, had taught school in a Vietnamese village while the war went on and on in the 1960s. He said, "Listen to your Syrian friends. They'll tell you if you should leave."

So in August we were back in Damascus. By then, Syria was receiving few visitors, but eight Iraqi refugees in their late teens were ready to begin a year of preparation for undergraduate study in the United States come summer 2012.

From Our April 27, 2011, Letter to Friends

A few days ago the *Washington Post* had this to say in an editorial:

> The administration has sat on its hands despite the fact that the Assad regime is one of the most implacable U.S. adversaries in the Middle East. It is Iran's closest ally; it supplies Iranian weapons to Hezbollah in Lebanon and Hamas in the Gaza Strip for use against Israel. Since 2003 it has helped thousands of jihadists from across the Arab world travel to Iraq to attack American soldiers. It sought to build a secret nuclear reactor with the help of North Korea and destabilized the pro-Western government of neighboring Lebanon by sponsoring a series of assassinations.

So "The administration has sat on its hands." What do they want? Another Afghanistan? Another Iraq? Another Libya? "From the halls of Montezuma"? The one thing the United States has not done enough of, in our opinion, is sitting on its hands.

In what ways is "the Assad regime...one of the most implacable U.S. adversaries in the Middle East"? The *Post* raises those same two specters of Hamas and Hezbollah. Can we never look in the mirror? Can we never recognize that life is moving on in Gaza (despite murderous attacks from Israel) and the West Bank, moving on in Lebanon in ways that might even break down the U.S.–supported sectarian government? Then they chide Syria for helping "thousands of jihadists from across the Arab world travel to Iraq to attack American soldiers." Do they pause to ask what were those American soldiers doing in Iraq? Do they ask why the United States can put its deadly forces and weapons anywhere we like, but other countries (no matter how poor or how long the border) must find ways to keep "jihadists" away from us?

This has been a year for us of reading about American exceptionalism, about perpetual war as a U.S. doctrine, about the abandonment of constitutional division of powers. Thanks to the *Post*, we can understand what these authors are talking about. Not to mention: We know of no proof for this statement about "thousands of jihadists." Is it one of those U.S. government/media truths that, repeated often enough, is universally accepted? Of course they fail to mention the Syrian civilians murdered when U.S. troops have crossed the border with Iraq. Again, little by little we all accept that no other life is worth what an American life is worth.

Israel kindly bombed that "nuclear reactor," by what authority no one knows. Ever since Colin Powell made such a fool of himself and George Bush by arguing at the UN for the administration's case for Iraq having nuclear weapons, we (United States/Israel) seem to avoid the UN.

We have lived here six years. We know a bit of what's wrong with Syria. We know what's wrong with the way the United States has handled this. If we have anything to say, it is: Be careful! You are shown only a distorted part of a whole. If you are really interested, go for the whole. These last days have been filled with alarmed-to-frantic parents in the United States and UK reacting not so much to the news from Syria as to the warnings from Foggy Bottom, that well-named area of Washington where the State Department lives. Why do they want all UK and U.S. citizens out of here? Happily we have never registered with the U.S. Embassy here so we don't receive their alarmist warnings to leave. But we know many of these young people who came here to study would gladly have stayed if Mom and Dad had kept calm. We don't hear of other countries in panic and believe it or not, there are lots of foreigners living here even if we do not count those who have been received as refugees.

So many asked what we are thinking. That's it.

Doing ISP in a Different Damascus 2011–12

For us, it was not an ordinary year. The usual volunteer teachers, many of them from the United States and UK in Syria to study Arabic, were not coming back; nor were new students, whose first language was English, arriving in Damascus as in past years. For the first time, we recruited an instructor whose first language was not English. Bjorn, a Norwegian, had married an Iraqi woman and they were staying put in Damascus. He was an effective teacher and a good friend to us.

We had begun to add math to the ISP curriculum after the first two groups told us they wished we had made them more familiar with English terminology and the skill level expected of first-year college students. For this 2011–12 year, we didn't expect to find a math teacher but one of our students, Taleen, had an uncle in Aleppo. His name was Dikran and he was trained in engineering. He accepted our invitation and came to live for a few months in Damascus, an excellent teacher for our students who seemed surprised to find math could be this interesting.

> ### Injustice Anywhere
> Iraqi students respond to *Eyes on the Prize*.
>
> Watching *Eyes on the Prize* opened my own eyes to the reality of how cruel and aggressive people can be. I had never known that all these events occurred in the United States. As a young Iraqi Arab, I drew a picture in my mind of America as a perfect country where everyone was equal and had the same rights. I was shocked to realize that the picture I had in mind was wrong and that America did not have equality as I thought.
>
> —Riyam
>
> Even if I were free, I should not stop demanding freedom for others, because freedom does not apply to certain people only. I remember during *Eyes on the Prize* one white college student, working with young children in the South, said, "If another person is not free, I'm not free. I'm fighting for my own freedom."
>
> —Awss

The institutions where we found resources and places for the ISP students to use libraries and to study over the years were closing one by one that fall and winter: British Council, Cervantes Institute, American Language Center. The U.S. Embassy and Consulate, where our students in past years applied for visas each summer, closed. Other cultural centers and embassies were closing also.

That fall, our students who lived further from central Damascus began to experience long travel times because checkpoints along *serveece* routes could create unpredictable delays. We encouraged our students to find small apartments to share closer to our apartment where all the classes took place. Throughout the year, we noticed the sadness of these Iraqis as they saw the Syrian people and government, who had offered a safe haven to so many Iraqis and other refugees before, now experiencing their own loss and suffering.

Theresa continued teaching Writers' Workshop and Literature Circles weekly all through that academic year. ISP students had fewer weekly sessions in the basic studies: academic writing, lecture listening, critical reading. Instead

Standing Up to Authority

Watching Diane Nash standing up to authority opened my eyes. It made me contemplate: Why in Iraq do we not have such people? I found a huge problem in the Iraqi society: People do not see the injustice they incur on a daily basis as unjust. Their justice standards have been trodden down. Post-war Iraqis are accustomed to military arrests, checkpoints, concrete walls separating one district from another, and being abused by politicians among hundreds of other injustices. Iraqis have grown accustomed to being submissive to an oppressive authority that separates itself from the public with thirteen-foot concrete anti-blast walls around the place called the Green Zone, whereas the rest of Iraqis live in the "red" zone.

—Hasan

We heard, "Oppression does not destroy people; the acceptance of it destroys them." Iraqis have not taken any action for their hope of a better future. Looking at the ideology of nonviolence as implemented by the civil rights movement, I see impressive results that can be achieved one day in Iraq. We need to inform people of nonviolence, so they will consider its power. Who knows the negative consequences of violence more than us, Iraqis? The time has come to realize that violence is a malignant disease.

—Mustafa

we built more on areas we had tried before but had never found enough time to explore, such as poetry seminars and history classes. These were focused studies where they might be challenged to think critically, to express their thoughts in written expression and in participation in discussion.

Film Study

Film and Discussion became a weekly event. Some films were one-time: *Il Postino* to introduce Neruda's poetry and the form of the ode, *Dr. Strangelove* (more than 50 years old then) to laugh and find out why it was funny. Other films were seen over a series of Wednesdays. *A Force More Powerful* had several separate episodes, each a story of how nonviolence triumphs in the twentieth century: in India, Poland, Chile, South Africa, United States.

That series became a context for watching and discussing ten of the fourteen one-hour episodes of PBS's *Eyes on the Prize* covering the civil rights movement from 1955 (the murder of Emmett Till) to the electoral and educational struggles of the '70s. We spent much time on this because we had learned in previous years that even watching and discussing a few of the episodes could be a profound introduction to a United States little known to them. The students, born in Iraq in the 1990s, knew little of the way slavery and Jim Crow laws, segregation, separate and unequal citizenship, and white privilege had shaped the United States despite its self-image of "liberty and justice for all." These documentaries gave some breadth to this as we saw, discussed, and wrote about what this meant, about the country where they would soon be attending university. And what had changed in all this struggle from the '50s until the present? History, literature, songs, religion (Who is this Malcolm X?). It was for us our own story being told, and together we had to figure out with the Iraqi students how some of the same elements had been experienced in their own lives. Written reflections on these films revealed the students' ability to understand better the struggles they have known and expect to know.

If somehow we were to gather again with those students, how would they relate what we studied of those earlier, nonviolent struggles for equality to what they have seen themselves of Americans? How have they seen issues of prejudice and racism, color and privilege, the new Jim Crow—real but obscured for white people because an African American was elected president? What do the police shootings of unarmed young black men mean to them? And what does it mean that Islam is blamed, hated, and ridiculed here? What would they tell us about the meaning of President Obama being accused of being a Muslim as if that were criminal?

Know History

That winter we had a dozen copies of the fine book by Jonathan Lyons, *House of Wisdom: How the Arabs Transformed Western Civilization*. Together with the students, we read and discussed this book over six weeks. The students had learned in high school what had taken place in the centuries following the spread of Islam. From the cities of southern Spain (Andalusia) to Persia and beyond, Arabs spread the teachings of the Qur'an even as they learned from the other "peoples of the book"—Jews and Christians and others. Arabic was the new common tongue, and Arabic showed itself able to handle the translating from ancient Greek and Latin, Persian and Hindi, then able to support the new scholarship in such areas as philosophy, the sciences, a host of art forms, medicine, mathematics, astronomy, map- and calendar-making.

The impetus for this age of scholarship came from the Muslim caliphs first in Damascus but then in Baghdad where *Beit al-Hikma*, the

---

The House of Wisdom

Dear Ali,

I read a book about how Arabs transformed the Western civilization, and I wanted to share one of its ideas that relates to the last discussion we had about the Arabian golden age and the current deterioration in the Arab civilization. *The House of Wisdom* by Jonathan Lyons was published in 2009. It brought my attention to important facts that I was not aware of before. My focus will be on the spread of knowledge from Arabs (Muslims mostly, but Christians and Jews and Zoroastrians also) to the West through pioneer scholars like Adelard of Bath who came from England, learned Arabic and traveled and studied in the Middle East in the 12th century.

Europeans were living in the age of darkness until that time. They remained too far away from civilization until they were exposed to Arab science and technology, especially in the cultural bridge of Andalusia in Spain. Europeans were not able to measure the hours of day or even keep the calendar. New devices from the Arabs, like the astrolabe, they exploited rather than fully understood. The West was "more invested in the how than in the why," wrote Lyons.

I feel sorry for the situation we are in now. We had a glorious civilization in the past. Now we use Western technology without even knowing how things were made. We must look forward to gain more knowledge in order to create a new glory some day. I end my letter with a quote from Adelard of Bath: "When I had thoroughly read one lesson, I desired the next with a greater passion, as if the one I had read would bring no benefit if what remained was lacking, hoping from this regime that I could keep in check my youth and console my old age."

Faithfully,
Mustafa

A Sonnet for the House of Wisdom

This House was built by Caliph al-Mansur.
Its walls and shelves and books: a place of pride.
A building? No, a planet full of cure
For minds, this house where wisdom once survived.

Alive that lovely Arab neighborhood
With concepts, colors, minds, ideas, aims.
To probe all nature, question all they could,
Thus yielding books of knowledge, hopeful claims.

Two truly distant cultures met at last
When West awoke within its cozy bed,
Translated precious books, our learning vast:
Soon grew this West and bit the hand that fed.

The House of Wisdom represents our pride!
This is a sonnet from an Arab's side.

—Rand, Hasan, Awss

House of Wisdom, became a sort of endowed center for the furthering of all these studies. The sense conveyed by Lyons is one of great excitement: absorbing learning from ancient times (Mesopotamian, Greek, Roman, Persian, African in all its variety), incorporating the new work of scholars, and—something we've lost to a great extent—grasping the relationships among all these fields of study.

In Andalusia (the south of what is now Spain) and in the Middle East, Muslims, Jews, and Christians were all part of this Arabic-speaking world. In Spain the three faiths were especially close as Arabic, Hebrew, and Latin met and mingled and eventually created the Spanish language. By the eleventh century, the rest of Europe was becoming aware that something had long been happening in the Arab world. Young European scholars traveled to Cordoba or to Antioch/Antakia or to Damascus to learn Arabic, to study with teachers—Muslims, Jews, Christians— that body of knowledge that embraced together what later was so often divided. They began to lift the long "dark ages" of Europe. The book tells this story. And it left us all with an eagerness to know more.

Another history study was an effort to go beyond easy answers and know the story of Palestine/Israel. We used two books that tell the Palestine/Israel story within the larger context of recent Middle East history: *The Unmaking of the Middle East: A History of Western Disorder in Arab Lands* by Jeremy Salt and *A History of the Modern Middle East* by William Cleveland (now in a fifth edition, updated by Martin Bunton after Cleveland's death). We also read from David Fromkin's book *A Peace to End All Peace* (Henry Holt, 1989). This tells the World War I story of Britain and France betraying their allies in the Middle East so they might redraw the map and install their own authorities once the Ottoman Empire was gone. Why they did this is basic to understanding the British commitment to a "Jewish homeland."

Perhaps the most crucial book we used was that of the Israeli historian Ilan Pappé, *The Ethnic Cleansing of Palestine*. Pappé tells nearly day-by-day the destruction of hundreds of Arab villages by the well-organized forces under Ben-Gurion's command. The "transfer" of the Palestinian population we would call today the war crime of ethnic cleansing. But the book is far more than this account based on archival documents. Pappé chronicles the emergence of strategies, some of which continue until today in the occupation of the West Bank. From the very beginning the Zionist leadership has known what they want and has known they are militarily capable of achieving it—a land cleansed of its indigenous people. But that leadership knows also the world must be told and believe a very different story.

We explored contemporary issues: one-state/two-state proposals, the right of return, settlements, nonviolent resistance in occupied Palestine (at the time of the hunger strike in Israel's prisons), the influence of Israeli lobbies on Americans as explored in the documentary film *Peace, Propaganda and the Promised Land*. And we used in this study the work of two Palestinian poets, Mahmoud Darwish and Taha Muhammad Ali.

In the final discussion we watched the documentary called *Forget Baghdad*, in which we meet several men in their early old age who grew up in Baghdad. The Jewish community in Iraq constituted an important minority, especially in Baghdad. That community had begun

> ### Andalusia, Ornament of the World
>
> "Ornament of the world" was how a 10th century Saxon writer and nun, Hroswitha, described Andalusia. How did she know anything of Cordoba or Seville? She was recounting what had been told her by a Christian bishop from Andalusia who came to far off Saxony as ambassador of the Muslim caliph. He was "a Latin- and Arabic-speaking Christian who came from a place where they not only knew the long-forgotten Greeks but where the bishop was an esteemed member of the caliph's diplomatic corps." (*Ornament*, page 34) His name was Racemundo to Latins, Rabi Ibn Zayd to the Arabic speakers. He had served already as the Al-Andalus ambassador to Constantinople when he met Hroswitha in the 960s. What Hroswitha learned about Andalusia she passed on to others when she wrote of this "ornament of the world" whose libraries and schools and architecture could barely be imagined in the rest of Europe, that is, in Christian Europe.
>
> The story of Andalusia is told by Maria Rosa Menocal in *The Ornament of the World: How Muslims, Jews and Christians Created a Culture of Tolerance in Medieval Spain*.

when Babylon conquered Jerusalem and took many captives back to Babylon. When Cyrus of Persia defeated the Babylonians several generations later, he allowed those who wished to return to Jerusalem. But not all chose to do so. In Iraq they were, as we heard often from older Iraqi friends, a vital part of the community. But in the early 1950s, the Israeli government, needing to increase the number of Jews in Israel, used various means that remain unclear to bring the Iraqi Jews to Israel. The filmmaker in the 1990s sought out a few of them and interviewed them about their lives in Iraq and in Israel. The Iraqi students, Muslims and Christians, knew this story from parents and grandparents. Now they heard it from people the age of their grandparents who still spoke Arabic with the filmmaker. The film had a strong impact on the Iraqi students.

He Talks Exactly Like My Uncle!

Here are lines from the written response two Iraqi students made after watching the documentary *Forget Baghdad*.

Only hearing those words of Iraqi places and foods was enough to burst out my tears. Every single character and story reminded me of this beautiful life my grandfather's stories carved in my brain. People were united. People loved each other. Iraqis were brothers and sisters.

—Rand

"There is one street in Baghdad, I think it's the most beautiful street in the world: Abu Nawas," said one of these Iraqi Jews, almost in tears. But I was in tears. This man! Had I seen him in a Baghdad neighborhood, I would not have distinguished him from any other Iraqi. How can I? His ancestors have been living there, by the Tigris, for two thousand years. He and his family have the memories, the lives, the language, the culture. They have it. Just like my father. In fact, he looks exactly like my uncle. He talks exactly like my uncle.

—Hasan

"Peace to You, O Damascus"

When Theresa left Damascus to welcome her first grandchild in California in November 2011, I (Gabe) would sometimes take long walks in the early dark during those days. Often I walked across the bridge that passes over the highway and the Barada, then becomes a street again before it passes Damascus University. Find the latter on the Central Damascus map (see page 34); the bridge comes as one moves north past the National Museum. I could see so much of Damascus, could see where the city gave up trying to climb Qassiun's slope, where it sprawls out to east toward the Old City and south toward Yarmouk, and to the west it enters Sahat Umawyeen's traffic circle or dips under it to head up the mountain beside the descending Barada. Most always the city stays low, letting its minarets be visible. Somehow it kept the intimacy of the narrow Old City lanes, not really knowing what to do with wide boulevards or airports. It made room for embassies just north and west of the bridge, but most were now locked and empty. Usually when I walk alone, I keep walking, but sometimes on those evenings I would just stand on that high bridge and think how Theresa and I had come to love this place and its ways and its people.

Decades before, I had heard a recording of Dylan Thomas reading his radio play "Under Milk Wood," and in it came those nursery rhyme–like lines that begin "And every evening at sun-down." Those lines came to mind on one of these nights as I walked on that bridge with city all around me. And after that, on other nights, they were what I wanted to say in other places on these walks. It seemed right in those evenings, in spite of and yet because our tourist visas still defined us as outsiders even after seven years:

And every evening at sun-down,
I ask a blessing on the town.
For whether we last the night or no
I'm sure is always touch-and-go.

244

That's how I felt looking at this city during these uncertain nights. This is home to several million people who at all their ages are suddenly more conscious about "whether we last the night or no...." Perhaps they are not so much thinking, "Will I see the morning?" but thinking that something has been coming apart and some Syrians are killing other Syrians day-by-day and this should not be.

By then, daily living had an even more precarious feel to it, and we knew we would be leaving when these Iraqi students of 2011–12 went off to universities in the summer. Tensions and prices rose, hours of no electricity rotated daily around the city, new checkpoints came and went, as did frequent pro-regime rallies and the disappearances of the canisters of cooking gas. People had access to various viewpoints and various tellings of the latest clashes, but each one would take what she/he chose. Perhaps contrary to what many Americans thought of Syria and the media, we could buy the *International Herald Tribune* at

> ## O Damascus!
>
> When the editor of this book, Ida Audeh, came to this point, she told us of a poem by Ahmad Shawqi (referred to by Arabs as the "prince of poetry"). In it, Shawqi speaks directly to Damascus after the revolt against French rule in Syria that began in 1925. Damascus was bombarded, thousands of Syrians died, and much of the center city was left in rubble when the French took control again in 1927.
>
> Ida then worked on and sent us the translation we use here. This is how Ahmed Shawqi's poem "Damascus" begins:
>
> Peace to you, O Damascus,
> more tender than the breeze of Barada,
> and uncontrollable tears.
> Forgive my rhyme and my pen,
> the enormity of your burden defies
> description....
>
> The hearts of colonizers, even at their
> most tender,
> are unrelenting stone....

many newsstands, and those who watch TV had access to news and opinions from anywhere. Syrian authorities, like the United States that Marcuse wrote about 50 years ago, seemed to have realized that most citizens will choose and be satisfied with easier priorities than liberty and justice for all.

In late 2002, just three months before the U.S. invasion of Iraq, we visited a university classroom in Baghdad where the students were reading and discussing *Waiting for Godot* as they did their own waiting for "shock and awe." What did Samuel Beckett's play mean to them as the United States was massing its bombers and missiles in neighboring client nations? Damascenes were waiting as the vague emergency came closer. The summer before I had read another "waiting" title, *Waiting for the Barbarians* by South African novelist J.M. Coetzee. Coetzee, in this short novel, tells a story set in no given place or time, except it happens in some frontier town where official fear of a vague and mighty enemy is forever encouraged by the distant authorities.

So it seemed in Damascus that winter and spring 2012. Waiting, but for what or for whom? Are all the photos taken with cameras the truth? Is there a government? Is there a resistance? Whose intelligence services and various other agencies are doing what to weaken or to save Syria? And for what reason?

The contradictions are so big we can't always see them. Here is Saudi Arabia and its smaller Gulf neighbors being holier-than-thou about protecting the innocent people of Syria from a government that fails to respect their human rights. Well, shame on Syria! And Turkey? At the same time they are attacking Kurds inside Iraq, they are sheltering Syrian dissidents who accuse the Syrian regime of similar human rights violations.

The Dylan Thomas "touch-and-go" prayer leads to several more verses. What brought Dylan Thomas, the master of the long and sonorous line, to write something so simple and on the edge, but only the edge, of boring?

> O let us see another day!
> Bless us all this night, I pray,
> And to the sun we all will bow
> And say, good-bye—but just for now!

Another poet, W.S. Merwin, might be speaking to such uncertainty in "A Message to Po Chu-I." Merwin's poem also plays with fantasy. The poet of our time is writing to a Chinese poet who lived 1,300 years ago. Po Chu-I was exiled in a time of war and, in his exile, lived among starving soldiers and civilians. Once the poet bought a goose that was about to be killed and eaten by soldiers. He kept the goose alive. What madness made the exiled poet do this? Without punctuation, the poem-letter from our century to Po Chu-I flows like thought. It crosses in and out of large and small matters and ends thus:

> I have been wanting to let you know
> the goose is well he is here with me
> you would recognize the old migrant
> he has been with me for a long time
> and is in no hurry to leave here
> the wars are bigger now than ever
> greed has reached numbers that you would not
> believe and I will not tell you what
> is done to geese before they kill them
> now we are melting the very poles
> of the earth but I have never known
> where he would go after he leaves me

Perhaps read these lines aloud and see how you pass from news of the goose to the matter-of-fact telling of that which concerns the contemporary poet as it did his long-ago and far-away predecessor who bought and saved the goose: "the wars are bigger now than ever" and "greed has reached numbers that you would not believe" and "we are melting the very poles of the earth" and so back to the goose.

Merwin was interviewed by Grace Cavalieri the year this poem was published and just after Merwin was inaugurated at the Library of Congress as Poet Laureate. After Merwin had read the poem, Cavalieri asked:

> When you say, "I have him here with me now," he is here with me now, it's enough to break the heart. Afghanistan, Iraq, Mozambique, Palestine; hear this poem. This is a global poem, isn't it? A prayer, and hope, still somewhere- hope?

> Merwin: It has to be. It's us.

> Cavalieri: It has to be. And as you said last night [in his acceptance speech], it's our imagination that is bigger than greed and conflict.

> Merwin: Yes.[1]

Spring 2012

A full year after the violence in Dara'a, we heard that Kofi Annan was in Damascus, appointed by the UN to mediate peace in Syria. He would resign in August, saying that the governments supporting al-Assad and those supporting the opposition were hindering any negotiation while Syrians suffered. That was very clear by then. It was not a civil war but the battle of others. Kofi Annan's successor as UN representative to bring the Syrian violence to an end was the Algerian diplomat Lakhdar Brahimi. But the proliferation of militias had begun.

U.S. officials, including Secretary of State Hillary Clinton, insisted that the United States supported the efforts of these mediators. But that support was no support at all as long as it was qualified, as it was by Secretary of State Clinton and President Obama. The United States would continue to insist that al-Assad must leave office before we would be party to negotiations. It took the new ISIS caliphate in 2014 to alter this U.S. stance. But it was clear in summer 2012 that wealthy Arab regimes, Saudi and Qatar especially, would send arms and money, the Turkish government would allow the arms and fighters to pass across their border into Syria, and they would offer areas for training to some who wished to enter the battle against the Syrian regime. As for the United States, it gave weapons and training to "approved" fighters like the Free Syrian Army.

---

1. For the whole poem, see: http://bit.ly/1XqKpFs.

Planting Seeds with the Guards at the Empty Embassy

When the French Embassy closed, the long arm-like barrier that had blocked the street to cars remained up, pointing to the cloudless sky, and the little guard shack not much bigger than a phone booth, remained open. Two or three Syrian men in ordinary work clothes stayed "on duty" as week after week passed, drinking tea that they brewed outside the guard booth on top of a blue tank of cooking gas.

Soon after, the guards began planting flowers in two dirt-filled cement barriers. Later they added thin bamboo poles and tied strings to form a trellis. We passed by almost daily on our way to the copy shop and exchanged greetings. They asked us if we were leaving too, indicating the deserted building they were guarding, not one car in the lot, not one French diplomat to be found. We assured them we would be staying as long as we had our students. Meantime, the guards kept adding to their garden: a few colorful primroses and some rosemary and thyme.

The trellis gave me (Theresa) a great idea, so the next time I was going past the vacant embassy I carried a bag of seeds: marigold seeds I had gathered our first year in the Old City, morning glories from our rooftop garden in Yarmouk, basil from our kitchen windowsill in Sahat Arnous, and sunflowers from our balcony in Jiser Abyad. I gave the seeds to the guards and told how high the morning glories would grow and how the beautiful purples and blues would look climbing the trellis in the months to come.

The guards accepted my seeds cheerfully and they invited me to come inside the little guard booth and join them for lunch. There we sat, three Syrian men and this foreign woman, sharing bread and hummus and stories about planting gardens. There was something magical about that moment, yet a sort of Waiting-for-Godot absurdity, planting seeds in the midst of the troubles that were hurting Syrians.

In March, a car bomb damaged one of the government's intelligence offices located in a residential neighborhood. Friends of ours lived nearby in a basement apartment, parents and four adult children. The explosion broke windows and twisted door frames so that doors wouldn't close or lock. Damascus was then being shaken by one or two of these major explosions each month. Outside Damascus, even if one doesn't believe all from any side of this conflict, the suffering was great as the government used heavy shells against civilian areas where "the rebels" might be hiding or finding support.

Perhaps it was our own sadness that made us aware what a sadness now settled over everyday life in this ancient city of Damascus, even though Damascus had yet to see such violence as was happening in Homs, Hama, and beginning in the northern areas near Syria's border with Turkey. Sadness, grief even, was a constant hum beneath daily life in Damascus. This seems not so much born of fear, but of loss: the images from cell phone/cameras, lives lost, and the deaths being counted day by day on the computers of distant observers.

But also faith was being lost, some conviction that people in Syria, often despite their government, can create and progress in true civility. By spring it was clear that the regime—whose one accomplishment had been a sort of stability since 1970—was not able to offer even that. That stability was worth something, but now it was vanishing, and little else could win loyalty. The government wasn't hearing that so-called "Arab street." They were, perhaps, waiting for something even more out of touch with the Syrian reality than they were. It would come.

The River, The Roof, The Palm Tree

Three years before all this, in spring 2009 as the second ISP group was applying for visas, we collected some of the best writing from these students and added writing from the 2008 class that we had kept when they went off to universities in the United States.

With these we made a book of the best writing from Writers' Workshop. The book's title named three things that seemed to make Iraq, in spite of dictators and invasions, a home these students loved. And, we realized, they loved Iraq in a way so different from the old "love it or leave it" of the United States in the Vietnam era. They had left, they were refugees in Damascus, but they wrote of the Dijla (Tigris) and of their families sleeping on the roof in the hot summers, and of the many kinds and many gifts of palm trees to Iraqis. So the book of their writings was named *The River, The Roof, The Palm Tree*.

The Foreword began, "These writings are offered so that you, the reader, may discover an Iraq you probably did not know and a love of Iraq you might never have imagined." Each student that year and the following years carried copies for their support groups and for the people who had overseen the admission process.

Something Is Already Being Reconstructed

Lissa Fecht, who volunteered as a teacher in 2008-09 with ISP in Damascus, designed the book containing the work of ISP students each year except 2011, when Anas Anees, a student with ISP in Damascus that year, was the artist. In summer 2012, she wrote part of the introduction which is quoted here:

These students have watched and felt the weight of destruction in their young lives. This is what they write about: loss, devastation. And yet, they write also about hope and renewal. They have found an ability to reconstruct their lives by pursuing not only education but a thoughtful conversion of their pain. Even if it is only in the simple act of telling their pain as a written story.

I've illustrated vignettes of deconstruction and reconstructing palm trees, and their inner structure. Perhaps through the written work of these students, something is already being reconstructed—a seed inside each of them that has the potential to grow larger and fuller than the great palm trees that they knew and loved in Iraq. And so, the vignettes both deconstruct and reconstruct throughout the book.

In spring 2010, we did a second edition, adding the best work of the next group now ready for university, and in June 2011 we added yet more pages from the third year of ISP's students. That summer we also left behind books created on copy machines. We found a wonderful third-generation printer who had real presses, real signatures for eight or 32 pages to be bound and covered. When we went to the United States that summer, we carried 120 copies of this 96-page hardbound book, beautifully printed. This edition of the book also added art work by one of the ISP students, Anas Anees, adding his drawings to those done the first years by Lissa Fecht, who designed the book.

In 2012, we knew this last edition had to travel with us to the United States. Instead of expanding the previous book, the 2012 writing became a book of its own, 32 pages and a soft cover. When we went to the printer that June, the sixteen months of protest and government violence were felt in the silent presses. The owner, like so many other business owners in Damascus, was trying to keep and pay all his workers despite the economy. They had been there for decades.

On July 2, we went with the students to the printing house to watch the pages being put on press, a process our students found fascinating. The company was founded in 1920 (the year the French marched in from Lebanon and the British-appointed king fled to become king of Iraq instead). One of the present workers had been employed there for 40 years and had seen the transitions of printing through that time. Here and there in this large basement were relics long replaced, a history of typesetting and printing. The employees seemed to enjoy having curious students visit. And when we all returned on July 4 to see the folding and binding done, the students helped in the work.

Some of the poems and prose written through the five years of ISP students have been in the sidebars of this book.

Summer 2012: Our Final Letter from Damascus

July 30, 2012

Greetings from Damascus to our friends and families!

We are on the final night of our seventh year in Damascus, but on the previous six departure eves we knew when we would return. This time we know only that we will return. Tomorrow we'll take a taxi from Damascus to the Lebanon border and on to Beirut.

Seven ISP students are in Baghdad. This weekend, three of them will leave Baghdad and one will leave Damascus, all heading to Chicago via Cairo. The final four will leave Baghdad on August 7. In previous years, the students have all had flights from Damascus to begin their university studies in the United States. But with no U.S. consulate in Syria now, the visa application and the long wait for the visa had to take place outside Syria.

The population of our building and of some other apartment buildings on this block seems to have doubled these weeks, if not in numbers then in volume and excitement. Families came from areas in the city where fighting was taking place. Lots of children. During these Ramadan days, despite the heat and the great length of the summer days, people are fasting from food and drink until the *iftar* meal after sunset. The sounds and smells of cooking start late in the afternoon and the hour before *iftar* is marked by lengthy and beautiful chanting from neighborhood mosques. The nights are loud, the mornings sleepy.

The Egyptian businessman in the apartment directly under ours moved out and a family from Homs moved in. When we went to greet them, the mother

Even the Palm Trees Seem Different

Check points, barriers, mourning flags were some of the sights I saw when I returned for the first time in five years to my homeland, Baghdad. I saw the cradle of my innocent dreams and childhood treasures, my beloved city, wounded with car bombs and bullet holes. My recent visit happened when I needed to change my passport and I found that the Iraqi Embassy in Syria is not issuing passports. The only solution was going back to Iraq and this was a difficult choice to make because I had to go alone.

With my friends' encouragement and my family's worried prayers, I started my fifteen-hour bus journey back to Mesopotamia. As I entered the Iraqi borders, an odd feeling that I had forgotten, a sense of belonging, came over me and I suddenly ran out of patience. I could not wait to arrive at my grandmother's house and see the stage on which my childhood's play had been acted.

I had been told by my friends in Iraq that Baghdad was not yet the safest or the most prosperous city as I might hope to see after five years, but no warning could have prepared me for what I saw. Everywhere I saw lines of high, cement barriers. Baghdad's wide streets that I used to brag about to my Syrian friends are now often reduced by checkpoints to a narrow margin that fits only one car, creating awful traffic jams. I saw the Tigris and I felt my heart skipping a beat. It flowed lower than before but was nevertheless as great and dignified as always. I started coughing and felt sick. The air was so polluted and not a green plant was in sight except for the few remaining palm trees. And dreadfully, even the palm trees seemed different.

Iraqis always take pride in their tremendous amount of resilience. This enabled us to live through several exhausting wars, hard sanctions and continuous loss of loved ones. However, the 2003 invasion seems to have drained every ounce of strength people had left. I witnessed a new feature shared by all who had stayed in Baghdad. They were numb, even the young. I watched children leaving their elementary schools after a nearby explosion. They seemed indifferent, only glad to have classes end early. All of this made me wonder if Iraqis will ever recover. Their hearts felt to me as icebergs. Like a frail candle, I could not melt them. I realized just how severe war trauma can be, especially for the budding generation. How else could people live absolute horrors and maintain their sanity?

My life-long goal is making a difference in the world, but I have not yet discovered how.

From *The River, The Roof, The Palm Tree*, 2012 edition,
by ISP student Taleen Dilanyan

introduced us to her four children. She had been a travel agent in Homs. She held up her cell phone and showed us a photo of the apartment in Homs as it is now, completely destroyed. They had with them just a few possessions.

Soon her sister moved in, bringing her children, escaping the city of Hama where their home was destroyed. And the third sister and her young children moved in from Midan, an area of Damascus that was experiencing intermittent conflict and violence. By our count, sixteen people were now living in an apartment the size of ours. The mothers were fasting as they kept Ramadan. This mostly quiet building now has wonderful noise! The children took over the hallways and stairs as play areas, singing schoolyard chants, bouncing balls, weaving "cat's cradle" with string on their hands. On the sidewalk by the building's entrance, girls play jump rope. They created an atmosphere of playfulness in the midst of all the loss and fear of worse.

We were surprised at sundown one night when there was a knock at our door and two little girls from that apartment below were standing there offering us plates of food their mothers had prepared for *iftar*, the meal to break the fast at sunset. We were so humbled by their Ramadan generosity

Hot afternoons were quiet during Ramadan, time spent resting at home. The girls downstairs sometimes sat on their balcony below ours, talking quietly. I (Theresa) prepared a basket, tied it to a rope and filled it with craft items, lowering it down slowly. This was very successful! Other days the basket was lowered filled with beads and string to make necklaces, or sketch pads and watercolors, or materials for collages that the ISP students had not used.

When we knew we were leaving Damascus, we brought our kitchen goods, housewares, and plants downstairs. Amid tears from all of us, one of the women murmured, "Don't forget us, don't forget us." She reached into her pocket and took out her cell phone. There was a green plastic bauble dangling on it. She yanked it off and gave it to me.

"I want to give you something. This is all I have."

Three days ago, with chaos inside our apartment as we were trying to pack and clean and distribute the goods accumulated in seven years here, there came a knock on the door. You have to know we live on the third floor of this building with two apartments on each floor. We open the door, and here is one of the young men who work at a tiny grocery store three doors away. He is holding a turtle—not a tiny turtle but a maybe four-inch diameter turtle. "Did you lose a turtle from your balcony?" We had not, but we thought, life and kindness go on.

We took our last walk this evening just before sunset. The streets grow completely deserted of traffic with only the occasional car or *serveece* hurrying people home to break the fast. Peaceful, but some evenings we hear both the chanting of prayers and the booms of some kind of artillery.

So we were out walking as the hour for *iftar* came on. We met one of the many people we had hoped to seek out to say goodbye. This tall young man manages a copy shop next to the now-abandoned French embassy and we had taken ISP materials to him several times a week for copying. We explained to him there on the street that we leave tomorrow and we thanked him for his good service and smiling presence. Every one of these goodbyes is part apology because both sides feel just a bit that to leave is to abandon. We told our friend we will go but we will return, God willing. He continued up the street, we down the street. Five minutes later, someone shouted behind us and we turned. He's hurrying after us, having purchased for us a bottle of the *tamer hindi* ("Indian Dates"), a delicious drink mainly for Ramadan and the daily breaking of the fast. We have had so many kind people like this in our lives here.

Over the years, we have come to love the call to prayer and the beautiful chanting that seems only in Ramadan. But we have never heard a woman chanting. On Tuesday at the public bath, I (Theresa) was just finishing dressing when Umm Mustafa, who works at the front desk, began disputing what Lina, the matriarch of the hammam, was saying about something in the Qur'an. Umm Mustafa insisted she was right and immediately pulled out a Qur'an from behind the coffee stand, directly found the page where her answer would be, and began chanting. I was mesmerized! The dome of the hammam and the stone floors accommodated her voice profoundly. After seven years, I witnessed my wish: to hear a woman chanting these beautiful sounds. What a final blessing as I prepare to leave this beloved city!

So this is the same Syria that you are reading about and watching day by day. Now Syria and its people have become a site where far more powerful and far wealthier nations are having it out. Iran vs. Saudi. United States vs. Russia. Israel looks on, hoping another neighboring country will be broken in pieces (and so no more complaining that the Golan Heights should be returned to Syria after 45 years of illegal occupation). Syrians and their everyday lives, their long history, their contributions to culture and science, their daily kindness and hospitality, their needs—such things mean nothing to the big players. The nonviolence that brought down the Shah and his police state in 1979 (only to see another oppression take over), the nonviolence that brought down Egypt's Mubarak—such nonviolence was hijacked early on as the Syrian regime's shameful turn to violence played into the hands of those who want to fight it out.

We will be mainly living in NYC now but we hope to see many friends on some short trips we'll take in this next year.

—Gabe and Theresa

And a Final Adventure

When we left Damascus in a taxi late in the morning on July 31, 2012, it was a Friday in Ramadan, the day of prayer, of rest, and lately of protest and fierce reaction. But for us it was a final and unexpected bit of bureaucracy the Syrian way. We had crossed easily into Lebanon or Jordan from Syria two or three times each of the seven years in Damascus. Passports. Residency. Stamped here and there, fees paid, and always on to the Jordanian or Lebanese entry place just down the road.

We had never been asked for our exit permission papers before, but that day the Syrian border officers were not about to let us cross the border into Lebanon without such a paper showing we could exit. And nothing would substitute. And it was Friday and though only an hour out of Damascus, it would be Sunday morning before the residency offices would open.

As we started back toward Damascus, we called a friend who called a friend who called us with a suggestion that we, still thinking in American, couldn't have imagined: "Go to the residency office. Sure I know today is Friday. But they're in there; some of the usual guys are in there. They aren't working, but they're in there. Go upstairs. The guys might be asleep because they're fasting for Ramadan. Wake them up and tell them the problem. Have the driver wait."

And so it happened. The stamp came down on this new paper. The driver was waiting outside for us. To us, it seemed Damascus was winking.

Appendix

In the sidebars of this book we have sometimes introduced short or long pieces from the letters and reflections of Hussein Maxos, our first Arabic teacher in Damascus. Hussein reflects on Damascus life, especially in his neighborhood near Souq al-Jouma'a.

We left Damascus at the end of July 2012. We need here the voice of a friend who is still there. We have chosen these texts and offer them with his permission.

Geneva Peace Talks, 2014

Geneva peace conference: 3–4 months of preparation, over 1,000 journalists, maybe over 30 countries, zero progress. The average people here look smarter than politicians, analysts, and an army of diplomats. The people I know, friends and relatives and neighbors, say that if world powers would like to stop the war, they would have done so two years ago. They also don't want one party to win. News says now that superpowers have just agreed on the amount of weapons delivered to all parties without agreeing on food and medicine to be given to the starving people.

People here are very frustrated as they see the international community caring about its own interests and not doing enough to stop the war or help the victims. Political analysis has become part of their daily conversations but with a polemic tone. I'm afraid that this frustration is feeding extremism, sectarianism, and terrorism.

January 2014

Herbs Collectors Defy Tragedies, Blur Pain and Joy

Since the beginning of the war in Syria, millions of people have become jobless, then later homeless. Umm Ahmad is 43. She lost her husband in the first year of the war. She heard that her husband was arrested after he participated in a demonstration. She went to all security agencies. She cried and slept at their gates, and guards put her out repeatedly.

Umm Ahmad has five children, all between 2 and 13. Her family is originally from the countryside west of Damascus. After she lost hope in finding her husband, she began asking her friends and relatives for help but it came as too little, too late. Very few people were able to offer help even for a limited time. She then became desperate and depressed.

They used to have a small house in the village, and her husband worked for a construction company. Then police brutality became military confrontations. Clashes, bombing, and shelling gradually approached their poor life and small home until it destroyed parts of it; destroyed part of their life when the father disappeared and destroyed part of their house in a neighborhood that soon was inhabited only by ghosts.

She rented one room with a shared kitchen and bathroom in a neighboring, relatively quiet village. The little money Abu Ahmad, her husband, had saved melted away like a piece of ice on a hot stove when prices rose sharply. Umm Ahmad became more depressed and worried and began to ask anyone for help. Still, she didn't give up.

Then a woman suggested to Umm Ahmad that she could join a group of women who collect herbs from nearby hills, then sell them in the streets of Damascus for a good price. She happily agreed and the next day she joined the group.

Syria enjoys a diverse geography with environments that produce a considerable variety of herbs. Umm Ahmad's group complain that the best herb-rich hills have become battlefields. Now they go to hills with fewer herbs. But even when they complain, these women will begin to sing and joke while they search for those misty green herbs. Their hands were soft before but are now rough and full of tiny cuts and bruises. But laughter is like a fuel they need to help them hold together mentally and physically. The poorest of the women or someone with a tragedy to face may begin to sing and dance wildly, as the others sing with her. The one who's most depressed looks more jubilant than others!

August 2014

Generosity and Hospitality Limits

We in the Arab world like to be generous and especially in receiving guests at home and taking care of them. Many Arabs used to work as traders and merchants who made long journeys in all directions. Their trade routes stretched from China and India to Europe and from central Asia to central Africa. Most imports to Europe during medieval times were brought by Arabs who invented it, grew it, or transferred it from far away.

Arabs needed khans, the medieval form of hotels or inns, but they enjoyed more staying in friends' houses along their routes. They reciprocally loved to host friends coming from far away. Even a few years ago, we would see some trader from Damascus having a friend from Alexandria or from Crete, from Isfahan or from as far as Bukhara in Uzbekistan.

Arabs also traveled for other reasons and always loved to stay with a friend, distant relative, or just an acquaintance of a father or cousin. In return, gifts are given. What is interesting is that the host friend doesn't have to be from the same religion or ethnic group. So we saw a Sunni Muslim Damascene staying in the home of a Druze, Jewish, or Yezidi friend. Naturally, the host of that person will be welcome at the guest's home another time. Nomadic Bedouins and shepherds could stop at the home of any friend or any friend of a friend for rest and water in a long journey through the desert.

So we Arabs are known for generosity and hospitality. This cultural characteristic is really rooted in necessity. Tolerance was not a choice; it was a matter of survival that has been inherited from one generation to another.

The main character of the Arab tales of generosity is Hatim from the Tayy tribe. One story of Hatim tells of when he slaughtered his horse to feed the guests because he had nothing else. He became the model of selflessness and Jesus-like sacrifice. The beautiful tradition of the Arabs is that any guest has the right to stay for three days before declaring the purpose of the visit. Should we extend that now to three months or three years with so many nations and militias making Syrians ask for hospitality?

December 2014

Don't Talk Politics!

We ran away from news of war and politics just to find it in every corner in our lives.

I need water. The water source from which part of Damascus takes drinking water is a *figeh,* a water spring, that has been occasionally a battlefield. Pipes carrying the water are damaged from time to time.

I need bread. The wheat imports are reduced by the sanctions on Syria and some of the wheat reserve in Syria is controlled by rebels.

I need electricity. The power generators feeding the capital are running on fuel that is becoming rare and expensive due to international sanctions. Oil fields in Syria are controlled by rebels. Many people don't pay the bills.

I need tomatoes. Many farms have been destroyed and most farmers fled their areas.

I need to repair the refrigerator (so if there is electricity it will keep food fresh). No spare parts. Or, if there are spare parts, they are very expensive. And no more are coming.

I need the things I must buy to work. But many things are faked here and sold publicly. No government control over the quality of products. The government is too busy with fighting.

No matter what you do to forget politics, it pops up in your face just to remind you 24 hours a day that we have a war and nothing can be normal no matter what we do to distract ourselves with daily issues.

Just don't talk about the war or politics, my neighbor says.

October 2014

Christmas in Damascus, 2014

I teach English occasionally, and during the war I have taught many people, especially poor students for their final exams of high school, for free. Actually, no matter how poor I am, they are poorer, and it's good to help someone during crucial stage of his/her future-building process. Well, nothing is more important than the final exam of high school for Syrian youth. Even when I'm paid, the fee has barely covered the taxi, otherwise the small intercity buses will take the whole day with too many checkpoints on the way. The rich who pay well seem to have left the town and the new rich don't care about languages or culture. The middle class, like the poor, has prioritized the basic survival needs.

However, teaching English for free has brought me to the Christian area in the east of Old Damascus. A small walk around that district will definitely show an obvious depression on all faces of people in the streets. It is

Christmastime! I greeted many people who recognized me with a big smile. Some were connected to the house-renting business so they hosted some of my foreign students. They love it when a Muslim like me, one who understands and respects their religion, contacts or visits them. They always have a desire for a dialogue with the Muslim majority. At a personal level, relations with Muslims are perfect with few exceptions, but a national dialogue is not encouraged by the government. Therefore it is absent.

Many people there have invited me for coffee, dinner, or a drink and offer a bed to sleep because transportation becomes risky at night with bad news from time to time. I happily accept almost all invitations. Conversations with my Christian friends were like any conversation with other Syrians. I enjoy it so much because most of them are liberal intellectuals with the occasional conservative.

This time is different. We were still good friends but the too many sensitive subjects about the war and the spread of sectarianism had an impact, especially because I had not seen many of them since the beginning of the war. What made things harder was the Christmas occasion and their obligation to celebrate and enjoy it. Like other Syrians, Christians have lost many of their beloved ones. Almost every family has lost a member or suffered, be it murder, kidnappings, arrest, or injury.

A large number of Christians have already left the country. The remaining population is also planning to leave, as living conditions are getting harder every day and particularly the severe power cuts covering most of the day and night. I was embarrassed for not being able to help them emigrate despite all my connections in the West. My brother's painful journey in the death boats from Libya to Italy with his wife and four young daughters is my example for being unable to help anyone wanting to seek refuge in the West. My brother Jamal, 42 years old, a mosaic artist, has finally made it to the Netherlands. They all are now recovering from the horrible journey.

More austere this year than the last year Christmas, most Christians here said that they will not have any celebration activities, not even a Christmas tree. They all told me, after I told them I'm writing about Christmas, that I have to tell the whole world that they feel abandoned. They say that they are the original Christians of the world who spread Christianity to Europe and elsewhere. They said they have been adhering exhaustingly to their religion for centuries while the whole world neglects them selfishly and neglects all Syria.

December 2014

Discussions in the Greengrocery

Abo Abdo, 42 years old, is a greengrocer in our neighborhood. I shop for my vegetables from him at least twice a week. I've known him for years and we used to exchange a smile or a simple greeting when our eyes met. At the beginning of the war, I began to complain about the high prices of food. Then our conversations expanded gradually. Abu Abdo keeps a cigarette held by his lips like my father did, and he has a cup of tea near the scale. He occasionally invites me to stay and talk when he's not very busy. He is politically neutral and cautious. That's what I pretend to be, which is the safest way.

As the time passes, our conversations became deeper and we somehow began to trust each other. I do trust him more than he trusts me. That was maybe due to our initial conversations. I used some complicated terminologies, which scared his modest education. I regret it but I was not aware of his contentment with his small world. The more we talk, the more private issues he tells and discusses with me.

One day he told me about his married daughter who fled her area in the eastern suburbs of Damascus. She came with her three children and husband to stay temporarily while they looked for a house to rent. The rents have risen sharply and her husband is unemployed most of the time. They stayed and stayed, and now, they are still there indefinitely. Divorce is becoming an option with Abo Abdo because of frustration with his uncomfortable life at home with his son-in-law, especially when he gets mad at his noisy grandsons and granddaughters.

Despite the sadness of the story of his daughter's family, I liked to listen to it more than to his elusive political analysis and his conspiracy theories that sometimes made me tired and want to leave.

He is a practicing Muslim, I am not. He thinks that in the tough times like in war, one has to resort more and more to religion. This explains why the uprising in Syria has turned religious to a large extent, especially in the eastern Syria where the tribal Bedouin community is dominant. It is interesting to consider the link between the ultra-conservative community that has been long marginalized and how it became the host of jihadist groups.

Beyond the puzzle of politics, he tells interesting stories on how they manage their daily life at the crowded home. The way they save bread in the freezer when they have power, the way they cook cheap food, and many other tactics are truly amazing. I often tell him how I invented several methods to save food and money. He likes some but others like mixing food he is still skeptical. I tell him that foods tastes are all a question of habit and as long as the food or the mixture is healthy, I have no problem in eating it.

His determination to stick to Islam is always confronting my evasive answers. I try to distract him and avoid his questions about my own practice of Islam. It helps me as well being armed with many verses calling for freedom of belief and respect of other religions from the Qur'an itself. Abo Abdo is a good-hearted and peaceful man in the neighborhood. I really enjoy his simple life, and I can't wait to finish my tomatoes, cucumber, and potatoes in order to go to his small shop and enjoy a chat. This guy represents many Syrian people in their peaceful, conservative, and yet innovative nature.

May 2014

Ramadan in Bad Times

The month of Ramadan in the lunar calendar is the holy month of fasting for Muslims all over the world. It is the time during which they are more religious, more sociable and more charitable. For Muslims, Ramadan is the month of compassion and empathy. The community solidarity is at its height and social inequality shrinks.

The suffering of abstaining from food and drink the whole day can help people feel how the poor and the needy live. That is what they taught us in school and at home when we were young. The fasting can strengthen personality and strengthen social bonds as well as getting the person out of his/her self-centered career circles. People here visit each other more often, help each other more.

Neighbors and relatives exchange plates of food during Ramadan. That is in Islam, if you cook something and your neighbors smell it, you should give them some. This year I haven't noticed any food exchange on my street yet. I will take the first step and send my neighbors a plate of food. I am sure it will be a very friendly and warm gesture and can never be rejected during Ramadan. The problem is that most of my food is basic or simple and maybe tastelessly healthy. The food that has to be given as a gift has to be homemade and traditional in a sense of being well known. Syrians hate strange food, and it would be impolite to buy them a ready-made food from restaurants.

What we miss here in Damascus since the beginning of the war is the big gatherings of Ramadan, especially the huge meals for the great crowds in mosques or parks. Such free meals are daily during Ramadan in normal times, basically an *iftar*, the meal that ends the long day's fasting from food and all liquids. These meals, open to all, are organized by charity organizations. If the meal takes place in the courtyard of a mosque, people wait together for the call to prayer that marks the end of the day's hunger and thirst. After *iftar*, all can participate in the *taraweeh* prayer that is an extended prayer during the holy month.

Now due to the war in Syria, a lot of Ramadan's joy has gone away. Families have been forced to scatter inside and outside of Syria, and many people live in refugee camps. Even those blessed to live with relatives or rent a house in the quiet areas suffer this uncomfortable life. We have ever fewer public services, including communication and transportation. Electricity is not available most of the day and now it not available during most of the night. The few hours when we have power, people rush to do too many things as they anxiously wash clothes, clean the home, cook, charge their electronic devices.

September 2014

Recommended Reading

Literature

Antoon, Sinan. *The Corpse Washer.* New Haven and London: Yale University Press, 2013. Roy Scranton wrote in *Kenyon Review:* "Anyone looking for easy lessons, moral uplift, or liberal satisfaction, however, will be disappointed. What *The Corpse Washer* does—with painstaking attention, narrative sophistication, and emotional restraint—is portray the evisceration of Iraq's middle class by despotism, sanctions, and three wars, and the final collapse of Iraqi society from a decade of brutal, mismanaged occupation, all through the story of one damaged life. *The Corpse Washer* is a powerful and important novel of the Iraq War, and a necessary counterpoint to American stories focused almost exclusively on the suffering and trauma of Iraq's occupiers. Historians and politicians will continue to argue over which lives 'count,' while the bodies pile higher and higher. Sinan Antoon's *The Corpse Washer* offers a moving literary elegy not only for the numberless Iraqi dead, but also for those who remain to bury them. It must be read."

Darwish, Mahmoud. *The Butterfly's Burden,* translated by Fady Joudah. Port Townsend, WA: Copper Canyon Press, 2007. Darwish, a Palestinian, wrote a poem that is a love song for Damascus: "The Damasene Collar of the Dove." It is included in this Arabic-English edition along with many other poems by Mahmoud Darwish.

Palestine

The script is still the same. The Israeli government is the special friend of the United States, and even when Desmond Tutu of South Africa, who knows apartheid well, calls Israel a worse apartheid case than South Africa ever was, what can we do? We can read the history. We can support in various ways the rights of Palestinians. We can educate ourselves and others about the violations of international law that continue daily against the Palestinians in Israel and the occupied territories. Online read: electronicintifada.net. In the United States, Jewish Voice for Peace has become a major force for education on "Boycott, Divestment, Sanctions." See jewishvoiceforpeace@org.

Falk, Richard. *Palestine: The Legitimacy of Hope.* Charlottesville, VA: Just World Publishing, 2014. Falk is emeritus professor of international law at Princeton and served from 2008 to 2014 as the UN Special Rapporteur on Human Rights in Occupied Palestine.

Pappé, Ilan. *The Ethnic Cleansing of Palestine.* Oxford, England: Oneworld, 2006. Pappé is an Israeli historian determined to tell the truth about 1948, the year that most of the Arab population of Palestine, Muslims and Christians, were forced to leave their homes and land. Syria received many of them in Yarmouk and other camps.

Iraq

The specific involvement that brought us to Syria began with our active opposition to the U.S. bombing of Iraq in 1991, which included the use of depleted uranium (DU) in shells and bullets, and our government's insistence that the UN sanctions, which may have caused the death of a million Iraqis, go on and on until in 2003 the United States invaded and occupied Iraq. The carnage and destruction of these sanctions is told in two important books, one by Hans van Sponeck and the other by Joy Gordon.

From Iraqi friends we hear again and again that the victim was their culture. What might reparations be? These books discuss the damage done to education at all levels, to museums and to libraries, but harder to measure is the loss of mutual respect and civility.

Baker, Raymond W., Shereen T. Ismael, and Tareq Y. Ismael, eds., *Cultural Cleansing in Iraq: Why Museums Were Looted, Libraries Burned and Academics Murdered.* London and New York: Pluto Press, 2010.

Gordon, Joy. *Invisible War: The United States and the Iraq Sanctions.* Boston: Harvard University Press, 2012.

Harding, Scott, and Kathryn Libal. "War and the Public Health Disaster in Iraq" in Merrill Singer and G. Derick Hodge, eds., *The War Machine and Global Health*, 59-87. Plymouth, United Kingdom: AltaMira Press, 2010.

Hills, Elaine A. and Dahlia S. Wasfi. "The Causes and Human Costs of Targeting Iraq," in Merrill Singer and G. Derick Hodge, eds., *The War Machine and Global Health*, 119-156. Plymouth, United Kingdom: AltaMira Press, 2010.

The International Seminar on the Situation of Iraqi Academics, *Beyond Educide: Sanctions, Occupation and the Struggle for Higher Education in Iraq,* eds. Dirk Adriaensens et al. Ghent: Academia Press, 2012. Entire text in English and Arabic.

Otterman, Michael, and Richard Hil, with Paul Wilson. *Erasing Iraq: The Human Costs of Carnage.* London and New York City: Pluto Press, 2010.

United Nations High Commissioner for Refugees, *Statistics on Displaced Iraqis around the World, September 2007,* www.unhcr.org/461f7cb92.html.

von Sponeck, Hans. *A Different Kind of War.* New York: Berghahn Books, 2006.

See also the novel by Sinan Antoon listed under "Literature."

Syria

Regarding Syria, one can say that Americans through these recent decades paid little attention. Now in 2016, half of Syria's 2010 population are refugees, 10 million of them, either outside Syria's borders or surviving inside Syria but away from their homes. The books suggested below have to do with Syria's past. The creation of Syria as a nation-state after World War I, its quarter century under French colonial rule, and an independent Syria after World War II: these are part of the larger history told in the books under the "Middle East" heading.

One year after the nonviolent beginnings of protest against the Syrian regime, the regime's violent response led to the organizing of the Free Syrian Army; Kofi Annan came to Syria on behalf of the UN. He called for a peace conference attended by the Syrian opposition, the al-Assad government and representatives of regional and world powers. The U.S. government said its acceptance would depend on the departure, beforehand, of the present regime. From that time, Syria had not a popular uprising or a civil war, but militias coming from beyond Syria to fight each other with weapons and salaries also from outside. One of these, Da'esh (also ISIS or ISIL) seems borne of revenge against the West for all that has befallen Arabs from the Crusades to the support of Zionists taking Palestine from its Arab residents in 1948.

The third and fourth titles deal with the ongoing tragedy in Syria. The others present the long and amazing history of Damascus and of Greater Syria.

Ball, Warwick. *Syria: A Historical and Architectural Guide,* 3rd ed. Northampton, MA: Interlink, 2010.

Burns, Ross. *Damascus: A History.* New York: Routledge, 2005. Ross Burns was Australia's ambassador to Syria from 1984 to 1987. He also wrote *Monuments of Syria: A Historical Guide.* The prose, the scholarship, and perhaps the love in these two books were a great gift to us.

Cockburn, Patrick. *The Jihadis Return: ISIS and the New Sunni Uprising.* New York: OR Books, 2015.

Glass, Charles. *Syria Burning: ISIS and the Death of the Arab Spring.* New York: OR Books, 2015.

Tergeman, Siham. *Daughter of Damascus.* Austin: Center for Middle Eastern Studies, University of Texas at Austin, 1994. A story of growing up in Damascus in the mid-twentieth century.

Middle East

Cleveland, William, and Martin Bunton. *A History of the Modern Middle East, 5th ed.* Boulder, CO: Westview Press, 2013. A very readable introduction.

Fromkin, David. *A Peace to End All Peace: The Fall of the Ottoman Empire and the Creation of the Modern Middle East.* New York: Henry Holt, 1989, with Afterword, 2009. It isn't only Sykes-Picot but all the broken promises and colonial habits of World War I victors from France and Britain.

Salt, Jeremy. *The Unmaking of the Middle East: A History of Western Disorder in Arab Lands.* University of California Press, 2008. With the Cleveland and Franklin books above, this will provide a context and a clarity for what is happening now. The author asks that crucial question, *"Cui bono?"* (Who profited?)

An Essential Part of the History

Lyons, Jonathan. *The House of Wisdom: How the Arabs Transformed Western Civilization.* New York: Bloomsbury Press, 2009. Our last year in Damascus we studied this book with our Iraqi students, and all of us learned what we two Americans should have been taught in high school.

Menocal, Maria Rosa. *The Ornament of the World: How Muslims, Jews and Christians Created a Culture of Tolerance in Medieval Spain.* Boston: Little, Brown, 2002. For five centuries after a prince from Damascus fled to Spain, something amazing happened in Andalusia. This book tells so well what its subtitle announces.

Schimmel, Annemarie. *Islam: An Introduction.* Albany: State University of New York Press, 1992. This is the work of a scholar who grew up in Germany and earned her first doctorate there at age 19. She taught Islamic studies at Harvard for 25 years. This small book is the best and most readable introduction we know to Islam.

Art and Culture

Bolman, Elizabeth S. "Review of *The Frescoes of Mar Musa al-Habashi: A Study in Medieval Painting in Syria.*" *Caa.reviews*, May 14, 2002, www.caareviews.org/reviews/414

Dodd, Erica Cruikshank. *The Frescoes of Mar Musa al-Habashi: A Study in Medieval Painting in Syria.* Toronto: Pontifical Institute of Mediaeval Studies, 2000.

Evans, Helen C., ed. *Byzantium and Islam: Age of Transition* (Exhibition Catalogue). New York: Metropolitan Museum of Art, 2012. Peter Brown's "The Great Transition" (a review of the exhibit itself and of this catalogue): *The New York Review of Books*, May 10, 2012, http://bit.ly/1OCMl85. Peter Brown's short essay brings excitement and clarity to understanding the gradual blossoming of Islam in the world of Byzantine Christianity.

Peña, Ignacio. *The Christian Art of Byzantine Syria.* West Berkshire, UK: Garnet, 1997. Magnificent photos and the learning of many years that Peña spent in Syria produced this book and brought us back again and again to the Dead Cities area west of Aleppo.

268

About the Authors

Theresa's Life So Far

Theresa Kubasak has braided literacy, arts, and social justice into her 40 years of teaching: from Hoover Street School in Los Angeles to rural Colorado, then Chicago and New York and on to Damascus. She wrote curriculum for the Woody Guthrie Archives and dropped out of a PhD program in 2001 to become more active with Neighbors for Peace. Her experiences in Iraq during the sanctions include flying in the no-fly zone, visiting schools in Baghdad, and using her squirrel puppet to stop border guards from threatening a friend. She resigned from New York Public Schools in 2005 to study Arabic in Damascus, where she founded Iraqi Student Project with her husband, Gabe Huck. Theresa taught Literature Circles and Writers' Workshop to Iraqis in Damascus and later to Syrian refugees in Istanbul in 2015-16.

Gabe's Life So Far

Gabe Huck attended Benedictine schools where he learned from one monk what literature is, and from another why we challenge power. He was a monk himself for four years but in 1965 caught a bus to Washington via Selma. A conscientious objector, he counseled COs, cheered Martin Luther King's Vietnam speech in 1967, and a year later walked as a mourner behind King's coffin. Then came 32 years of putting books together as a publisher, loving alphabets and words and art. With Theresa, he made four journeys to Iraq and post-9/11 was part of Neighbors for Peace in Evanston. In Damascus with Theresa for seven years, they found a home among Syrians who were well practiced in kindness to refugees. They returned to the U.S. in 2012, convinced that here is where the problems originate.

And Now

Four years after leaving Damascus, we live in New York City. We have seen many of the Iraqi students with whom we worked in Damascus. In 2016, all of them will have completed undergraduate studies and some already have advanced degrees. We went to Istanbul in summer 2015 and for two months worked with Syrian refugees there, including a few with whom we have continued to work from afar. We may be able to welcome them to college studies in the U.S. If you could help with this in any way, let us know. You can contact us at gabeandtheresa@gmail.com

We thank you for your time spent with us in this book. We all, especially here in the United States, have much to do.

Theresa and Gabe on Straight Street in Damascus.

دمشق، ليست صورة منقولة عن الجنة
إنها الجنة
وليست نسخة ثانية للقصيدة..
إنها القصيدة

نزار قباني

Damascus, it's not a picture from paradise.
It is paradise.
And it's not a copy of the poem.
It is the poem.

NIZAR QABBANI